PETERLOO

JACQUELINE RIDING is the author of *Jacobites: A New History of the '45 Rebellion*. Former curator of the Palace of Westminster and Director of the Handel House Museum, she is a historical adviser on feature films, including Mike Leigh's *Mr. Turner* and *Peterloo*.

Victory at Peterloo by George Cruikshank, from William Hone's
A Slap at Slop and the Bridge-Street Gang, 1822.
(The John Rylands Library, Manchester)

THE STORY OF THE MANCHESTER MASSACRE

PETERLOO

Jacqueline Riding

FOREWORD BY MIKE LEIGH

HEAD
ZEUS

An Apollo Book

This is an Apollo book, first published in the UK in 2018
by Head of Zeus Ltd

Copyright © Jacqueline Riding, 2018

The moral right of Jacqueline Riding to be identified as the
author of this work has been asserted in accordance with the
Copyright, Designs and Patents Act of 1988.

All rights reserved. No part of this publication may be reproduced,
stored in a retrieval system, or transmitted in any form or by any
means, electronic, mechanical, photocopying, recording, or
otherwise, without the prior permission of both the copyright
owner and the above publisher of this book.

Chapter opener images taken from William Hone's *The Political
House that Jack Built* (London, 1819), and *The Man in the Moon,
a speech from the throne, to the senate of Lunataria* (London, 1820).
(Author's own)

9 7 5 3 1 2 4 6 8

A catalogue record for this book is available from
the British Library.

ISBN (HB): 9781786695833
ISBN (E): 9781786695826

Typeset by e-type

Printed and bound in Great Britain by
CPI Group (UK) Ltd, Croydon CR0 .

Head of Zeus Ltd
First Floor East
5–8 Hardwick Street
London EC1R 4RG

WWW.HEADOFZEUS.COM

DISCARDED

London Borough of Richmond
Upon Thames

RTTE   RUI

90710 000 371 547

Askews & Holts   RICHMOND UPON THAMES

942.733 RID   £25.00

LIBRARY SERVICE
                 9781786695833

For Lancashire Witches,
past, present and future

CONTENTS

'At Waterloo there was man to man, but at Manchester it was downright murder.'

FOREWORD

by Mike Leigh

As we worked on the film *Peterloo*, all of us, on both sides of the camera, were continually struck by the ever-increasing contemporary relevance of the story. Despite the spread of universal suffrage across large parts of the globe – poverty, inequality, suppression of press freedom, indiscriminate surveillance and attacks on legitimate protest by brutal regimes are all on the rise.

Peterloo is of seminal importance, yet many people have never heard of it, including, curiously, generations of native Mancunians and Lancastrians. I myself grew up in Salford. As a boy, I trod the streets that stand where St Peter's Field once was. The Midland Hotel occupies the site of Buxton's house, from where the misguided magistrates watched the massacre unfold. Next door is the Central Library, where I received my early theatrical education at the tiny Library Theatre, the local professional repertory company. As a teenager, I attended meetings of the Manchester Branch of the Gilbert and Sullivan Society, which took place at the (Quaker) Friends' Meeting House, dating from 1795, which played such a critical role at Peterloo.

And then there was the Free Trade Hall, now the Radisson Hotel, which these days boasts a newish red plaque commemorating Peterloo. It was here that I attended Hallé Orchestra, jazz and folk concerts, heard Bertrand Russell address CND rallies and delighted to see Tom Lehrer perform, and where I directed *Big Basil*, an early play of mine, for the Manchester Youth Theatre in 1968.

Early in our research, when Jacqueline Riding and I walked the Peterloo site with expert Robert Poole, I was shocked to realise how ignorant I had once been about the bloody events that had taken place on that very spot less than a century before my parents were born.

My primary school was next to Cromwell Bridge, which crosses the River Irwell. There, we were repeatedly told about the Siege of Manchester in 1642, during the Civil War – but Peterloo was never mentioned. Why, during our educational visits to cotton mills and soapworks and bread factories, were we never marched around the Peter Street area, and made to picture and re-live what was the most important event – apart from the Blitz – ever to take place in these streets? And why, in 'O' Level History, was Peterloo dismissed as a mere footnote?

A lifetime later, as we approach its bicentenary, the whole world can now learn the truth about Peterloo. This splendid book will bring a new freshness and clarity to the story; and so too, I hope, will *Peterloo* the movie, albeit in a different way. Jacqueline's book is a comprehensive, detailed and accurate history, whereas my film is a dramatic distillation – not a documentary, but nonetheless, I hope, true to the spirit of Peterloo.

The film and the book complement each other. Please enjoy them, but do be sure to be both moved and horrified by them, too.

"A distant age asks where the fabric stood."

Prelude

TWO FIELDS

'The scene of misery'

On Sunday 18 June 1815, two armies, numbering 140,000 men and boys, faced each other across open fields and low-rising arable land, fourteen miles south of Brussels in the Kingdom of the Netherlands (now Belgium).[1] They would decide, once and for all, Europe's fate after twenty-two years of catastrophic war. The rain had been pouring down for several days, making a swamp of the terrain that the Commander-in-Chief of the combined British, Dutch and Hanoverian (or 'Allied') army, Field Marshal His Grace the Duke of Wellington, had selected as the field of battle.

Among those waiting in tense anticipation for his commanding officer's signal was John Lees, a cotton factory owner's son from Oldham in the northern English county of Lancashire.[2] John was five feet four inches in height with a 'fresh' complexion, grey eyes and brown hair. He had enlisted into the British army at Manchester, one of the country's major textile-producing towns, on 23 September 1812 aged fourteen.[3] What possessed him to take such a step is not known. 1812 was the year when Great Britain commenced war with the United States of America and when Napoleon Bonaparte's hubristic decision to march on Moscow turned into a decimating retreat through a bitter Russian winter. In faraway Lancashire, the weavers were experiencing mass unemployment and terrible deprivation. There were some in Britain, landowners and farmers for example, who profited from the war, but many more who had been and continued to be brought to their knees by it. Taxation was one burden from which no one was immune, regardless of how small or irregular their wages, whether direct (via property or earnings) or indirect (via goods). Income tax had been devised in 1798 by William Pitt the Younger to finance the ongoing war effort. At the resumption of the war after the short peace between 1802 and 1803, the then prime minister, Henry Addington (in office until 1806, afterwards elevated to the peerage as Lord Sidmouth), revised the system, doubling those liable to pay it while significantly reducing evasion through collection at source. For the majority of Britons, who had no vote in national parliamentary elections, this was taxation without representation. And as national government did little beyond fighting wars – no poor relief, policing, medical care, schooling – for most citizens the return on decades of taxation, beyond more war and deeper national debt, was negligible.

1812 was also infamous for the assassination of Prime Minister Spencer Perceval – shot in the lobby of the House of Commons by a disgruntled merchant, John Bellingham – and for the violent Luddite Revolt, when handloom weavers vented their frustration and despair, exaggerated by wartime hardships, on the water and steam-powered machines that were transforming textile production, uprooting thousands of the working and labouring class from individual cottage industries to the vast weaving and spinning sheds of the cotton mills that have come to symbolize the 'Industrial Revolution' of England's Midlands and North. Both events appeared to signal that a general rising against the government was about to break out, or even revolution against the state itself, as in the American colonies in 1776 and then, more terrifyingly, France in 1789. Fears that enduring revolutionary zeal was spreading to the United Kingdom, fuelled by the writings of the English republican radical Thomas Paine (*Common Sense*, 1776, and *The Rights of Man*, 1791), left the longstanding Tory government, in power since 1783, on constant alert. Paine's message of liberty, equality and the potential of a government based on a true representation of the people, rather than the Old European systems founded on hereditary privilege and monarchical rule – as Paine himself put it, 'to begin the world over again'[4] – seemed to be moving from theory to reality.[5]

Initially the Whig opposition in Parliament, led in the House of Commons until his death in 1806 by Charles James Fox, delighted in the political transformations across the Channel. But on the commencement of the Reign of Terror and the trial and execution of King Louis XVI and then his queen in 1793, at the instigation of Maximilien Robespierre and his fellow militant revolutionaries or Jacobins, many British radicals rejected the direction in which France's new republican government was heading. The constant threat of invasion from France, which turned into an imminent danger in the years 1798 and 1803, was finally allayed by Lord Nelson's decisive victory at Trafalgar in 1805, establishing the Royal Navy's dominance of the seas. However, reports of the blood-stained guillotine and rampaging working-class *'sans culottes'* mobs, women and men, provided fresh impetus to the propaganda of the government and its supporters. The term 'Jacobin' was levelled at anyone who advocated even modest reformation in the British Parliament while their national leadership, particularly Fox and the playwright and politician Richard Brinsley Sheridan, were portrayed in the popular caricatures of James Gillray as bloodthirsty, regicidal nihilists in revolutionary garb, including red Caps of Liberty – originally the symbol of freedom for former slaves in ancient Rome, now used to signify a French-style febrile republican spirit. The result was a polarization the length and breadth of Great Britain into two distinct political parties representing irreconcilable stances.

The British government's response to the immediate crisis commencing in 1812 was to pass the Frame Breaking Act, making machine breaking a capital crime, then to round up as many Luddites as possible, to try them and, if found guilty, to hang them.

The Corn Laws introduced by Lord Liverpool (prime minister on Perceval's death), which passed through Parliament in early 1815, were designed to maintain artificially high profits on grain by banning cheaper imports from North America, in order, it was generally understood, to pay off the monumental national debt accrued by years of military and naval conflict. One result was the inflation of prices for basic foodstuffs like bread, while, at the same time, the wages of the labouring man and woman fell. Thus, their means of survival doubly and devastatingly assaulted, they prayed that with Peace would come Plenty, whilst rallying increasingly behind the constitutionally-based parliamentary reform movement for redress, led predominantly by the middle classes. This shift in attitude and behaviour within the labouring class – from illegal, indiscriminate violent action against the symptom of their troubles, easily condemned and dealt with by the authorities as with the Luddites, to (largely) legal, disciplined and peaceable methods to address the source, i.e. the absence of representation in parliament – was barely acknowledged by the government. Lord Liverpool's Home Secretary, Lord Sidmouth, judged that, whatever the appearance and method used, nothing short of revolution and constitutional devastation was intended.[6]

Sidmouth believed, fundamentally, in the vesting of political power in landownership and property, as well as the existing balance between Crown, Church and Parliament. The apparently tempered and constitutional behaviour of the lower orders in the cause of social change that must, inevitably, come with political enfranchisement, with the encouragement of those from the middling sort, like the political pamphleteer and agricultural reformer William Cobbett, who sought to harness their collective strength, was simply a front for more nefarious activity, in Sidmouth's opinion, and would always be treated with suspicion and, when necessary, crushed. A steady flow of intelligence, gleaned by spies and agents of varying credibility from all quarters of the country, but all supporting the accuracy of this presumption, was collated and then circulated by Sidmouth's increasingly pressurized Whitehall department, the Home Office.

Paranoia undoubtedly played a part, but Sidmouth's perception that a shift to violence was only a matter of time was not wholly inaccurate. For although it is generally the case that old-style rioting had been replaced by peaceful political agitation, at the same time the pressure to resort to such measures continued, repression from the Home Office and local magistrates notwithstanding. During the post-war years, radicals utilized a repertoire of agitation, validated by notions of popular constitutionalism and a commonly-held understanding of English and British history, to mount a display of ever greater numbers demanding parliamentary reform. This included the process of mass petitioning and, more powerful still, the concept of 'monster' meetings (what we would now call mass demonstrations). There were strains and disagreements among reformers about when and how agitation could be moved to the next level, or even into physical force. It would take a deft and charismatic leader to manipulate the threat posed by a multitude of the people collectively demanding an end to the corruption and incompetence of the old order, while maintaining a tempering influence over them. Hopelessness could so easily turn into violence.[7]

Perhaps desperation, allied to the certainty of a regular wage and employment, had driven John Lees to enlist, like so many of his comrades-in-arms. Or perhaps he yearned for adventure, fearing he might miss out on the Europe-wide military struggle, the great crisis of the Age, which had dominated the whole of his young life. Whatever his reasons, on joining up he was posted to Major Robert Bull's 'I' troop of the Royal Horse Artillery and, three years later, found himself on a battlefield named after the nearby village of Waterloo.[8] Once the definitive nature of this battle had become clear, the British nation – and particularly its military power, regardless of the successes of the earlier Peninsular War (1807–14) – would be divided between those who were at the battle of Waterloo, and those who were not: as Captain Thomas Dyneley, also of the Royal Horse Artillery, later observed, 'John Bull is always pleased with his last toy.'[9]

On that June day, John Lees, with his troop, was in the heat of the combat, as they fired their guns above the large and strategically important farmhouse of Hougoumont.[10] Below them was Major-General Sir John Byng, commander of the 2nd Brigade of the 1st (or Guards) Division who were defending the farmhouse against relentless enemy attack: the desperate struggle over Hougoumont is often described as a battle within the battle. Byng, now in his early forties, had been commander of the Southern Irish District during the suppression of the 1798 uprising, inspired by the revolutions in America and France, and had then served with great distinction under Wellington in the Peninsular War, becoming, as a result, a Knight Commander of the Order of the Bath. In the event, Waterloo and its immediate aftermath would be the last period of active military service for this seasoned soldier. He aimed to live out his days in uneventful semi-retirement, leaving ample time for his first love, horse racing, as commander of England's Northern District. Located in the heart of this district was Manchester.

Captain Dyneley's Royal Horse Artillery 'E' troop was attached to Lieutenant General Sir Hussey Vivian's cavalry brigade. Dyneley, a veteran of the battles of Salamanca and Vitoria and the sieges of Burgos and Ciudad Rodrigo (he was wounded at the latter), had been part of the force covering the retreat from Quatre Bras two days earlier, during which his brigade had been attacked by French cuirassiers, lancers and artillery. He later wrote, with classic British officer *sang-froid*, 'Vivian sent me in advance with a couple of guns and I blazed away at them furiously; the practice was good, but they dashed on with as much unconcern as if I had only been pointing my finger at them.'[11] On 18 June, Captain Dyneley's troop was located at the extreme left of the Allied line, with the order not to engage until the arrival of the Prussian army under Field Marshal Gebhard Leberecht von Blücher.

Earlier that morning, the 5th Brigade of Cavalry, including the 15th The King's Regiment of Light Dragoons (Hussars), had formed up less than half a mile to the rear of Hougoumont, tasked with protecting the Allied army's right wing, while one and a half squadrons were watching the valley leading from Braine-L'Alleud.[12] The entire cavalry was under the command of Henry William Paget, Earl of Uxbridge, who was famously injured, losing a leg, while at Wellington's side. Major-General Colquhoun Grant was at the head of the 5th Brigade, with the 15th Hussars under the command of Lieutenant Colonel Leighton Cathcart Dalrymple and Major Edwin Griffiths, 'officers', according to the regiment's medical officer, William Gibney, 'who had distinguished themselves at Vittoria [sic], Tarbes and Toulouse, and had for commanders of troops, officers second to none in the service', including Captains Joseph Thackwell, Skinner Hancox and Lieutenant John Whiteford.[13] Despite being considered, most notably amongst themselves, as the elite of the British cavalry, the 15th had had a few rough nights in advance of the battle. The day before, according to Captain Thackwell, as the rain thundered down, his regiment was 'bivouacked in a field of rye on the right of the village of Mont St Jean', which they endured as best they could, despite having 'No rations or supplies of any description'.[14]

The battle commenced with a bombardment from the French artillery just before midday, Captain Dyneley observing that 'the rascals did this beautifully'.[15] The 15th Hussars immediately suffered casualties. Major-General Grant had no fewer than five horses shot from under him during the course of the battle. One was killed by a cannon ball that had just passed through Lieutenant Colonel Dalrymple's left leg, as described by Dr Gibney, leaving the limb 'only suspended by a few muscles and the bone in splinters'.[16] Dalrymple was quickly patched up on the battlefield by Gibney and then carried, on a plank, the few miles to Waterloo village for the necessary amputation. As the lieutenant colonel wrote in his journal, 'I was placed in a room with an officer of the 33rd desperately' – as it turned out, mortally – 'hurt in the neck… his groans were most melancholy. Particularly to a person in my situation.'[17]

Meanwhile, as the battle raged on, Major Griffiths, commanding officer in Dalrymple's place, was killed, leaving Captain Thackwell to lead the final charges. He was shot through the bridle hand, but, having placed the reins in his teeth, was then shot in the left arm, the bone shattered between the elbow and shoulder. He would remain on the battlefield, in agony, for some time. His wounded arm was later amputated to the shoulder. This left Captain Hancox to take over command and lead the 15th out of action.[18]

Captain Dyneley recalled that some Royal Horse Artillery troops had 'suffered most dreadfully in men and horses' and although his troop had lost one sergeant, around twelve other men dead or wounded plus about fifteen horses killed, he considered them fortunate to have had 'not an officer touched'.[19] Describing the battlefield, he continues: 'The slaughter throughout the day had been dreadful and the ground was so completely covered with killed and wounded that it was with great difficulty we could pick our way so as to prevent driving over them, and I saw hundreds of poor fellows ridden over.'[20]

Lieutenant Colonel Dalrymple was transported to Brussels with Dr Gibney, who wrote in his journal that 'we quitted the scene of misery together. The road was rough and terribly monotonous, cut up by artillery, waggons, carts, and everything with wheels on which wounded men could be conveyed. Much of it lay in the forest of Soignies, which was in many parts yet thickly strewn with dead horses and dead soldiers, lying unburied.'[21] The rank and file, like John Lees, who were not required as part of the army of occupation, were left to shift for themselves, many making the long and arduous journey home on foot. This rapid influx into Great Britain of thousands of disbanded veterans aggravated an already strained labour market. John Lees, at least, had a family in Oldham and the prospect of employment in his father's factory.[22]

Captain Dyneley was promoted to the rank of major and, after the battle, joked to a friend, 'I remember being laughed at... and told I had better remain a Captain, as being called a Major would make me look old; now I beg leave to state that it has had quite the contrary effect and that I look 20 years younger and am on uncommonly good terms with myself.'[23] He was posted to near Beauvais, where 'we have excellent shooting', an 'abundance of hares, partridges and quails', although, he concludes, 'It seems quite uncertain how long we are to be kept in this country.'[24] The 15th Hussars returned to Canterbury and, as no war was in the offing, they remained in England, moving between the new barracks that were springing up all over the country, while undertaking tedious but necessary domestic duties, quelling riots and breaking up political meetings, in support of the Civil Powers. The Duke of Wellington as 'the valiant leader of such a signal victory' was voted in parliament a sum of £200,000, in addition to the £500,000 already granted to him, as 'farther proof of the opinion entertained by Parliament of his transcendent services, and of the gratitude of the British nation'.[25]

★

Less than two years after Waterloo, the twenty-nine-year-old silk weaver, poet and champion of radical parliamentary reform, Samuel Bamford, in the company of his like-minded friend Joseph Healey, a quack doctor, was hastening across the Lancashire moors, 'this wild region' as he later described it, from his native Middleton, a small township six miles north of Manchester. Samuel was five feet ten inches tall, strong, with brown hair, grey eyes that were, in his own words, 'lively, and observant', nose 'rather snubby', his profile 'of rude good nature, with some intelligence'.[26] The 'Doctor', as he liked to be addressed, was a few years older and a little shorter, with dark hair and whiskers, and 'an air of bravado that was richly grotesque'.[27] Like his devout Methodist father before him, Dr Healey was 'a firm believer in witches and witchcraft', for which the county of Lancashire, scene of the Pendle witch trials of 1612, was famed.[28] Both men had been forced to leave their homes to avoid arbitrary arrest on suspicion of high treason. Such was the life of a radical in these skittish post-war times: branded, by those who sought to undermine their cause, as being hell-bent on transplanting the mob-rule terrors of republican France to the United Kingdom and destroying the current balanced perfection (as some, like Lord Sidmouth, saw it) of the British constitution. The post-war period was made more volatile still when, in 1815, Mount Tambora in the Dutch East Indies (now Indonesia) erupted, causing extreme weather conditions across Europe. This single natural disaster devastated the harvest the following year, known as the 'Year without a Summer', causing mass starvation and food riots in Great Britain. That same black summer, in a villa near Lake Geneva, Mary Shelley's novel *Frankenstein* was born.

Bamford later humorously compared his and the doctor's immediate travails in the March of 1817 to the progress of John Bunyan's Pilgrim, 'Christian and Faithful, at the hill, Difficulty', but after ascending Knowe (or 'Knowl') Hill, the two friends surveyed, with silent delight, the vista that stretched out before them.

In his autobiography, published twenty-five years later, Bamford refers to the ancient and mythical as well as modern features within this rugged landscape.[29] In the distance were the moors towards Todmorden and Walsden. Then 'following the horizon, we next saw the ridge of Blackstone-edge, streaked with sungleams and dark shadows; then the moors of Saddleworth, particularly Oaphin with his white drifts still lingering, and Odermon with his venerable relics of druidism, his "Pots an' Pons".' To the east and south respectively, the hills of the adjoining counties of Derbyshire and Cheshire 'rose like a region of congealed waves', whilst the countryside towards Lancashire's great trading seaport, Liverpool, 'was bounded by a bright streak, probably the Irish sea'. A 'dim white vapour' rising into the clear blue sky 'indicated the site of Preston or Blackburn'. The towns of Bolton and Bury seemed very close by, while 'Manchester, Stockport, Ashton, Oldham, and Rochdale, were distinctly visible'. Finally, 'neither last nor least',

Bamford and Healey spied 'one small speck – it was the white end of a house at Heabers, which directed our looks to the misty vapour of Middleton, rising beside dark woods from the vale in which the town is situated'.[30]

Thoughts of the family he had left behind, of hearth and home, triggered a pang of melancholy and the two men were left 'feeling we were cut off and outcast'. But they endeavoured to take solace in the glorious prospect of their homeland and their faith in the tender care of 'a bounteous Creator'. At this moment, Bamford recalled, a 'beautiful spring of water, pure as a cup from heaven's banquet, was gently brimming over a bason [sic] of white sand and pebbles into which it arose. A sward of sweet green grass lined the margin of a silvery band that lay glimmering and trickling on the sunny side of the hill; whilst here and there were tufts or rushes, glistering with liquid pearls.'[31] Taking this sacred water in their cupped hands, they drank to family and friends; to their brethren who suffered, whoever and wherever they might be; to the imminent downfall of tyranny, and, above all, to Liberty. On these toasts, they gave three energetic 'Huzzas!' at which an 'old black-faced tup', gently grazing nearby, 'lifted his horns from the heather, looked gravely at us, and giving a significant bleat, scampered off, followed by such of his acquaintance as were browsing near'.[32]

Bamford's reminiscences might seem whimsically bucolic at best, at worst mawkishly sentimental to a cynical modern ear. But here – in language and rhythms inspired by Bunyan, Alexander Pope and John Milton, 'my old Homeric Pope, and my divine Milton',[33] brought to vivid life by the communal theatre of the Protestant pulpit – Bamford is setting out his personal suffering and sacrifice, as well as the impact on his loved ones and community, in his determined pursuit of the cause for parliamentary reform: demands that, to us, seem so straightforward. One man, one vote; secret ballots; equal representation; regular parliaments. Yet, at this present time, the situation, from the perspective of a modern democracy, was very far from balanced perfection. The entire county of Lancashire was represented by only two Members of Parliament; Manchester had none. Borough-mongering, the buying and selling of parliamentary seats, continued unabated alongside the representational perversion of 'rotten boroughs', constituencies with few voters and where, invariably, the choice of representative was in the hands of a single family. The most infamous example was Old Sarum in Wiltshire, a hill with no inhabitants, which had, like Lancashire, two Members of Parliament. If all adult male Britons – those who were neither criminals nor insane – had the vote, then the nation's families too would have a voice in Parliament. And further, if the constituencies of the United Kingdom were equally apportioned according to size and population, then all parts of the nation would have a say over who could speak for them and how. Then, and only then, would the common man be truly represented by the House of Commons within the national parliament. (It would take another century before the common woman joining him in the vote became a serious proposition.)

The agitation for parliamentary reform was a nationwide movement, encompassing the whole of Great Britain and Ireland. The emphasis here is events local to Lancashire and, particularly, Manchester, but the significance was national. What follows is the story of how, on 16 August 1819, the lives of Samuel Bamford and Joseph Healey, in pursuit of their vision for themselves and their country, would become inextricably linked with those of John Lees, Major Thomas Dyneley, Major-General Sir John Byng and Lieutenant Colonel Leighton Dalrymple. It is a sequence of events that culminated, on that day, in the death of at least fifteen people and the injury of hundreds more, some at the hands of Waterloo heroes, during an immense but peaceful gathering of men, women and children on open ground in Manchester, known as St Peter's Field. This mass meeting was intended as the glorious regional climax of a national mobilization or 'union' of underrepresented people. It ended in carnage and national shame. It is also the story of how another veteran of Waterloo, John Lees, would survive a bloody battle fought on a foreign field, only to face greater peril at this pro-democracy meeting on home soil: what was quickly and strikingly branded the massacre not on St Peter's Field, but on the field of Peterloo.

1

MANCHESTER

'The second town in the kingdom'

The town of Manchester is in the southern district of the Palatine County of Lancaster, or Lancashire, 185 miles northwest of London. It sits at the confluence of the Rivers Irk, Medlock and Irwell. Local historians writing in the eighteenth and early nineteenth centuries believed that this site was first occupied by the Ancient Britons, five hundred years before the birth of Jesus, but that the foundations of a settlement could be dated to the Roman invasion of Britain in AD 43, during which, to defend themselves, the Britons came together and formed 'a place of tents' or 'Mancenion'. The name changed to 'Mancunium' at the time of Agricola in AD 79, then, by the medieval period, to 'Mancestre', from which, these local sages conclude, the town's modern name springs.[1]

Except to the south, where peat or turf can be found, early-nineteenth-century Manchester was surrounded by coal mines, some of them worked since the seventeenth century, on the estates of, among others, the Dukes and Earls of Bridgewater and Balcarres (Haigh Hall) and the Hultons of Hulton Park. The Old Bridge to the northwest of the town, spanning the River Irwell, was the ancient link between Manchester and her sister township of Salford. The nearby River Mersey was one route connecting the citizens and trades of these towns to Liverpool. The Medlock, running into the Irwell to the south, supplied water to the Bridgewater Canal, a

Lithograph of Blackfriars Bridge, Manchester, by Henry Gould, 1821.
(Chetham's Library, Manchester)

superb example of eighteenth-century civil engineering created to ship Lancastrian coal to the remainder of the county and around Great Britain. The Bridgewater Canal had then been extended, by the 'Ship Canal', to connect Manchester and its surrounding areas directly to the Irish Sea to the west. By such means, the cotton bales on which the town and county's textile industry relied, arriving at Liverpool from the plantations of North America, were then delivered to Manchester's cotton-spinning mills and, beyond, to the factories of Cheshire, Derbyshire and the West Riding of Yorkshire. The Abolition of the Slave Trade Act of 1807 made participating in the trade illegal in the United Kingdom and its colonies, but Britain continued to import the American cotton picked by the descendants of enslaved Africans for decades to come.

In 1801 the combined population of Manchester and Salford, including the conjoined townships of Hulme, Chorlton Row, Ardwick and Cheetham, was calculated as 108,460. Ten years later it was thought that this number had increased by at least twenty thousand, allowing locals to consider Manchester, in population alone, as 'the second town in the Kingdom'.[2] At this time, according to the Manchester historian and journalist Joseph Aston, 'between one third and one half of the adult population were not native to the town and the whole parish of Manchester by 1811 contained 22,759 inhabited houses, occupied by 28,282 families, of whom 1,110 families are employed in agriculture, the vast majority, that is 25,338 families, in trade, manufactures and commerce, and a final 1,834, Aston declares, 'not appertaining to an industrious employment'.[3] Aston observes that an Act of Parliament, dated 1791, 'was obtained for the purpose of lighting, watching, and cleaning the town'.[4] The first gas lamp was introduced in 1807. By 1816, the town was lit in the winter months by 2,758 lamps while the streets were swept and 'the soil carried off' twice a week.

The growth in population can be explained by the expansion of the textile industry. Through the technological innovations of Richard Arkwright, James Hargreaves and Samuel Crompton, the processes of spinning and weaving were centralized within large factories, with an associated expansion of supporting trades such as machine component manufacture. This brought an influx of workers from the outlying areas of Lancashire and the North, and, further still, from Ireland (via Liverpool). In the second half of the eighteenth century, water-powered factories sprang up along the river banks and canal sides of Manchester, such as Thackeray & Whitehead's Garratt Mill (1760) and David Holt's works (1785) on the Medlock, and Bank Mill (1782) on the Irwell. However, the irregular nature of water power in Manchester encouraged the mill owners to experiment with a new concept: steam power. The enthusiastic adoption of this technology was the basis of Manchester's dominance, signalling the step change required for the full transition from market town to industrial capital of 'Cottonopolis'.[5]

In 1816, the district of Ancoats, four hundred acres lying within the northeastern region of the town, reflected this significant change in the townscape. One of the oldest and most distinguished buildings in Manchester was Ancoats Hall, a house of late Tudor vintage set within a sizable plot beside the River Medlock, with formal gardens rolling down to the water's edge. It was described in 1795 as 'a very ancient building of wood and plaister, but in some parts re-built with brick and stone'.[6] By this date the hall, once the residence of the Mosley Lords of the Manor, was occupied by William Rawlinson, 'an eminent merchant in Manchester', one of the new-breed citizens of wealth and influence. The hall no doubt maintained an elegant air of antiquity and even tranquillity, in dramatic contrast to the area lying to the west.

As described by *The Times*, the Ancoats district 'consists of four great streets, Oldham-street, Great Ancoat-street, Great Newton-street, and Swan-street, from which innumerable narrow streets or lanes branch off'.[7] Small mills already existed here by the 1790s, including Shooters Brook Mill, Ancoats Lane Mill and Salvin's Factory, but by 1816 the sheer number, scale and proximity of the new steam-powered mills that were being built here made the area distinctive, even within a rapidly industrializing town like Manchester.[8] The network of canals, including the Ashton and Rochdale canals (completed in 1796 and 1804 respectively) with additional smaller offshoots, and the presence of Shooters Brook – a tributary of the Medlock – made it an attractive area for investment and expansion. In the late 1790s two major spinning mills were built near the then incomplete Rochdale canal by Scotsmen James McConnel, John Kennedy and brothers Adam and George Murray. The seven-storey McConnel & Kennedy Mill on Union Street, known as the Old Mill, contained two steam engines of forty and sixty horse-power.[9] The partners then built Long Mill next door, completed in 1806, with a forty-five-horse-power steam engine.[10] Murrays' Mill, also on Union Street, was a monumental eight storeys high.

Although the power from water was limited and had, in any case, been usurped by steam, the waterways in Ancoats facilitated the delivery of coal (which powered the engines) and the movement of finished goods. Two of the many coal mines encircling Manchester were located on the northern edge of this area, including the Bradford Colliery. The presence of the factories encouraged the building of associated businesses, workshops and warehouses. The Canal Street Dye Works was built on a branch of the Ashton Canal, while the Soho Foundry (Peel, Williams & Co.), making components for steam engines and boilers amongst other things, was established on Pollard Street, adjoining the Ashton Canal, in about 1810.

According to Joseph Aston, by 1816 Salford and Manchester had, collectively, eighty-two steam-powered spinning factories, mainly found in the Ancoats, Oxford Street, New Cross and Beswick areas.[11] These 'astonishing monuments of human industry' were so famous that, as Aston continues, 'it is become a fashion for strangers to visit'.[12]

The temporary peace in 1814 (prior to Bonaparte's escape from the island of Elba, which led to the Waterloo campaign) encouraged visitors from mainland Europe to travel to Great Britain to inspect the recent technological developments. Several arrived in Manchester, noting down their impressions of the town in letters, journals and official reports. Johann Georg May, a factory commissioner from Prussia, described England as 'this land of efficiency' where 'there is a superfluity of interesting things to be seen. There is something new to catch the eye in every step that one takes.'[13] Manchester, he noted, is 'known throughout the world as the centre of the cotton industry'. Adjoining each factory, which, by this date, were usually of at least five storeys, 'there is a great chimney which belches forth black smoke and indicates the presence of the powerful steam engines. The smoke from the chimneys forms a great cloud which can be seen for miles around the town' and, as a result, the 'houses have become black'. May also recalled that one of the rivers 'upon which Manchester stands is so tainted with colouring matter that the water resembles the contents of a dye vat'.[14]

The Swiss industrialist Hans Caspar Escher, in August 1814, also observed the effects of the pollution created by the textile industry: 'In Manchester there is no sun and no dust. Here there is always a dense cloud of smoke to cover the sun while the light rain – which seldom lasts all day – turns the dust into a fine paste

which makes it unnecessary to polish one's shoes.' That aside, he
marvelled at the fact that, within a fifteen-minute walk, he had
counted over sixty spinning mills. 'I might have arrived in Egypt
since so many factory chimneys… stretched upwards towards the
sky like great obelisks.'[15] He also noted the tremendous speed at
which new factories were being built, observing the construction
of one power loom factory measuring about 130 feet in length and
fifty feet in width, with a total of six floors. 'Not a stick of wood',
he declared in awe, 'is being used in the whole building. All the
beams and girders are made of cast iron and are joined together.
The pillars are hollow iron columns which can be heated by steam.
There are 270 such pillars in this factory.'[16]

Johann Conrad Fischer, a Swiss inventor and steel manufacturer,
first visited Manchester and Salford in the September of 1814. He
described the Philips and Lee spinning mill on Chapel Street in
Salford as 'so large that there can be few to equal it in size'.[17] Built
between 1799 and 1801, the mill was seven storeys high, employed
over nine hundred operatives, and was one of the first factories
to be heated by steam and lit by gas, the latter installed in 1805.[18]
The co-owner, George Augustus Lee, had been the manager of
Peter Drinkwater's relatively modest four-storey spinning mill in
Auburn Street, Piccadilly (founded in 1789), the first such mill to be
built in the centre of Manchester.

Hans Escher, meanwhile, recalled a factory where the manager
speaks to his colleagues throughout the site, while sitting in his
private office, 'by means of tubes and he hears their replies by the
same means'.[19] He continues: 'The spinning mills are now working
until 8 p.m. by (gas)light. Unless one has seen it for oneself it is
impossible to imagine how grand is the sight of a big cotton mill
when a facade of 256 windows is lit as if the brightest sunshine
were streaming through the windows. The light comes from a

sort of inflammable air which is conducted all over the building by means of pipes.'[20] Further, 'the Manchester manufacturers are much more advanced than their Glasgow rivals. To reach Manchester standards of efficiency in Swiss factories we should have to sack all our operatives and train up a new generation of apprentices.'[21] Escher reflects on the awesome power created by such machines: 'One shudders when one sees the piston of an engine going up and one realises that a force of 60 to 80 horse power is being generated... A single steam engine frequently operates 40,000 to 50,000 spindles in a mill which has eight or nine floors and 30 windows. In a single street in Manchester there are more spindles than in the whole of Switzerland.'[22]

The visitors also made observations about the man, woman and even child power that was required to work the machines. Johann May visited Chadwick, Clegg & Co. (two establishments on Oxford Road and 10 Marsden Square) and in one mill he observed a '14 horse power steam engine which drove 240 looms, two shearing machines and six sizing machines. One adult worker operated each shearing and sizing machine.'[23] May also recorded that to save wages 'mule jennies have actually been built so that no less than 600 spindles can be operated by one adult and two children. Two mules, each with 300 spindles, face each other. The carriages of these machines are moved in one direction by steam and in the other direction by hand. This is done by an adult worker who stands in between the two mules. Broken threads are repaired by children (piecers) who stand at either end of the mules.'[24]

The events around 1812, known as the Luddite Revolt, were clearly still uppermost in people's minds, as Johann Fischer recalled while visiting one mechanical spinning and weaving shed: 'when one sees these power looms for oneself it is easy to appreciate the bitter feelings of the men who have been thrown out of work (by them). Fifty of these looms – operated by one and the same steam engine – stood in a medium-sized room. Each was no more than about four feet in height, length and width. They were operated by fifteen artisans and one foreman.'[25] He recalled that the movement of the shuttle and the passing of the thread into the machine was executed much faster than could be done by hand, therefore improving output. Moreover, as the foreman observed to Fischer, power looms do not get tired in the same way that a handloom weaver does. 'Consequently the cloth produced by the power loom is more uniform – and therefore of higher quality – than the cloth made by hand.'[26] Fischer left Manchester 'delighted with the new and remarkable things that I had seen'.[27]

In a report submitted to the House of Commons to support a petition 'praying for a limitation of the hours of labour in Cotton Mills' and signed by six thousand factory workers from Manchester and its environs, many of them parents of child workers, the authors draw attention to the fact that by the mid-1810s children of six and seven years of age, and sometimes even as young as five, were employed in the mills. A working day at this time was around fourteen hours, often without a break. In some factories the temperatures reached an unbearable seventy-eight or eighty degrees. In July 1816 John Mitchell, a physician, visited the Methodist Sunday School in Brawley Street, Bank Top, to assess the number of students that were employed in mill work and the state of their health. Of the 818 children present, almost equal numbers of girls and boys, 269 were factory workers and 116 of those were sickly. The general appearance of the factory children was 'pale and inanimate... There is a very peculiar hoarseness and hollowness of voice... which seems to indicate that the lungs are affected.'[28] Thomas Bellot, a Manchester surgeon, attested that it was not uncommon for factory children 'to be checked in their growth, to

Lithograph of Market Street, Manchester, by Henry Gould, 1821.
(Chetham's Library, Manchester)

become lame and deformed in their legs... and eventually to die of consumption' as a result of 'their long confinement in heated and ill-ventilated rooms, and of their being constantly on their legs during their long hours of labour'.[29] He also describes the factory workers among the Sunday School children of St John's district as 'for the most part, low, slender, and in general much emaciated'.[30] All the medical men commenting on the health and appearance of the factory children were struck and, in many cases, openly distressed by the dramatic contrast in the condition of these children and those who worked in other trades. If the children survived, they would continue in the factories as adult workers.

With the factories and associated services came housing.[31] The Ancoats area quickly achieved equal distinction, alongside the density and scale of its factories, for its large expanses of terraced houses for the workers. Factory owners tended to house only their key employees, while the average worker lived in housing built by speculators. There were two typical designs. The first model involved two rows of housing back to back, as seen on Portugal Street and Silk Street, and the second consisted of one-up, one-down terraces, literally houses of two storeys with a single room on each. With the back-to-backs, windows and doors were in the front facade, while the rear shared wall was solid, allowing only limited natural light to enter the rooms. Ancoats housing usually had two main floors, although attic workshops also existed. The rapid rise in rents between 1807 and 1815 meant that basements were often let to separate families. To help make ends meet, families or couples often took in lodgers. Housing was, therefore, cheek by jowl, with individual properties crammed with family and strangers. One small benefit of a concentration of workers' housing within a small area was that the watchmen who patrolled the streets of Manchester at night, would, for a small fee, wake the workers for their daily shifts with a call or a tap on the window.[32]

The contemporary report in *The Times* (quoted earlier) also states that Ancoats, 'created by the success of the cotton-trade', 'swarms with inhabitants, who all share its vicissitudes. It is occupied chiefly by spinners, weavers, and Irish of the lowest description, and may be called the St Giles's of Manchester,' the last a reference to the notorious slum area in London made famous by William Hogarth's image of urban horror, *Gin Lane* (1751). *The Times* continues: 'Indeed, no part of the metropolis presents scenes of more squalid wretchedness, or more repulsive depravity, its natural concomitant, than this... its present situation is truly heart-rending and overpowering. The streets are confined and dirty; the houses neglected, and the windows often without glass. Out of these windows, or in the most airy situation, the miserable rags of the family... were hung up to dry.'[33] Hans Escher, pondering on the impact of industrialization as it had developed in England, observed: 'How lucky we are in Switzerland where we have a balance of agriculture and just a little industry. In England a heavy fall in the sale of manufactured goods would have the most frightful consequences. Not one of all the many thousand English factory workers has a square yard of land on which to grow food if he is out of work and draws no wages.'[34]

From 1810 onwards, male 'coarse spinners' (as opposed to fine thread spinners) in Manchester earned between one shilling and eight pence and two shillings and four pence per day, while the women earned between 15s. 7d. and 17s. a year.* Between 1810 and

---

* The abbreviation 'd.' for a penny derives from the Roman *denarius* coin, plural *denarii*. A farthing was one quarter of a penny. There were twelve pence to the shilling, twenty shillings to the pound and twenty-one shillings to the guinea.

1816, the best calico weavers' wages fluctuated from 9s. 6d. to a peak at 13s. 8d. in 1814 and then down to 9s. 2d. The following year they dropped again to 8s. 4d. Calico printers consistently earned £1 6s. a week.[35] To put this into context, the average retail price for flour (per twelve-pound weight) was 3s. 9d. in 1810, 4s. 9d. in 1812, falling to 3s. in 1816. Potatoes (per twenty-pound weight) over the same period moved from ten pence to twenty-two pence and down to eleven pence in 1815. The price then fluctuated during the year 1816 between eight and fourteen pence. Irish butter per pound weight dropped from 1s. 1d. in 1810 to 11d. in 1816, while the same weight in cheese stayed at 8½d. until 1816 when it dropped to 6¾d.[36]

Although the dramatic increase in factory building, and the associated housing for workers, was radically transforming the spread, environment and character of Manchester, there were still areas in the town, particularly around the Collegiate Church (now the cathedral), Hanging Ditch and Chetham's Hospital (commonly called the College), which, like Ancoats Hall, retained some of their medieval and Tudor appearance. And in addition to factories, the wealth and income derived from the textile industry had funded, throughout the eighteenth and early nineteenth centuries, the construction of many magnificent civic and religious buildings, as well as elegant private houses and squares where the merchants and businessmen resided. In 1814 Hans Escher observed that 'Everybody who is well off in Manchester has a greenhouse in which he grows considerable quantities of grapes, peaches, etc. These fruits are finer and riper than ours but they do not last so long. The fruit trees in gardens and parks flourish in a remarkable way.'[37]

The warehouses and offices were located in the centre of the town, around St Ann's Church (completed in the 1720s) and where the News Room and Library called the Portico (opened in 1805) and the New Exchange (completed a few years later) could also be found. During business hours the town centre, according to May, 'resembles that of a permanent fair. The warehouses have long windows but they are not high. This is partly due to the window tax and partly because it is convenient to store goods in rooms with low ceilings. Sometimes,' he continues, 'when I stopped in the street to find out the name of the firm occupying particular premises I was surrounded by a number of brokers offering twist and calico for sale. The cotton exchange in the market place is very busy.' He concludes, 'As in London, so in Manchester it is possible to get the news from all over the world at the exchange. The building is open all day. All the English newspapers and the leading foreign newspapers are available. Visitors are admitted without charge.'[38] Other notable buildings in the centre of Manchester included the Theatre Royal, the Assembly Rooms, the Infirmary, the Lunatic Hospital and Asylum, and the Public Baths.[39]

Building work continued southwards. The foundation stone of St Peter's Church, built by subscription and located at the lower end of Mosley Street, was laid in 1788. The church was consecrated in 1794. Designed by the renowned architect James Wyatt and built in Runcorn stone in the Doric order, it had the overall appearance of a Grecian temple.[40] The altarpiece is recorded as a 'Descent from the Cross' by the celebrated late-sixteenth-century Bolognese artist Annibale Carracci.[41] The church gave its name to an adjoining area of rough open ground which, by the 1810s, was in the process of being developed but was still used by the locals as a meeting place. Peter Street had been marked out to cross the field from the church towards Deansgate (a main thoroughfare running north to south) in the west. On the north side, on Dickinson Street, the old Quaker or Friends Meeting House was being extended and updated. As described by Joseph Aston: 'Like the respectable members of the sect which here worship, it is plain, but substantial.' The building had a burial place attached.[42]

In 1816, then, the town of Manchester was a visible mix of old and new, standing on the cusp of the full transformation to the industrial city as vividly described by Elizabeth Gaskell and dissected by Friedrich Engels. Although industry had brought riches and employment, there were obvious winners and losers and, in the years following Waterloo, this disparity would become more extreme, feeding an already volatile political and social environment.

THE CLERICAL MAGISTRATE.

2

THE NEW BAILEY

'The real ruler of Manchester'

Manchester supported Oliver Cromwell and Parliament against the Stuart king Charles I during the mid-seventeenth-century Civil Wars (the Wars of the Three Kingdoms). However, after the Glorious Revolution of 1688–9, many of the citizens of Manchester and, more broadly, Lancashire (with its sizable Roman Catholic population) felt a loyalty to the deposed and exiled 'legitimate' Catholic Stuart monarch, James II (Charles I's second son), and his male heirs. James's successor or usurper, depending on your view, his nephew the Protestant William III, signed the Bill of Rights in 1689 which, among other things, enshrined the right of the people to petition the monarch (or his/her regent) as a keystone of the English constitution. The bill eventually ushered in, after the death of William's heir Queen Anne in 1714, a tentative form of constitutional monarchy within the now united kingdoms of England and Scotland – since 1707, named Great Britain – under the Protestant Hanoverian Georges. But many of Manchester's leading citizens still maintained a devotion to the Stuarts, if only of the sentimental variety. It was over the Old Bridge, via Salford, that the Young Pretender, Charles Edward Stuart (James II's grandson), and his Jacobite[*] or

---

[*] From the Latin for James, *Jacobus*.

'rebel' army entered Manchester in the late November of 1745, drawn to the town by its reputation as a Jacobite enclave and his desperate need for recruits to fight for this final attempt to restore the exiled House of Stuart.[1]

In reality Lancashire and Manchester were divided, like much of Great Britain, as Samuel Bamford recalled in his autobiography. His great-grandfather, Samuel Cheetham, during 'the troubles in 1745... loaded his gun, and swore he would blow out the brains of any rebel who interfered with him'.[2] His maternal grandfather, meanwhile, was ably assisting the Jacobite army in the collecting of local taxes. This ancestor just avoided execution for his part in the rebellion. As Samuel's fond recollections suggest, such ancestral loyalties and family divisions were remembered long after the precise details of the events had been forgotten, although it is also true that the '45 rising was still, just, within living memory and Charles Edward's brother Henry Benedict Stuart (1725–1807), the Jacobite 'King Henry IX', continued the direct male Stuart line into the new century. As Bamford proudly concludes, 'Such were the men and women from whom I derived my being. The rebel blood, it would seem, after all, was the more impulsive; it got the ascendency – and I was born a Radical.'[3]

The peaceful accession of a third Hanoverian King George in 1760 signalled that Jacobite hopes were effectively dead. At George III's coronation in September 1761 the loyalist *Manchester Mercury* described a parade of all the principal trades through the town centre, organized by the local magistrates, and a ball at the old Exchange attended by seven hundred people.[4] By this date a gradual acceptance of the Hanoverian monarchy had occurred across the political spectrum. Archibald Prentice was a partner in Thomas Grahame's textile firm which had moved from Glasgow to Manchester, at Prentice's instigation, in 1815.[5] A proud radical, his thoughts on this acclimatization to the Hanoverian dynasty reflect his politics:

> the doctrines of passive obedience and non-resistance, which had made them continue Jacobites, reconciled them to the reigning family, which had, in its turn, become legitimate, and had shown no great disposition to extend popular rights or religious liberty, or to innovate upon the previously existing relations between Church and King. While the Church had a defender it mattered not much to them whether he was a James or a George; and, until the dawn of the French revolution, which awakened a hope that every governmental institution throughout Europe was about to receive beneficial renovations, Jacobites and Hanoverians, Churchmen, and Dissenters, lived together in tolerable harmony, smoking their pipes and drinking their ale in peace and quiet converse about the progress of their new machinery and the widening prospects of manufactures and trade.[6]

If local Whigs and Tories, in essence the ancestors of the later nineteenth-century Liberal and Conservative parties respectively, had indeed dispensed with party politics, and if religious differences between Anglican 'Churchmen' and 'Dissenters'* had indeed been put aside, for the sake of domestic peace and the betterment of local trade and commerce, then the seismic tremors caused by the French Revolution of 1789, as Prentice goes on to observe, would have put paid to any such amity.

The political divisions within society existed on a local as well as

---

* Dissenters, or non-conformists, in Manchester were mainly Quakers, Baptists, Unitarians and Methodists.

national level, but took on a particular slant in Lancashire.[7] In Manchester, Archibald Prentice wrote: 'There are numbers of persons now alive who recollect hanging in Manchester taverns, boards stuck up with the inscription – "NO JACOBINS ADMITTED HERE."' He firmly believed that the 'putting up of these articles-of-peace boards was part of a plan to prevent the discussion of reform principles in bar-parlours', the tavern being, throughout the Georgian period, the forum for political debate and the spread of ideas.[8]

In nearby Middleton Samuel Bamford recalled his own father reading Thomas Paine's *Rights of Man* and *Age of Reason*, but at 'the commencement of the French Revolution, a small band only, of readers and enquirers after Truth was to be found in Middleton. They were called "Jacobins," and "Painites," and were treated with much obloquy, by such of their bigotted [*sic*] neighbours, as could not, or would not, understand that other truths existed in the world.'[9] This situation would only get worse as the events in Paris escalated. In 1793, in Archibald Prentice's words,

> [A] shriek of horror arose when Louis XVI was executed, not by the infuriate mob, but by deliberate judicial sentence; and another when Marie-Antoinette was led to the scaffold; and all England's chivalry was roused to revenge the wrong to royalty and beauty. George the Third is recorded to have said, 'If a stop be not put to French principles, there will not be a king left in Europe in a few years;' and the nation joined in his fear of such a calamity.

As a result, the 'war spirit was kindled, and it flamed up as fiercely as King, or Aristocracy, or Church could desire'.[10] The effect, according to Prentice, in Manchester was extreme and pernicious:

'Even in assemblies for music and dancing the "Jacobin" and his wife and daughters were liable to insult and vulgar abuse. The reformers were excluded from all society but that around their own firesides, and even there they had carefully to guard against the introduction of the insidious spy; and in business transactions, none who could help it would deal with them. Throughout Lancashire the same coarse manners and intolerant spirit prevailed.'[11]

Bamford also recalled such intimidation and partisanship. As a child, while sitting on the front steps of his home and watching the annual community rush-cart parade through Middleton (a subject we shall return to), young Samuel noted 'a cart more richly decked than others' on which 'was placed the figure of a man, which I thought was a real living being'. A rabble, he recalled, was following the cart and throwing stones at the figure, clearly a type of Guy Fawkes effigy, while shouting (in the local dialect), '"Tum Pain a Jacobin" – "Tum Pain a thief" – "Deawn wi' o'th Jacobins" – "Deawn wi'th' Painites," – whilst others with guns and pistols kept discharging them at the figure.' 'They took care,' he continues, 'to stop when they came to the residence of a reformer; the shouting and the firing renewed, and then they moved on. Poor Pain was thus shot in effigy on Saturday; repaired, re-embellished, and again set upright on Sunday; and "murdered out-and-out" on Monday – being again riddled with shot, and finally burned. I, of course,' he concludes, 'became a friend of Thomas Pain's.'[12]

In 1816, on a day-to-day basis, Manchester was governed by a boroughreeve (or 'reve') and two constables chosen by a jury 'impanneled', as Joseph Aston describes it, by the steward of the manor. By tradition, the boroughreeve was selected from those who had already served as constables, but by the early nineteenth century it was largely an honorary position. As Aston observed in 1816: 'He does not appear to have many duties to discharge, since the actual superintendence of the police is performed, under the direction of the two Constables, by their deputy, who has a salary of £350 per annum, and has under his command four beadles to assist him in the laborious duty of constable in so populous a township.'[13] The boroughreeve, however, did preside at all public meetings, including those where politics and parliamentary reform were discussed, 'which are convened by himself and the Constables, at the requisition of respectable inhabitants, who notify the nature of the business intended to be brought forward'. He therefore had the ability to permit or forbid a meeting, officially at least. To aid the constables, there were around two hundred special constables 'who, residing in different quarters of the town, tend very much to the conservation of the peace'.[14]

Archibald Prentice, inevitably perhaps, offers a different impression of Manchester's civil power, describing it as run by 'the self-styled "friends of social order", who swore by "Church and King", and thought that they better served God and their country by punishing the discontented than by endeavouring to remove the causes of discontent'.[15]

The protection of property was the most important element of law and order – property, among other things, being the basis for eligibility to vote and to sit in the House of Commons – which resulted in a judicial system with extreme penalties against, in modern terms, the most minor thefts by those who owned little or nothing. Transportation, hard labour, whippings and custodial sentences were commonplace punishments. The New Bailey Prison, where the Petty and Quarter Sessions magistrate courts sat, was located just across the River Irwell (at the western end of Bridge Street) on Stanley Street, Salford.[16] Bamford described the prison as a 'Golgotha', a 'building of sombre appearance; with flanking towers, and shot-holes, and iron spikes jutting above high walls; and ponderous black fetters, hung above the barred window, and grated portal'.[17]

The magistrates who presided at the Petty and Quarter Sessions included two Anglican churchmen, the Reverend William Robert Hay (b. 1761) and the Reverend Charles Wicksted Ethelston (b. 1767). William Hay lived in Yorkshire, where he was Rector of Ackworth, but he also held the important position of the chairman of the Salford Quarter Sessions. Unlike many of the magistrates, who tended to be either landowners or, as fewer such persons took up this onerous office, from the middling professional class, Hay had legal training, although he had given up the law in preference for the church. Charles Ethelston (sometimes spelt Ethelstone), a tall man of 'large proportions' who 'spoke deliberately and with much pomp of manner',[18] had been a pupil at Manchester Grammar School, attended Trinity College Cambridge and, by 1804, was a published poet*, the Rector of Worthenbury and a fellow of the Collegiate Church.[19] In regard to his role as magistrate, William Hay 'had formed a high opinion of Mr. Ethelstone's firmness, decision, and temper, and considered him a valuable magistrate. Their views agreed on all important subjects connected with the administration of the law.'[20]

In 1814, Ethelston was actively supporting 'The Book Repository', wishing 'to circulate on a large scale in Manchester and the neighbourhood, amongst the lower classes, at a reduced price, the publications of the Christian Knowledge and Prayer Book and Homily Societies', no doubt an attempt to wean the working man off the radical literature which, as will become clear, was habitual reading material for some. He was also active in developing the concept of schools based on the principle that 'the national

---

* Notably his volume entitled *The Suicide: with other poems*, London, 1803.

religion should be made the foundation of national education'.[21] In 1817 he attended the annual meeting of the Tory 'Manchester Pitt Club', 'where 200 gentlemen dined in the Exchange Buildings, decorated for the occasion with banners, flags, busts, &c., under the presidency of William Hulton of Hulton Park, Esq.'[22] William Hulton, of the wealthy coal-mining family and the chairman of the Lancashire and Cheshire magistrates, also sat on the Grand Jury at the Lancaster Assizes, which covered cases committed at Manchester, Liverpool, Royton and elsewhere.

Ethelston apparently 'advocated the union of Church and State' while lamenting 'the bad effects on the popular mind of Sir Francis Burdett's and Lord Cochrane's political proceedings'. Burdett and Cochrane, the two Members of Parliament for the City of Westminster, were both advocates of reform, Burdett being one of the leading national figures.[23]

There is a description of the Reverend Charles Ethelston in court at the New Bailey, offered by its author F. R. Raines as an indication of his wit, which, Raines declares, 'was generally fertile in coarse humour after the manner of Rabelais and Hogarth':[24]

A servant girl was brought before the magistrates at the New Bailey for having robbed her mistress of wine, and for being found drunk and incapable in the cellar at midnight. Being asked what she was doing there at such an untimely hour, she replied she was frightened, for she had seen a spirit, and had gone there to hide herself. 'No doubt, girl,' said Mr. Ethelstone, with great gravity, 'you met with the *spirit of the cellar!*'[25]

By tradition, most of the magistrates, like Ethelston and Colonel Ralph Fletcher of Bolton, provided their services without fee, considering it payment enough that they were performing their civic and moral duty. But by 1816 a magistrate who was a barrister, called a stipendiary magistrate, was appointed by government 'and with a salary of £1,000 per year sits every day except Sunday in the courtroom of the New Bayley'. This position was first occupied by William David Evans and then, from 1818, by James Norris.[26] In 1816 Aston commented that the Quarter Sessions 'are so busy that they sometimes run for two weeks at a time'. The introduction of a paid magistrate indicates the issues around the appointment and retention of unpaid volunteers, as well as the dramatic increase in workload.

The lists of offenders and their respective crimes and sentences from the most recent Quarter Sessions were immediately published in the *Manchester Mercury*. On 30 January 1816, for example, the newspaper reported that Mary Dalton, 'for receiving cloth stolen from T. Brough', would be imprisoned for two years at Lancaster Castle, while Betty Mitchell received a nine-month sentence for stealing butter from J. Newton of Manchester.[27] On 14 May 1816 the paper listed nineteen people who had been sentenced to be transported for seven years, including William Hart and Michael Mar 'for stealing a blanket, &c. from Mr. T. Proctor', and one individual, William Major, found guilty of stealing treacle from a Mr. J. Chadwick, who was to be transported for fourteen years.[28] The same hefty sentence was handed down to Edward Wild, as reported by the paper, 'for stealing a watch from J. Arnold'.[29] Transportation was usually to the new penal colony at Port Jackson, near Botany Bay, Australia (this term was now in general usage, officially replacing Terra Australis in the 1820s).

One case from the Quarter Sessions even warranted editorial comment, under the title 'Modern Reformers', as follows: 'At the present Salford Session, James Mahon was convicted, on Tuesday, of feloniously stealing a coat, a shirt, and a pair of stockings, the property of his master.' The report observes that Mahon 'urged in his defence, that he was a *Reformer*, and that the prosecutor having two coats, both better than his own, he had a natural right to one of them.' The editorial asks, 'Could the principles of their system have been more clearly elucidated, by the longest harangue, from the ablest orator of the party, than by this simple avowal.'[30] In all instances the likely chairman would have been the Reverend William Hay.

These 'miserable rulers', as Archibald Prentice describes the magistrates, 'were in their turn ruled by one of their own servants, the noted Joseph Nadin, the deputy constable of Manchester', the officer who, Aston records, was earning £350 per year. Prentice goes so far as to say that to 'this man's rule, strengthened, it is said, by seasonable loans to some of the magistracy, for he had contrived to make his office one of great profit, may be attributed much of the jealousy and hatred with which the working classes in this town and neighbourhood regarded their employers, the local authorities, and the general government of the country'.[31] Nadin's character and behaviour, as described by his less favourable critics, has the air of a corrupt and bullying lawman of America's Wild West.[32] Nadin had taken over the role of deputy constable in 1802, having previously been a mill manager in Stockport. At that time the annual salary of the deputy constable was a mere £150.[33] The constables under his command, in imitation of Henry Fielding's mid-eighteenth-century Bow Street Runners, were known as 'Nadin's Runners'.[34]

Joseph Nadin certainly made a powerful impression on anyone who had the misfortune to cross his path. Samuel Bamford described him as 'I should suppose, about six feet one inch in height, with an uncommon breadth and solidity of frame. He was also as well, as he was strongly built; upright in gait, and active in motion. His head was full sized, his complexion sallow, his hair dark and slightly grey; his features were broad and non-intellectual, his voice loud, his language coarse and illiterate, and his manner rude and overbearing to equals or inferiors.'[35] William Harrison, a cotton spinner from Oldham, when asked whether he knew Joseph Nadin, replied, 'No, and I don't wish to know him.' When pressed further and asked whether Nadin was 'much feared in this country?' Harrison retorted, 'I believe he is, and with good reason.'[36] In turn Archibald Prentice declared Nadin 'the real ruler of Manchester', who was instrumental in repressing, 'by every means of coercion, the rising demand for political and social rights'.[37]

One local reformer whose activity was rigorously monitored was John Knight, who had been a committed supporter of universal manhood suffrage and, more broadly, the rights of the labouring class since the 1790s.[38] His family were from the area of Saddleworth, on the Lancashire–Yorkshire border; John's uncle ran a woollen mill in Stonebreaks, but his father, Joseph, was a handloom weaver. John and his brother William were inspired by the French Revolution and the ensuing Napoleonic Wars to enter local politics. By 1812, at the height of the Luddite riots and the hardships brought on by the war, John Knight was living in Hanover Street, Shudehill, Manchester and was central to the formation of a local Reform Society in that year. The immediate purpose of the new society was to petition the House of Commons and submit an address to the Prince Regent, as set out in the Bill of Rights of 1689, calling for parliamentary reform. As Knight recalled, 'The labouring classes of the community, especially those employed in the cotton manufacture, who are almost literally crushed to the earth by the increase of taxation, and the price of every necessary of life, with a concomitant reduction in their earnings, gladly hailed this meeting, as affording them an opportunity of expressing to the executive power, their real sentiments as to that ruinous and destructive system of policy.'[39]

A meeting was called on 11 June 1812 at the Elephant Tavern in Tib Street to discuss next steps. But before it had even begun, Knight was informed that Nadin was on his way with a military force to break up the gathering, upon which they moved to the Prince Regent's Arms in Ancoats. The address and petition had been prepared and the meeting proceeded. The petition to the House of Commons highlighted the futility of the war and the burdens it placed on the populace, and stated that 'the object of all political institutions ought to be the general good, the equal protection, and security of the person and property of each individual, and therefore labour (the poor man's only property) ought to be held as sacred as any other'.[40] It made a number of demands in order to avert 'the annihilation either of the government or of the people... to restore cordiality and confidence between the government and the people; to diminish the national expenditure; to restore to the people their constitutional share in the disposal of their labours, their liberties and their lives; to give them that liberty, practically, which is now only enjoyed nominally, to conciliate and unite the will of the government and that of the people'. And it concluded:

we earnestly and zealously pray that your honourable House will adopt the most speedy and effectual means to restore to this afflicted nation the BLESSINGS OF PEACE! To diffuse the elective franchise as far as taxation; to divide the population of the United Kingdoms into equal parts, those parts to equal the number of representatives, each representative to be an inhabitant of the district which he represents, each man, not confined for crime nor insane, to be intitled to vote for a representative, and to cause Parliaments to be elected annually.[41]

As these eminently reasonable proposals were being discussed, Nadin suddenly burst into the room, armed with a blunderbuss and accompanied by a large number of soldiers with guns and bayonets. Knight and thirty-seven fellows were searched, bound and then taken to the New Bailey, where twenty-four men were put in a single cell 'and crowded almost to suffocation, for sixteen or seventeen hours. We requested fresh air, water, and an immediate examination. The last, however, we could not obtain, nor were we permitted to see either our friends or solicitors.'[42]

They were charged, simply on Nadin's oath, with 'holding an unlawful meeting, combining for seditious purposes, tending to overthrow the government; which he could bring a witness to prove'.[43] They were eventually sent to Lancaster Castle, fifty-five miles away, 'ironed [shackled] together... without any other refreshment than a coffee breakfast, and a glass of beer each; and on our arrival we were put among persons accused of robbery, murder, and almost every species of crime.'[44] At one point Knight was placed in solitary confinement 'in a dungeon, in the tower, where I remained upwards of fifty hours'.[45] During his confinement, Knight came to understand that the authorities were prejudiced against him and his fellow prisoners because they represented lower-class interference in politics. Yet, he later wrote, the 'poor, I am persuaded, feel no wish to usurp the place of their superiors, in an expression of their political sentiments'. Rather 'so acute, so long continued and severe have been their sufferings, that the apathy and indifference of the middle and higher classes, on subjects of the most vital importance to their welfare, and even existence, have rendered it imperiously necessary for them to come forwards.'[46] The thirty-eight arrested and imprisoned were eventually acquitted when the testimony of a paid informer was exposed in court.

While in prison Knight was contacted by the veteran reformer Major John Cartwright (b. 1740), an early proponent of the reform fraternities initially called Hampden Clubs (after John Hampden, one of the five MPs whom Charles I attempted to arrest in the House of Commons in 1642, precipitating the Civil War) and later known as Political Unions. The first Hampden Club had been established in London by Thomas Northmore in 1811.[47] Soon after Major Cartwright began to tour the North of England to encourage the creation of branches in the region, with the aim of bringing the working and middle classes together in a formidable alliance for the purpose of parliamentary reform. The first club in Lancashire was formed in 1816 at Royton by William Fitton, a local surgeon, and others were set up at Oldham, Rochdale, Stockport, Middleton and Manchester in the same year, with standard membership subscription set at a penny a week. Major Cartwright's key innovation, to be rolled out through the expanding Hampden Club network, was the production of the mass petition, a document signed by thousands or even tens of thousands of men to signal the scale of support for reform.

Samuel Bamford was instrumental in the formation of the Middleton Hampden Club and was elected secretary as he was 'a tolerable reader… and a rather expert writer'.[48] In his autobiography he summarizes the extraordinary impact of the Hampden Clubs and the fraternity's founding principles on the working class:

Instead of riots and destruction of property, Hampden clubs were now established in many of our large towns, and the villages and districts around them; Cobbett's books were printed in a cheap form; the labourers read them, and thenceforward became deliberate and systematic in their proceedings... by such means, anxious listeners at first, and then zealous proselytes, were drawn from the cottages of quiet nooks and dingles, to the weekly readings and discussions of the Hampden clubs.[49]

As Bamford recalls, the key reading material was William Cobbett's *Weekly Political Register*, printed by T. C. Hansard, which Cobbett established in 1801, initially as an anti-Jacobin journal but thereafter increasingly critical of the Pitt government. By the 1810s Cobbett and Sir Francis Burdett were the leaders of the reform movement and both venerated Major Cartwright. Burdett was now also the chairman of the London Hampden Club.

In 1816, in addition to the main journal, Cobbett began producing his *Weekly Political Register* in a cheaper format targeting the working man, selling it for two pence a copy. It became the most widely read paper among the working class, as Bamford testifies:

At this time the writings of William Cobbett suddenly became of great authority; they were read on nearly every cottage hearth in manufacturing districts of South Lancashire, in those of Leicester, Derby, and Nottingham; also in many of the Scottish manufacturing towns. Their influence was speedily visible; he directed his readers to the true cause of their sufferings – misgovernment; and to its proper corrective – parliamentary reform.[50]

The power of print, as the Reverend Charles Ethelston understood, coupled with opportunities for basic education – in essence, reading and writing – was crucial to this transformation in working-class empowerment and identity. And just as crucial was who provided this education.

As the reading material of Samuel Bamford and his father suggests, working people's ability to read and write meant that they could not only judge for themselves the radical literature which was targeted at them, but also disseminate their own ideas and interpretation through writing, publishing and public speaking.[51] As the author of two autobiographies, poetry and much more besides, Samuel Bamford is an interesting case in point. First taught by a Methodist tutor, then at the Middleton Free Grammar School and the Manchester Grammar School, Bamford recalled that in his youth 'the Methodists of Middleton kept a Sunday School in their chapel at Bottom of Barrow-fields, and this school we young folks all attended. I was probably a far better speller and reader than any teacher in the place, and I had not gone there very long when I was set to writing.'[52] He continues, 'The church party', in other words the Anglican Church, 'never undertook to instruct in writing on Sundays; the old "Armenian Wesleyans" did undertake it, and succeeded wonderfully.'[53] 'For the real old Armenian Methodists', the descendants of the reforming Anglican ministers John and Charles Wesley, 'thought it no desecration of the Sabbath to enable the rising generation, on that day, to write the Word of God as well as to read it.' Bamford describes the usual timetable:

Every Sunday morning at half-past eight o'clock was this old Methodists' school opened for the instruction of whatever child crossed its threshold. A hymn was first led out and sung by the scholars and teachers. An extempore prayer followed, all the scholars and teachers kneeling at their places; the classes, ranging from those of the spelling-book to those of the bible, then commenced their lessons, girls in the gallery above, and boys below... Whilst the bible and testament classes were reading their first lesson, the desks were got ready, inkstands and copy-books... and when the lesson was concluded, the writers took their places... and so continued their instruction. When the copy was finished, the book was shut and left on the desk, a lesson of spelling was gone through, and at twelve o'clock singing and prayer again took place, and the scholars were dismissed. At one o'clock there was service in the chapel; and soon after two, the school reassembled, girls now occupying the writing desks, as boys had done in the forenoon; and at four, or half-past, the scholars were sent home for the week.[54]

This description sets out the melding of the basic schooling with Bible instruction and Christian worship. As Bamford recalls, the Middleton Sunday School 'was well attended', not just by local children and youths, 'but by young men and women from distant localities. Big collier-lads and their sisters from Siddal Moor were regular in their attendance.' From all around, places like Whittle-le-Woods, Bowlee, White Moss, Chadderton and Thornham, 'came groups of boys and girls with their substantial dinners tied in clean napkins, and the little chapel was so crowded that when the teachers moved they had to wade, as it were, through the close-ranked youngsters.'[55]

Bamford confirms the confidence that such learning instilled, as working men became not only open to the reform movement, but enthusiastic advocates thereof:

Nor were there wanting men of their own class, to encourage and direct the new converts; the Sunday Schools of the preceding thirty years, had produced many working men of sufficient talent to become readers, writers, and speakers in the village meetings for parliamentary reform; some also were found to possess a rude poetic talent, which rendered their effusions popular, and bestowed an additional charm on their assemblages.[56]

The notion that the Methodist-led Sunday Schools were acting, whether by design or accident, as a hotbed for radical thought, as well as encouraging religious non-conformity, finally stirred the Church of England to reconsider their opposition to writing on the Sabbath. By 1816, according to Joseph Aston, fears expressed in Manchester of 'an undue influence, on the part of the Methodists, over the minds of the children, in the formation of their religious opinions' led to a split in the town's Sunday Schools. The schools now fell 'under the direction of two distinct Committees, and are supported by two separate subscriptions', that is, the children of Church of England parents and the children of all the other denominations. Aston believed the two committees 'are active in the cause of humanity, and have many rooms in different parts of the town appropriated to the benevolent purpose of pointing the infant thought to virtue, and teaching "the young idea how to shoot". Near EIGHT THOUSAND children are attenders of the schools supported by the Establishment,'[57] while, Aston calculated, those within Manchester taught by the other denominations numbered around five thousand.

Of the eight thousand educated by the Church of England, Aston describes 'the most amiable… heart-gratifying sights' of these children, 'clean, and in many instances, neatly-dressed', on Whit-Monday gathered in St Ann's Square, 'attended by the Clergy of the Established Church and the acting committee, in order to proceed to the Collegiate Church, to hear the annual sermon which is preached to them'. He concludes, 'For the heart must be cold indeed, must be wanting in the most essential of human energies, which does not swell with pleasure at the sight of so many of the rising generation rescued from ignorance, and its, too often, consequent depravity, by the hand of Charity.'[58] Bamford's account suggests the Methodists' approach was a less patronizing, authoritarian one, focused on equipping children for both the spiritual and practical aspects of life. The gift of learning, however, had already created a generation of well-read, confident and devoted advocates of parliamentary reform from the labouring class, who were now in the habit of gathering to agitate for change.

3

DORSET HOUSE

'The Web of Villainy'

Both the Reverend William Hay and the Reverend Charles Ethelston used informants and spies to gather intelligence on the activities of reformers in Manchester and beyond. They despatched this information to the Home Office in London on a regular basis, for the delectation of the clerks and the under-secretaries, including Parliamentary Under-Secretary John Hiley Addington (known as Hiley) – Sidmouth's beloved younger brother and confidant – and the hard-working John Beckett, the Permanent Under-Secretary. The two under-secretaries each commanded salaries of £2,000 rising to £2,500 after three years' service, and the Chief Clerk, from 1816 Mr T. H. Plasket, a salary of £1,000 rising to £1,250 after five years. In 1803 the number of clerks had increased to a total of thirteen. Among their key activities was the methodical copying for the record of all correspondence generated by the department, including letters from Lord Sidmouth and his under-secretaries, and the filing of all correspondence and documentation, including depositions, coming into the Home Office.[1]

The Home Office occupied Dorset House on Whitehall, a building with origins in Henry VIII's tennis courts, part of the old Palace of Whitehall, later converted into lodgings for Charles II's favourite and ill-fated illegitimate son, James Scott, Duke of Monmouth (executed by his uncle, James II, after the Monmouth rebellion of

1685). By the late seventeenth century it was the office of the Lord Chamberlain, the Duke of Dorset, and remained in the family until the early nineteenth century when the leasehold was purchased by the Crown for occupancy by a relatively new department in Whitehall terms, the Home Office, created in 1782.[2] By 1815 large stones were coming loose from the facade and landing in the street, which led to the encasing of the entire frontage in brick, much to the irritation of some contemporaneous architects.[3] However, the building maintained an appearance of antiquity, with buttresses and corner turrets still visible. Within, the Home Secretary occupied a large office with a generous bay window. Maintaining this increasingly busy and understaffed department in some semblance of domestic order was the 'necessary woman' or housekeeper, Mrs Anne Moss, who commanded a combined annual salary and allowance of £140.[4]

The central role of the department was the keeping of the King's Peace, for although day-to-day responsibility rested with the constables and magistrates of each district and town, ultimately the Home Secretary, as one former occupant declared, 'exercises a general controlling and co-ordinating authority over the whole country'.[5] In addition, during the nineteenth century, the Home Office was responsible for industrial laws, including the various Factory Acts.[6]

By late 1816, information was arriving at Dorset House that would have done little to allay the Home Secretary's fears of an imminent uprising in the northwest. And the leaders of the local Hampden Clubs were accused of being the main agitators.

Like Hay and Ethelston, Colonel Ralph Fletcher, who had jurisdiction in Bolton, maintained a regular correspondence with the Home Office. Notable among the spies and informers he used was one William Chippindale, a manufacturer from Oldham. In December 1816 Chippindale reported details of a strike by weavers at Denton, near Ashton, and Newton Land, near Manchester, which 'has excited a great Sensation throughout the whole of this neighbourhood & it would not at all surprise me if the example was immediately followed throughout the whole of the District of which Manchester is the focus'. He considered the matter to be of such importance – 'if the contagion should spread, many days cannot elapse before the Country [region] becomes a scene of outrage' – that he wanted to alert General Sir John Byng, now happily ensconced at Pontefract, Yorkshire, as the commander of the Northern District. Chippindale had perceived a sudden rise in activity among the reformers,

> & their spirits appear to have experienced a sudden Revival. They <u>have taken four or five empty Rooms for the Purpose of reading Cobbett in</u>. – The lower class are invited to attend & admission is gratuitous. One or more of the Leaders attend & perform the office of reading which is generally accompanied with a short commentary. Every thing connected with them & their Proceedings in my opinion indicate that the[y] are rapidly advancing to an Insurrection & I hope you do not fail to impress this upon the mind of the Secretary of State. They appear to have given up every Expectation of bringing over the middling & higher Classes & all their Efforts are consequently directed to corrupt the minds & inflame the Passions of the working class, whom they now urge to trust to their own Exertions without looking for bid to those above them. The instruments chiefly employed by them for effecting this purpose are Cobbett & the Statesman.*

---

* Unsurprisingly, a few years before William Cobbett described the pro-reform *Statesman* as 'the very best daily news-paper that we have' (*Cobbett's Weekly Political Register*, Vol. XXIII, No. 16, 17 April 1813, p. 578). In 1822 he bought a sizable share in it.

The reformers, Chippindale concludes, consider the 'Great day is now near at hand. – This is again industriously circulated & operates no little upon the minds of the People in the way of alarm.'[7] What the 'Great day' actually meant is not explained, but Chippindale's inference is revolution.

Just over a month later, John Lloyd, secretary of the Stockport magistrates, was reporting on a future meeting of the local Hampden Club, and another meeting he had attended at Macclesfield at which a petition to the Prince Regent was discussed. One of the speakers at Macclesfield was John Knight, whose words Lloyd characterized as an invitation to 'farther & support revolutionary Principles'. Knight had described the response of 'the late King of France' to the principles of reform: 'The King refused Gentlemen – & what was the consequence? Why – He lost his Head!!' The insinuation, stated Lloyd, 'was obvious – The Prince [Regent] refuses & he is to be impeached by his subjects! Such I believe to be within their sapient speculations... They wish to see distress and poverty because they derive specious arguments from misery. They wou'd increase it with the same cold blooded design.'[8] The language here attributed to John Knight flies in the face of his reputation as a promoter of protest by peaceful means, of open public meetings (as opposed to secret ones), and his advice that 'the Language used should be mild and constitutional, but firm and clear'.[9]

Nine days after Lloyd's report, on 16 January, Charles Ethelston wrote to Lord Sidmouth to confirm that he had employed 'Campbell' and 'Fleming', who were considered useful to the government *pro tempore*. Ethelston emphasized that he was 'paying due attention to the caution given me to do this' – that is, to employ spies – 'on a moderate scale', and he alluded to 'a development of the plans & Machinations of the disaffected as I conceive will not be deem'd trifling... when the enclos'd Depositions taken before me are consid[ered]'. He had compared the enclosed document with 'other collateral Testimony procur'd by secret Agents in the pay of the Constable of Manchester' and, as their accounts tallied, he was confident that they presented a true reflection of what had occurred. He also refers to 'seditious & inflammatory publications... preparing the populace for riot & Insurrection'. The magistrates were vigilant and already adopting measures to counter these evils. In the meantime, Ethelston adds, 'I hope I shall not be deem'd obtrusive or acting the part of an Alarmist in endeavouring to afford Government, as far as my humble efforts may extend, such a Clue to the Web of Villainy' in the area, which he is determined 'to unravel'.[10]

The enclosure Ethelston refers to was entitled 'The Information of Peter Campbell of Manchester'. On 13 January, according to his testimony, Campbell had attended a Hampden Club meeting in Eccles, to the west of Manchester. He recalled that one Jones, formerly a Methodist preacher from nearby Flixton,

after a very labour'd & most inflammatory speech, highly calculated to excite sedition, ask'd the multitude what they wou'd do provided the Prince Regent did not listen to this petition – wou'd they lie down & die – The answer was No – No – And the result was to form a Committee to determine upon a plan in conjunction with their Brethren in Manchester to be ripe for execution after they had receiv'd their answer from the House of Commons.

Campbell made particular note of an eighteen-year-old machine maker called John Bagguley, who 'declar'd with vehemence, the country was govern'd by a bad Government & a bad King & a bad ministry – that the said Baguley [sic] vociferated repeatedly the

King Government & Ministry were hellish, damnable & infernal'. Campbell reported also 'that a load of abuse was pour'd upon the Prince Regent'.

Following this meeting, Campbell had returned to Manchester arm in arm with Bagguley, talking of politics. Campbell ventured to say that 'you are well aware, Baguley [*sic*] that Parliament will not grant your petition', to which Bagguley replied, 'I know... but all the multitude who join us are not to know that secret.' 'How', Campbell pondered out loud, 'shall we manage when our petition is rejected – we have not an organis'd body,' to which Bagguley apparently responded that 'three fourths of us are already organis'd for we have been in the Militia in volunteer corps & in the regular Army'. But, said Campbell, 'where are your arms?' Bagguley answered, 'Independent of the Depot in Chester there are 3 places in Manch[este]ʳ where we can procure them; & from our Brethren in Sheffield we can get any quantity as well as from Birmingham where we have Friends in great numbers with whom we are in constant & regular correspondences.'

That evening, Campbell attended another meeting at New Islington, in 'the Garretts', where 'a very numerous Body were collected'. John Bagguley spoke at length 'of the enormous revenue of the Prince, whom he abus'd as the most infamous of Characters'. Other speakers, more measured in their language, 'blam'd Baguley [*sic*] for his openness & said he shou'd be sly & cautious tho' they allow'd what he said to be right & proper.'[11]

All this signalled to Sidmouth and his helpers that the Hampden Clubs, active purveyors and disseminators of Cobbett's revolutionary rantings, as they saw it, were a new and significant threat to the nation's tranquillity. Cobbett himself decried the lies, in his opinion, that were being viciously and perniciously circulated against the fraternities:

It is also a very scandalous falsehood to say, that the HAMPDEN CLUBS, or any of the Reformers, endeavour to urge the people to compel the *state* (the *parliament*, is meant, I suppose) by *force of arms*, to an immediate submission to their demands. We have uniformly, and, hitherto, most successfully, exhorted the people to adhere to a peaceable and orderly conduct. Such a falsehood as this, therefore, merits public execration, though the promulgation of it cannot fail to shew the badness of the cause of our enemies, who, unless their cause were desperate, would not resort to any falsehood at all.[12]

An event would soon occur that would bring these tensions to a head.

4

WESTMINSTER

'The great Babylon'

Sir Francis Burdett, chairman of the London Hampden Club, called upon delegates from affiliated clubs to meet at the Crown and Anchor Tavern, a regular venue for radical meetings situated on the Strand in Westminster, on 24 January 1817. The purpose was to discuss and agree what reforms they should collectively be petitioning for. Printed petitions had been organized in advance by Major Cartwright, to be presented to the House of Commons at the State Opening of Parliament later that month.

Samuel Bamford was chosen to be the Middleton delegate and proceeded south to the great Metropolis, or, as he called it, 'the great Babylon'.[1] He arrived by coach at the Elephant and Castle and was immediately escorted to his lodgings in Buckingham Gate* by William Benbow, a shoemaker from Birch near Middleton and himself a leading radical. Having refreshed himself after his journey, Bamford and his companion walked through St James's Park, passing the tree-lined canal populated by pelicans (originally a gift from the Russian ambassador to Charles II), and then east along the Strand to the Crown and Anchor. Here, Bamford wrote, 'whilst I stood gazing around a large hall, which seemed wonderfully

---

* Buckingham Gate runs alongside what was then Buckingham House – now Palace.

grand and silent in a tavern, a gentleman came out of a room and accosted my companion, who increased my curiosity, and awe by pronouncing the name of Mr. Hunt… This was an event in my life. Of Mr. Hunt I had imbibed a high opinion; and his first appearance did not diminish my expectations.'[2]

The gentleman concerned, Henry 'Orator' Hunt,* was undoubtedly one of the most gifted, charismatic and persistent of all the late Georgian radicals. Bamford recalled his first encounter with this famous individual:

> He was gentlemanly in his manner and attire; six feet and better in height, and extremely well formed. He was dressed in a blue lapelled coat, light waistcoat and kerseys, and topped boots; his leg and foot were about the firmest and neatest I ever saw. He wore his own hair; it was in moderate quantity, and a little grey. His features were regular, and there was a kind of youthful blandness about them which, in amicable discussion, gave his face a most agreeable expression. His lips were delicately thin, and receding; but there was a dumb[†] utterance about them which in all the portraits I have seen of him was never truly copied.[3]

In January 1817 Henry Hunt was in his mid-forties and at the height of his political powers as a leading exponent of a new and powerful tactic in the cause of radical reform: the mass meeting. Hunt had demonstrated at Spa Fields, within the Islington district of London, in November and December 1816 that very large

---

* The nickname was coined by the poet Robert Southey in 1816.
† The use of 'blandness' and 'dumb' might seem harsh, if interpreted in the modern sense, but in period parlance the former meant 'suavity, mild or soothing quality' and the latter simply 'silent' or 'unspoken'. See the *Oxford English Dictionary*.

gatherings of people – as many as one hundred thousand by some calculations – could assemble, peaceably, to hear invited speakers. Public meetings held on open ground, rather than in privately hired rooms, were, by their nature, available to all and therefore far from clandestine. Yet, at the same time, Hunt and other organizers of these mass or 'monster' meetings were deliberately exploiting the laws on political gatherings and the people's rights, as stated in the constitution, with the intention of intimidating, through the demonstrable scale of support, an increasingly intransigent government into a programme of reform.[4] In December 1816, Hunt had managed to stop the extreme radical or revolutionary element of the reform movement led by Arthur Thistlewood, called 'Spenceans' after Thomas Spence (d. 1814) – who had arranged this particular meeting at Spa Fields (2 December) – from turning into a violent disturbance, which would inevitably have led to repression by the state and a backlash in public opinion against the reformers.[5] In the event, the little violence that did occur happened some distance from Hunt, so that he could safely describe those present as a gathering of empowered citizens, rather than an unfocused and uncontrollable mob. That Hunt was able to maintain this discipline while exerting such pressure on the authorities is remarkable, particularly given the growing pressure from within the broader reform movement to consider the use of physical force.

In his autobiography Samuel Bamford gives the following picture of Hunt as a mesmerizing speaker:

> His eyes were blue or light grey – not very clear, nor quick, but rather heavy; except as I afterwards had opportunities for observing, when he was excited in speaking; at which times they seemed to distend and protrude; and if he worked himself furious, as he sometimes would, they became blood-streaked,

and almost started from their sockets. Then it was that the expression of his lip was to be observed – the kind smile was exchanged for the curl of scorn, or the curse of indignation. His voice was bellowing; his face swollen and flushed; his grip[p]ed hand beat as if it were to pulverise; and his whole manner gave token of a painful energy, struggling for utterance.[6]

There is a grudging admiration in Bamford's pen portrait, despite the fact that it was written several decades later, by which time his regard had diminished, and Hunt himself was long dead. It captures the subject's fervent self-belief, striking physical appearance and magnetic oratorical delivery, through which Hunt had quickly attracted a huge following and an even greater reputation. Tall, athletic and with a full head of lustrous hair (a little grey adding distinction), atop of which, when he was not addressing an assembly, rested a dapper white-beaver hat set at a jaunty angle, Henry Hunt was every inch the fashionable gentleman. But in action, when worked up to a passion, a raised clenched fist punching emphasis at each and every well-chosen phrase, all delivered in a lilting Wiltshire accent, here was a man who could not only draw the crowds but hold them in thrall.

History, on the whole, has not been kind to Henry Hunt, probably because he does not fit the modern template of the working-class hero: indeed, in terms of social background he was far from it.*

---

* For example, E. P. Thompson states: 'Hunt voiced not principle nor even well-formulated Radical strategy, but the emotions of the movement. Striving always to say whatever would provoke the loudest cheer, he was not the leader but the captive of the least stable portion of the crowd' (E. P. Thompson, *The Making of the English Working Class*, London, 1968, p. 690). John Belchem's work provides a vital corrective to such dismissive assessments; see Bibliography.

Credit should be given to him for not choosing an easy path in life, but rather the hazardous road to parliamentary reform. After all, many of his background and upbringing did absolutely nothing to improve the lot of the labouring class. In this sense Hunt should be celebrated, as he was in his lifetime and the decades immediately after his death, notably by the Chartist movement, as a working man's – and, later, in his support for female suffrage in the House of Commons, woman's – hero.

Rejecting a life of leisure, the young Henry, as the owner of three thousand acres in the West Country, had applied himself to an active and purposeful career as a gentleman farmer, with the occasional external investment, including the Jacob's Well Brewery in Bristol. The income from his land made him more able than most to pursue his political agenda. His private life was unconventional, even by the notoriously loose standards of the Regency era. By 1817 he was formally separated from his wife, with whom he had two sons, and living openly with the spouse of a former friend, Mrs Catherine Vince. The couple were devoted to one another, but this arrangement left both open to ridicule and the – often hypocritical – censure of their peers. This harsh criticism, particularly meted out by the local West Country gentry, was a significant driver for Hunt's wholehearted immersion in radical politics. His admiration for the writings of William Cobbett would lead to a close, if turbulent, friendship with the pamphleteer and journalist.[7] Up until this time, Hunt had been loyal to Sir Francis Burdett, the key advocate, along with Lord Cochrane, for reform in the House of Commons. However, events at this meeting would highlight divisions within the reform movement, both in respect of aims and methods.

Chairing the Hampden Club meeting in January 1817 was the old reform warhorse, Major John Cartwright, 'that venerable patriot' as described by Bamford, in his plain brown wig and long brown surtout, 'walking up the room, and seating himself placidly in the head seat. A mild smile played on his features, as a simultaneous cheer burst from the meeting.'[8] Through the Hampden Clubs Cartwright had led the national petitioning campaign to present to Parliament the signatures of tens of thousands of disenfranchised adult males in support of reform. But he opposed the concept of universal suffrage, preferring, like Burdett, to restrict the vote to householders and those who paid direct 'income' tax.

William Cobbett was also in attendance at the Crown and Anchor. It was Bamford's first encounter with his great hero, and he had this to say of Cobbett:

> Had I met him anywhere save in that room and on that occasion, I should have taken him for a gentleman farming his own broad estate. He seemed to have that kind of self-possession and ease about him, together with a certain bantering jollity, which are so natural to fast-handed and well-housed lords of the soil. He was, I should suppose, not less than six feet in height; portly, with a fresh, clear, and round cheek, and a small grey eye, twinkling with good-humoured archness. He was dressed in a blue coat, yellow swansdown waistcoat, drab kersey small-clothes, and top boots. His hair was grey, and his cravat and linen was fine, and very white. In short, he was the perfect representation of what he always wished to be : an English gentleman farmer.[9]

The one person who was not present was the worthy Baronet himself, Francis Burdett, a fact of some interest to the assembled delegates. Burdett, realizing that voices might be raised in support of universal suffrage, had chosen to stay away. But the meeting could still proceed with Cartwright, Cobbett and Hunt at the helm.

A journalist from the *Morning Chronicle* reported that the 'Delegates, in point of number, were under fifty, and, in respect of character, with the exception of the Political Gentlemen already named, were the Deputies of manufacturing districts, and from the very worthy class of mechanics in towns', among them Middleton's own Samuel Bamford and William Fitton, the Royton surgeon. The report goes on, 'To speak of conduct during the whole period of the discussion, it was orderly, calm, and deliberative.'[10] Major Cartwright explained to the assembly the practical reasoning behind extending the vote to 'householders' only, in that the details of named householders were readily available, and that the term would include those, for example, who dwelt in cottages, houses or 'flats' (a term used in Edinburgh), whether they paid rates or not. To that end, Burdett had requested that a resolution be presented, by Cobbett in his absence, whereby suffrage should be limited to householders. 'This', observed Bamford, 'was opposed by many, and especially by the delegates from the manufacturing district.'

Henry Hunt, Bamford recalled, 'treated the idea with little respect, and I thought he felt no discomfort at obtaining a sarcastic fling or two at the baronet'.[11] The *Morning Chronicle* journalist reported Hunt's response, which was to make a joke of the term 'housekeeper' for, in the West of England, 'it was understood to mean the old lady who took care of the house (*a laugh*)'. Having thrown this restriction out, Hunt continued in a more serious tone:

What, he would ask, has called forth the animation that now, like an electric shock, pervaded the Empire, on the great question of Reform? What but the feeling of universal suffrage? It is this sentiment that has given the tone to nearly 600,000 petitioners

– that is still spreading, like wildfire, in the extremest points of this Island, and has already burst out in Ireland (*hear, hear!*) Will you, by the adoption of a limit such as proposed, damp the spirit of the whole nations? Why, one-fourth of the worthy persons who have signed these petitions would be excluded. They are not householders. Such a proposition must, and he knew would, shock them – the thousands he was delegated from, the men of the West of England, would withdraw.[12]

The issue was how a full list of all British males over the age of twenty-one could be easily drawn up. The answer was provided by Samuel Bamford, as Cobbett recalled in the *Weekly Political Register*. During the discussion 'a very sensible and modest man... from *Middleton*' stood up and said:

I have seen how much exactness the lists of all male inhabitants, in every parish, *inmates* [i.e. occupants] as well as *householders*, have been made out under the *militia laws*, and I see no reason why regulations, which have been put in force universally for calling us forth to bear arms in defence of the country and of the estates and property of the country, should not be put in force again, and by the very same officers, for calling us forth to exercise our right of suffrage at elections.

'This', observed Cobbett, 'was enough for me. The thing had never struck me before.'[13]

With such a simple solution the tide turned, but not without evident internal bickering, according to Bamford: 'Hunt took up the idea, in a way which I thought rather annoyed Cobbett, who at length arose, and expressed his conviction of its practicability, giving me all the merit of his conversion.' However, resolutions in favour of universal suffrage and annual parliaments 'were thereupon carried'.

As Burdett had refused to present the delegates' petitions to Parliament, another MP was needed. The name Lord Cochrane was aired, although his lordship had refused to act in defiance of Burdett, his fellow member for Westminster. The meeting was then adjourned until the following day. Bamford was introduced to Cobbett, as he later recalled, but his hopes of a face-to-face meeting with Henry Hunt were not realized: 'I was not... introduced to the great man, and soon after he left the room.'[14]

By 1817 the Prince Regent had, for over a decade, taken his father's place at the ceremonial opening and closing (or 'prorogation') of Parliament. Both ceremonies usually entailed a speech, addressing both Lords (or Peers) and Commons, delivered by the monarch – or his representative – from the throne in the House of Lords debating chamber. At the state opening, members of the House of Commons, having been requested to join the monarch and peers, would stand at the bar of the house as the speech was being read out. Now a corpulent fifty-four-year-old, unsteady on his gouty legs, with a chestnut wig artfully teased into youthful modishness, a dab of powder and rouge about his fleshy face, George had been granted the title of Prince Regent since 5 February 1811, in response to his father King George III's debilitating condition, today thought to have been bouts of acute mania associated with bipolar disorder. But Parliament, fearing the prince's general interference if he were in possession of full regency powers, had imposed significant restrictions on him until the following year (1812), when the king's incapacity was deemed to be irrefutably permanent. His Majesty would spend the rest of his days in tormented isolation at Windsor Castle. The Whig party had thought that, once Regent, the prince would support them in forming a government, given his close association in the recent past with leading members such as Charles James Fox. This did not happen and the Tories remained firmly in power.

From 1812 the government had been led from the 'upper' House of Lords by Robert Jenkinson, second Earl of Liverpool. In 1817, Lord Liverpool was forty-seven years old and had previously held the positions of Secretary of State for Foreign Affairs, Secretary for War and Home Secretary. The leader of the government in the House of Commons was Robert Stewart, second Marquess of Londonderry, known as Lord Castlereagh, who had been Chief Secretary for Ireland during the rising of 1798, had been instrumental in forging the parliamentary union between Great Britain and Ireland in 1800 which had created the United Kingdom and, since 1812, had been Secretary of State for Foreign Affairs, alongside Lord Sidmouth as Home Secretary.[15]

Despite his best efforts, since 1795 the Prince Regent had been married to Princess Caroline (of Brunswick), whom he hated with a passion. From 1807 he had sought solace and love, maternal as well as romantic, from his mistress Lady Isabella Seymour-Conway, Marchioness of Hertford. The Marchioness was a staunch Tory who regularly organized political soirées at her London mansion, Hertford House (now home to the Wallace Collection). Such was her power over her needy lover that the prince's political realignment, leading to the dashing of Whig hopes, was universally credited to her. Lady Hertford would be replaced in 1819 by the prince's new favourite, Lady Elizabeth Conyngham, who, the Duke of Wellington believed, had fixed her beady eye on the position of royal mistress as early as 1806.[16] George's daughter, the twenty-one-year-old Princess Charlotte, had recently married Prince Leopold of Saxe-Coburg-Saalfeld. Charlotte was the sole legitimate child produced by any of George III's six surviving sons and, as a result, was hailed – in the words of one courtier – as the nation's 'brightest hope'.[17]

The death of the Whig politician Richard Brinsley Sheridan in 1816, according to the Prince Regent's first biographer Robert Huish (writing in 1830), left him isolated – bereft of companions who were both intelligent, stimulating company and a source of sage political advice. There was no one to encourage him towards a useful role in national life, or to guide him in exercising his increased power and influence. For a while, in the orbit of Fox, Sheridan and, earlier, the great orator and political theorist Edmund Burke (d. 1797), 'his ideas of men and things were not allowed to sink into littleness and insignificance'. Less flattering still, Huish continues, while he associated with 'deep-thinking persons, he was himself obliged to think'. Indeed, observes Huish, warming to his theme, in 'the company of such men, the veriest dolt must have risen some degrees in the scale of human learning'.[18] With these political giants dead, the Prince Regent was now surrounded by intellectual 'pigmies' and 'sycophants', who, Huish declares, 'taking their tone from the royal taste, descanted in rhapsodical language on the manifest improvement which had taken place in style of dress, since that momentous subject had occupied the attention of the royal mind'. Rather than considering issues of importance – such as, for example, the consequences of the Congress of Vienna, which had met in 1814 to consider Europe's future after decades of war – George focused on the 'question of the superiority in point of elegance of the buckle over the shoe-tie... the natural fit of a wig, and the graceful adjustment of its curls, were the topic of conversation, where once were heard the glowing patriotism and constitutional knowledge of a Fox, the extensive learning and impassioned oratory of a Burke, and the splendid wit and elegant language of a Sheridan.'[19] Huish was not alone in these judgements. Even in its report of George's funeral in 1830, *The Times* observed that 'there never was an individual less regretted by his fellow-creatures than this deceased King. What eye has wept for him? What heart has heaved one throb of unmercenary sorrow?'[20]

In recent years, there have been attempts to rehabilitate the Prince Regent, to present a counter-narrative to his dismal reputation as epitomized by Huish's damning assessment. Some point to his lavish patronage of the arts and architecture, for example the Royal Pavilion at Brighton.[21] The pavilion is indeed wonderful and it is the business of princes to be princely. Yet, as the 'father' of his people, in the absence of the king, it remains difficult to defend his behaviour, particularly (even for a prince) his extraordinary self-indulgence and gluttony (the root of his debilitating gout) during a period when hundreds of thousands, if not millions of Britons were suffering acutely. As John Bagguley's passionate, largely critical and well-received addresses to his fellow workers reveal, the king's lowliest half-starved subjects had no faith in and even less respect for His Royal Highness.

Nothing better represents the gulf between prince and people, nor with greater irony, than the events surrounding the State Opening of Parliament in 1817. On that Tuesday, 28 January, the Prince Regent breakfasted at his London abode, the magnificent Carlton House located on the Mall a few hundred yards from the Royal Palace and Court of St James's. Although famed for the magnitude of his repasts, this particular morning he seems to have had a frugal meal, just the one pullet, but with the promise of an opulent dinner on his return. Aside from copious levels of rich food and strong liquor, the Regent was also addicted to laudanum, a tincture of opium, which he took to dull the pain from his various ailments, including gout. By 1817 he was taking 1,200 drops a day.[22]

To offer some context to this remarkable dosage, William Buchan's popular book, *Domestic Medicine*, recommended, for extreme headaches, 'twenty drops of laudanum, in a cup of valerian or penny-royal tea, twice or thrice a-day', only increasing the dose if 'the pain is very violent'.[23] Trussed into his parliamentary robes and regalia, a small mountain of ermine, velvet, gold and silk, with a high black hat supporting three tall, fluffy white feathers, the emblem of the Prince of Wales, His Royal Highness clambered into the ornate state coach, commissioned and habitually used by his father, and set off on the short journey to the Palace of Westminster. The processional route passed through St James's Park and Horse Guards to Parliament Street and the royal entrance at the southern end of the palace.

The Old Royal Palace of Westminster, in which the business of Parliament was conducted, was a collection of medieval, Tudor and more modern buildings gathered around the great eleventh-century hall of William Rufus, remodelled with a spectacular hammer-beam ceiling by King Richard II (r. 1377–99).[24] The chamber of the House of Lords, formerly where the Court of Requests had met, was hung with the Armada Tapestries,* woven in the 1590s and sited here by Oliver Cromwell in 1644 as a reminder of England's resistance to foreign invasion. At one end of the chamber was the throne and cloth of state, under a simple red canopy. During parliamentary sessions the throne was left vacant as symbolic of the monarch's presence, while in front of it stood a clerk's table and woolsacks, on which the Lord Chancellor sat and where the Mace, the symbol of royal authority, was displayed. As

---

* They celebrated England's defeat of the Spanish invasion fleet in 1588 during the reign of Elizabeth I. The tapestries were destroyed, along with much of the old palace, in the great fire of 1834.

the State Opening proceeded the Prince Regent was enthroned, surrounded by the assembled peers in their red parliamentary robes. Perched on the government's front bench, to the Regent's right, were Lords Liverpool and Sidmouth.

The Lord Chancellor, kneeling before the Prince Regent, handed the speech to His Royal Highness, and the prince as usual commenced with an update on his father's current state of health: 'It is with deep regret that I am again obliged to announce to you, that no alteration has occurred in the state of his Majesty's lamented indisposition.' He then set out the broad financial requirements for debate in the House of Commons, and offered his opinion on the state of the nation, observing that the 'distresses consequent upon the termination of a war of such unusual extent and duration have been felt, with greater or less severity, throughout all the nations of Europe; and have been considerably aggravated by the unfavourable state of the season', a reference to the disastrous harvest of 1816. He continued:

Deeply as I lament the pressure of these evils upon the country, I am sensible that they are of a nature not to admit of an immediate remedy; but whilst I observe with peculiar satisfaction the fortitude with which so many privations have been borne, and the active benevolence which has been employed to mitigate them, I am persuaded that the great sources of our national prosperity are essentially unimpaired; and I entertain a confident expectation that the native energy of the country will at no distant period surmount all the difficulties in which we are involved.

What privations His Royal Highness had been forced to bear personally is not immediately apparent. However, he went on to state, in a less buoyant manner, that these admirable native energies had been expended in support of darker forces, insurrection and revolution: 'considering our internal situation, you will, I doubt not, feel a just indignation at the attempts which have been made to take advantage of the distresses of the country, for the purpose of exciting a spirit of sedition and violence.'

He ended his address to the assembled Lords and Commons:

I am too well convinced of the loyalty and good sense of the great body of his majesty's subjects, to believe them capable of being perverted by the arts which are employed to seduce them; but I am determined to omit no precautions for preserving the public peace, and for counteracting the designs of the disaffected. And I rely with the utmost confidence on your cordial support and co-operation, in upholding a system of law and government, from which we have derived inestimable advantages, which has enabled us to conclude, with unexampled glory, a contest whereon depended the best interests of mankind, and which has been hitherto felt by ourselves, as it is acknowledged by other nations, to be the most perfect that has ever fallen to the lot of any people.[25]

It is difficult to argue with Robert Huish's verdict on this speech: 'There is not, perhaps, any official document which contains a greater number of political falsehoods, or which has a more direct tendency to mislead the people, in regard to the real state of the country, than that deceptive compilation.'[26]

After the parliamentary session had been duly opened, having done his duty, the Prince Regent tottered off in his robes and plumed hat to the state coach, where he was joined by Lord James Murray and began the short journey back to the Mall, escorted once more by constables and cavalry guardsmen. According to the next day's *Morning Chronicle*, 'An immense body of people had assembled in St James's Park, at Whitehall, and in Parliament-street to see the procession of his Royal Highness the Prince Regent to and from the House.' The reporter observes that the 'multitude was vociferous', hurling 'the most outrageous epithets' at the Prince Regent *en route* to the Palace of Westminster. On his return, the 'crowing, clamour, and insults increased... cries of "God save the King," and huzzas were mixed with the vociferations personally offensive to the Prince Regent.' To a cacophony of loyal and, mainly, not so loyal shouts and cries, the coach and its escort passed through Horse Guards once more and was proceeding along the Mall when, suddenly, one of the windows of the coach 'was shattered in two places by stones or some missiles, from a hand unseen. It was nearly opposite the Park wall of Carlton House.' It was initially thought, from the manner of the crack in the glass, that a member of the cavalry escort had accidentally knocked a sword against the window, 'but these ideas were discountenanced: an alarm was therefore excited that it might have proceeded from an air-gun. No bullets nor stones were found in the carriage, the opposite window was not broken, nor was any person taken into custody; and his Royal Highness was safely set down at St James's Palace, from which he had set out.'[27]

Later that day, after recovering from this unprovoked attack from an ungrateful people, the prince, presumably, would have consoled himself, in light-hearted company, with the dinner his chef had prepared for him, including four entrées, a second course of chicken and duck, accompanied, if there was still room, by a sideboard laden with beef, mutton, ham, partridges and, a royal favourite, pullets.[28]

Unaware of the events that had occurred nearby, a group of Hampden Club delegates, led by Henry Hunt, were determined to present their petitions. Knowing that great numbers of people would be collected around Parliament Street to catch a glimpse of the Prince Regent, Hunt had arranged to meet these delegates at a quarter to two at the Golden Cross in nearby Charing Cross.[29] The aim was to march down Whitehall to Lord Cochrane's house in Palace Yard, adjoining the Palace of Westminster, and hand his lordship the cache of signed petitions from the North of England and Bristol for presentation to the prince.[30] Lord Cochrane had not been informed of this in advance; Hunt simply believed that he might be amenable, with a little nudge. As they marched ostentatiously towards Parliament, passers-by were told that they were carrying petitions to Lord Cochrane. Cheers then went up, 'and the people ran forward to communicate the intelligence to others, so that before we got to Horse Guards, we were attended by several thousand people, cheering us as they went along'.[31]

As Hunt had predicted, a large crowd had already gathered in Palace Yard. Samuel Bamford observed:

> I beheld Hunt in his element… He seemed to know almost every man of them, and his confidence in, and entire mastery over them, made him quite at ease. A louder huzza than common was music to him; and when the questions were asked eagerly, 'Who is he?' 'What are they about?' and the reply was, 'Hunt! Hunt! Huzza!' his gratification was expressed by a stern smile. He might be likened to the genius of commotion, calling forth its elements, and controlling them at will.

According to Hunt, after some persuasion (and the size of the well-primed and expectant crowd gathered outside his house would certainly have helped in this respect), Lord Cochrane accepted the petitions. Seated in a chair, he was lifted up and, with

Hunt leading, his lordship was carried through the throng into Westminster Hall, 'the old rafters of which rung with the shouts of the vast multitude outside'.[32]

Sadly, events earlier that day had created a convenient distraction. Hunt wrote in his memoirs that the Regent's carriage window had been cracked by nothing more ominous than 'some gravel or a potatoe [sic]' and that the 'venal press' had 'made a great noise' about it. The alarm was carried through to Parliament where 'the outrage was attributed to the Reformers, not one of whom do I believe was present'.[33] For those against reform, the timing of this 'outrage' was providential, with so many infamous Hampden Club delegates from across the country in the immediate vicinity. The debates that should have commenced on the return of the peers that afternoon, 'the great national business of the day', so the *Morning Chronicle* concludes, 'was suspended to make room for the institution of an inquiry into the tumult and outrageous attempt made on the life of his Royal Highness'.[34]

As the Lords' session resumed, Lord Sidmouth stood up and declared to the assembled peers that 'he had one of the most important communications to make to them, that had ever been made to parliament'. At this juncture 'Strangers' – that is, all those who were not members of the House – were ordered to withdraw and were not readmitted. Lord Sidmouth then confirmed, no doubt to murmurs of disbelief, that the Prince Regent's carriage had been damaged 'by a stone, as some represented it, or by two balls, fired from an air-gun, as others stated it, which appeared to have been aimed at his royal highness'. An address to the Prince Regent was agreed, congratulating him on a near escape from what was now being characterized by Sidmouth, and circulating through the loyal press, as an assassination attempt. All usual business was postponed until the following day.[35]

That same day, 150 miles to the northwest, Samuel Fleming, now under the cypher 'S.F.', was providing information on oath before the Reverend Charles Ethelston, which was immediately forwarded to the Home Office. Fleming describes attending a Hampden Club meeting on 3 January at Hayley Bridge near Manchester. Here one John Johnston, 'the Famous Orator' and friend of John Bagguley, made a speech in which he 'observed the Prince will not hearken to our Petitions, but We will punish him by taking his Head off as was done formerly by Charles 1st'. Johnston asked that 'every one amongst you who is desirous of extricating himself from an odious and tyrannicle [sic] Government signify his intentions by holding up his Hand'. All hands were held up; 'the Company were unanimous and said they were all ready & determined in the cause.' After this, according to Fleming, John Knight and others spoke 'to the same effect', referring to the government as 'an infernal Damnable Crew' in a manner 'very fierce & savage'. Against the backdrop of the assault on the Prince Regent's coach, such reports fed into the government's narrative of attempted regicide and imminent revolution.

Fleming then describes attending a meeting in Eccles ten days later with Ethelston's other informant, Peter Campbell, and backs up his companion's recollections already quoted – almost word for word – particularly the striking reference, here attributed to John Bagguley, to the beheading of King Charles I and the like penance happening to the Prince Regent. He also refers to 'old disbanded soldiers' who were now supporting the aims of the Hampden Club by training raw recruits in military discipline. Following the meeting Fleming walked home with 'Ogden the Printer' – William Ogden was a longstanding reformer and well-known speaker. According to the informer, Ogden 'compar'd the Parliament to an Anchor, and the Hampden Club to Men pulling at it – that the different meetings would all join soon and would have a pull all together & pull the House down', by which, Fleming inferred, Ogden meant that they would 'take off the Heads of all the Members of it whom they did not like'.[36]

Further information, also provided by Ethelston, directly concerned the Prince Regent's speech. On 31 January one John England, adjutant of the Newton and Failsworth Militia in the Parish of Manchester – also known as informer 'E.H.' – described walking through Salford between six and eight o'clock the previous evening (Thursday 30 January) when:

he saw several men in the street who were raging [against] the Prince Regent['s] speech, that one of them in particular had collected a crowd round him – that he called out in a tone of derision, 'here is _your_ Prince Regent's speech; and what does he say; what will he do for you? if you are not content to be starv'd at home, he will cut your heads off – there is your Prince Regent' – saith that he endeavoured to inflame the mob and to make the Prince contemptible and odious – saith that the state of the public mind is very bad – that they talk of nothing but a general _Row_ & a division of property.

England also recalled seeing groups of disaffected people hanging around street corners, who, as he passed them, called out menacingly, 'That man has not long to live!' On the way to a Middleton Hampden Club meeting, he reported, some of his neighbours who were attending declared that 'we are quiet enough going – when we return we'll clear all before us'. The 'mob', England concluded, were 'quite furious & determined on Acts of Violence'.[37]

On the same day, informant 'A.B.', a former member of the Manchester local militia otherwise known as John Oldham, swore on oath before Ethelston that threats were being used against those who did not sign up to the Hampden Clubs:

> one Darlington, a Tailor living in Chancery Lane, Ardwick near Manchester said that every one of the King's party who refused to subscribe a penny per week to the Hampden Club would, when the Reformers rose _be hung at his own door_ – saith that in Gorton & Denton, near Manchester, nothing is spoken of but Reform, & that those who would not back them, the Jacobin party marked & declared they would all be murdered at their own doors... that Cobbett's journal is regularly circulated and read; that a number of them are taken to the Clubs and about the Country – that they are exposed to sale as publicly as penny rolls... that the Jacobins are more determined than ever, either to have what they want, or to shed the blood of those who oppose them.[38]

A few days later, at a meeting chaired by William Benbow on 3 February in New Islington and immediately reported back to the Home Office, the informer quotes Samuel Drummond raging against the exorbitant sums of money, from the public purse, allocated to members of the Royal Family and their hangers-on. Drummond rhetorically demanded to know what business one man had with £39,000 a year, another with £38,000, another (surely the king, 'who had lost his senses if ever he had any') with £2 million, and yet another – 'our illustrious, gracious, good or rather shall I say big fat man', which strongly suggests the Prince Regent – with £1,500,000. 'What right', Drummond asked, 'have they with this money – whilst those whom they have robbed are starving for want?' John Bagguley, meanwhile, was using Magna Carta to justify 'the seizure of the King', at which William Benbow swiftly called him to order.[39]

The government acted quickly. Dossiers containing these and similar reports from all over the country, including intelligence gleaned from William Chippindale and John Lloyd, alongside copies of offending publications such as Cobbett's two penny *Weekly Political Register*, were collected and presented to the secret committees which had been formed to report back to both Lords and Commons regarding the incident on 28 January. Less than a month later, the second reading occurred of what became known as the Habeas Corpus Suspension Bill,* 'to empower his majesty to secure and detain such persons as his majesty shall suspect are conspiring against his person and government'.[40]

Lord Sidmouth, as Home Secretary, led the debate in the House of Lords on the findings of the official report into the attack on the Prince Regent. He observed that, whatever the differing opinions, no one could read it 'without the deepest regret, calculated as it was to shock every feeling of loyalty to the throne and of affection for the illustrious individual exercising its functions, and to cast a loathsome stigma upon the character and disposition of the country'. In his opinion, the report contained three key points: firstly, 'that a traitorous conspiracy had been formed in the metropolis for the purpose of overthrowing, by means of a general insurrection, the established government, laws, and constitution of this kingdom, and of effecting a general plunder and division of property'. Secondly, 'that designs of this nature... have been extended, and are still extending widely in many other parts of Great Britain, particularly in some of the most populous and manufacturing

---

* Habeas Corpus – literally, 'you may have the body' – is a fundamental right in English law (a similar act, the Criminal Procedure Act, was passed in Scotland in 1701) ensuring that no one could be imprisoned illegally or detained without charge.

districts'. And thirdly, that 'such a state of things cannot be suffered to continue without hazarding the most imminent and dreadful evils'. Therefore, it was the government's decided opinion 'that further provisions are necessary for the preservation of the public peace, and for the protection of interests in which the happiness of every class of the community is deeply and equally involved'.

Sidmouth also lamented that 'for a long series of years, but more especially since the commencement of the French revolution, a malignant spirit had been abroad in the country, seeking to ally itself with every cause of national difficulty and distress' and that after the Peace, while the people suffered unprecedented strain, 'it had employed itself in exaggerating calamity, and fomenting discontent'. The purpose of 'that malignant spirit' was:

> to avail itself of the reduced and burthened state of the country, and to apply it to its own desperate purposes; for evidence had been laid before the committee, by which it unquestionably appeared, that the whole physical strength of the population was to the destruction of the most sacred establishments. That the distress arose, in a great degree, from unavoidable causes, he apprehended would be denied by few; yet this malignant spirit had represented to the ignorant and credulous, that their sufferings were to be attributed not merely to the ministers of the day, but to defects! in the constitution: the efforts that had been made, and nobly made, to mitigate every cause of complaint, had been treated as worse than nothing, and as increasing the evil they were intended to remedy; and this evil agent, whose deliberate purpose seemed to be to destroy all that was valuable, had at length plainly told the people, that peaceable entreaties were vain, and that by open violence alone could their grievances be redressed.

Attempts had been made in the past to prosecute the authors, printers or publishers of these 'infamous libels', Cobbett's most notably, but these publications were drawn up 'with so much dexterity – the authors had so profited by former lessons of experience, that greater difficulties to conviction presented themselves than at any former time'. Sidmouth cited evidence from the diligent Lancastrian magistrates, among others around the country, to show that in the manufacturing districts seditions 'had been circulated by every possible contrivance; every town was overflowed by them; in every village they were almost innumerable, and scarcely a cottage had escaped the perseverance of the agents of mischief; hawkers of all kinds had been employed, and the public mind had, in a manner been saturated with the odious poison'. With direct reference to the Hampden Club fraternities, he continued: 'Clubs had also been established in every quarter under the ostensible object of parliamentary reform... a very large proportion of them indeed had parliamentary reform in their mouths, but rebellion and revolution in their hearts.'

The Pitt government had successfully introduced new legislation, the Treason Act (clarifying the definition of high treason) and the Seditious Meetings Act (prohibiting public meetings of more than fifty persons without a magistrate's licence), after George III was himself attacked *en route* to the State Opening of Parliament in 1795, when fears of a French-inspired revolution and regicide were at their height. Surely, the Home Secretary observed, the same strictures should be applied after the assault on the Prince Regent? The true question, he believed, was whether it was more dangerous 'to strengthen the hand of ministers for the general protection, or to refuse it, and thereby to hazard every right that was dear and sacred?' Thus, with a heavy heart, he required the suspension of the Habeas Corpus Act, 'to obstruct the commission of the most flagrant crimes, and check the hands of sacrilegious despoilers of the sacred fabric of the constitution'. He asked that this power 'be communicated without delay', for to procrastinate would mean ruin. Accompanying the act to suspend Habeas Corpus was a more constraining Seditious Meetings Act and a new Treason Act, specifically making it high treason to assassinate the Prince Regent. These acts were collectively known by those who opposed them as the Gagging Acts. With the ongoing use of the laws on seditious libel to target political publications and public addresses, the clampdown would be complete.

The suspension of Habeas Corpus – infringing a fundamental liberty of every Englishman, indeed every Briton – met profound resistance as it moved through Parliament. Thomas Wooler, in his new radical journal *Black Dwarf*, one of the publications Lord Sidmouth was determined to pursue, fulminated:

> It is not ENOUGH, that the House of Commons is not chosen by the people – that the nation is racked to the vitals to furnish sinecures and pensions to the most worthless – that we are *forced to complain*, and unable to relieve our present distress – that ruin has enveloped millions on all sides, and threatened to enter the dwellings of all but the minions of a court, and the host of its exactors – are these things not ENOUGH, but we must have more weights added to the burthen.[41]

Even the infamous Inquisition, he declared, showed more compassion towards its victims than the people of England can now expect, 'should THEY SUFFER the Habeas Corpus Act to be suspended… But the Ministers of the English Crown, because they will not lighten the burthens, and redress the monstrous injuries of the people, would forbid them to complain, and punish them for complaining.'

'But', Wooler continues, 'AGAINST WHOM is the Habeas Corpus to be now suspended? Against whom is the ministerial vengeance to be now directed. Is it against traitors?... Is it against the robbers of the country?... No! it is against the people. It is against the LAST RIGHT of the people, that the measure is aimed.' The intention was obvious: 'to destroy public meetings, to suppress the language of remonstrance and complaint – to reduce us below the worst condition of human slavery – to restrain even our *feelings*; and make us like the damned, *"believe, and tremble".*'[42]

The act suspending Habeas Corpus was passed on 3 March 1817.

5

BIBBY'S ROOMS

'Extreme measures'

William Benbow, Samuel Bamford's companion at the Hampden Club meeting in Westminster, had kept a low profile during the month after the incident with the Prince Regent. By the beginning of March, however, he was busy organizing a major new event, in which he asked Bamford to join him. Bamford refused, considering it to be a foolhardy enterprise, 'our first great absurdity', which had little hope of success. The plan was for thousands of men to walk to London, carrying kit for the journey including blankets, from which the march and its participants took their names – respectively the Blanket March and the Blanketeers. In London they would present hundreds of signed copies of a petition to the Prince Regent. The maxim of the Hampden Club reformers, as Bamford recalled, was 'Hold fast by the laws'; with the suspension of Habeas Corpus, it was more vital than ever that this display of mass agitation for parliamentary reform should be legal and peaceful. What worried Bamford, aside from what he saw as the futility and absurdity of this gesture, was the nature of its leaders. He observed that these men, including John Bagguley and his friends John Johnston (a tailor) and Samuel Drummond, 'had recently come into notice as speakers' and 'being in favour of extreme measures, were much listened to and applauded'.[1] All three were part of a new breed of labouring-class radical, products, one might say, of the Sunday School system.

Since passing the Gagging Acts, the government had had a list of reformers drawn up for monitoring purposes and possible action. The names of those from Lancashire, including Bagguley, Drummond, Johnston and John Knight, were provided by the spies and informants John Lloyd and William Chippindale. General Sir John Byng, military commander of the district, was abreast of the situation and would be ready to act.

It seems that the idea of a march to London was suggested by George Bradbury during a meeting at Stockport on 10 February 1817, before the Gagging Acts had been passed. The legal viability of the march depended on a little-known law from the reign of Charles II which stipulated that up to ten people could carry a petition, but eleven would be considered a 'tumultuous assembly'.[2] This appeared to restrict any march to ten individuals – but what if thousands were divided into small groups, each carrying a petition?

Bagguley, Drummond, Johnston and Benbow took this idea and ran with it. By Monday 3 March their plan was fully formed. The petition to the Prince Regent, written by Bagguley and Drummond on behalf of the undersigned inhabitants of Manchester, declared:

> That your Petitioners before the last War, neither felt nor feared either difficulty or privations; but during its continuance, have frequently experienced both; and have repeatedly applied to your Royal Father, your Royal Highness, and the House of Commons for redress, which applications, we are sorry to say, have in our humble, but firm belief, not received that attention, which their importance merited, so that now, when the waste of war is over, our sufferings are become both more general and deeper than ever.

These 'sufferings' were attributed to the rapid increase in taxation and rents, which 'leave a quantity very far short of being sufficient to keep your Petitioners in existence, and therefore their lives are now become a burden, and a plague to them'. The petitioners argued that if the House of Commons was truly representative of the people at large, then the war would not have been permitted to go on for so long, and the resulting increases in taxation would have been checked accordingly. The Corn Laws, the Law of Libel ('which subjects the publishers of Truth itself, in some instances, to great pains and penalties, therefore preventing the publication of the most important Truths') and the bill to suspend the Habeas Corpus Act ('empowering Ministers to imprison without proof of guilt, whomsoever they please, and for an unknown length of time') would not have been necessary.

The petitioners therefore called upon the Prince Regent to dismiss the ministers responsible and to appoint, in their stead, men who were genuinely committed to conciliatory measures for parliamentary reform, who would also economize in every department of national expenditure, reducing the burden of taxation. 'Our lives', the petitioners declared, 'are in your hands – our happiness in a great measure depends on you if you procure the adoption of measures calculated to relieve us, you may then safely rely upon our support and gratitude – without this, we can neither support you nor ourselves.' This petition was reprinted three thousand times and sold to participants at a penny a copy.[3]

The constitutional nature of the petition was crucial. It drew attention to the people's grievances, it offered a means by which the grievances could be addressed, and it highlighted the role the Crown was expected to play in resolving the situation. The Prince Regent was put under notice: if he did not respond as the petitioners desired, then he could not be supported, with the implication that the people would then have the right to act as they saw fit. This petition, setting out the causes of popular discontent and the likely effects of any failure to address it, had its echoes in the speeches attributed to Johnston, Knight and Bagguley that were reported to the magistrates by spies and informants.[4]

Even though the right to petition the throne had been enshrined in the Bill of Rights, it could not be relied upon, especially given the failure of Major Cartwright's efforts so far. Ignoring or rejecting the demands of the people must have consequences. A few weeks before the Blanketeers' petition was printed, this was clearly set out by Thomas Wooler in *Black Dwarf*, a publication John Johnston, at least, is known to have read. 'You have the *right* of petitioning, have you?' Wooler poses. Yet 'while you possess the *right of petitioning*, and they possess the right of *neglecting your petitions*, it is just the same thing as if you had no right at all'. Our ancestors, Wooler reminds his readers, exercised their right to petition the monarch, 'but then they carried arms in their hands to support them'. The petition was only the first step, the second was the determination to enforce it. He offers some historical perspective to support his point: the circumstances that led to the Barons' War (1215–17) straddling the reigns of King John and Henry III of England, and the Civil Wars and Glorious Revolution of the seventeenth century. 'Would *petitioning* have ever obtained the constitution?' he asks. 'How then can petitioning be expected to preserve it. Was John *petitioned* to sign Magna Charta [*sic*]: Was Charles *petitioned* to lay down his head upon the block: – was James *petitioned* to abdicate his throne? Or was William *petitioned* to accept the Bill of Rights? No! No!' He concludes that 'the *right* of *petitioning* with our ancestors meant the right of laying their grievances before the *highest authority*, and demanding, or ENFORCING an attention to their wrongs.'[5] For publishing this article, Wooler was arrested, not for the first nor the last time, for seditious libel.

John Bagguley and his companions had clearly taken such arguments to heart, in a step away from the peaceful petitioning advocated by Major Cartwright and the Hampden Club founders. As Bamford recalled, the new stance appealed to their growing audiences and body of followers. In fact, the relentless rejection of the people's petitions lent increasing legitimacy to alternative forms of mass action.

By early 1817 Bagguley was regularly speaking to thousands of fellow working men at Bibby's Rooms, the upper floor or garrets of an old spinning shed in New Islington, Manchester, accompanied by Samuel Drummond and John Johnston. As described by one attendee, John Livesey, a coach proprietor in Turner Street in Manchester, 'a small part of the Room at one end is occupied by Looms... There was a Table by way of Hustings* and a Bench as a seat on which People got up to speak.' The room itself was 'near 50 Yards long and 9 Yards wide' and, in Livesey's words, invariably 'very crowded'.[6] During the period before the suspension of Habeas Corpus, Bagguley and his companions had been using language more radical in both tone and content, and this continued, according to the spies, even after that legal protection had been removed. It is impossible that Bagguley *et al* were unaware that they were being regularly watched and reported on; evidently, they either courted danger or had come to disregard it.

---

* Hustings: the temporary platform from which a speaker addressed a crowd, and, more specifically, where the nomination of candidates for Parliament was made and where the candidate addressed the electorate. See *OED*.

John Livesey was also present at a preparatory meeting, held on St Peter's Field at midday on Monday 3 March, to make plans for the journey to London. Livesey's testimony gives some sense of the manner in which these meetings were organized, as well as the rhetoric used. He says that Samuel Drummond, alongside Bagguley on the hustings, 'appeared to be rather intoxicated and principally spoke against the Police'. It appears that Bradbury, who had suggested the march in the first place, 'was drunk also'.[7] (It is not clear whether Livesey means that they were literally 'in liquor' or, given the occasion, euphoric.) Bagguley rose to his feet and declaimed, 'Gentlemen you have met here different times, and what you have resolved will have no effect, therefore I think it is high time to come to a determination. I now propose that you meet here at 9 o'clock on Monday morning this day week, in order to go to London with your Petitions… as many of you as are willing to undertake this journey.' He requested the gathering to 'signify the same by holding up your hands', and the majority did so to loud cheers. To test their resolve, Bagguley proceeded to set out the difficulties facing the marchers. The spring weather was decidedly inclement. And what of their loved ones? 'Can you leave your Wives and Children and tear yourselves from all Friends to go and claim those Rights your Ancestors got for you?' He paused, looking around, and continued, 'I say will you turn back when you go to Stockport or when you come to face those high and cold Hills in Derbyshire?' This met with the universal response of, 'No, No', Bagguley then asked: 'will you stick fast to your Leaders?' Came the answer, 'We will, We will.'

Bagguley paused again, pleased and encouraged by the response. So, he went on, 'you must bring each of you a Blanket, you must consider it will take each of you 6 days to go, and your Number will be too great for any accommodation on the Road. Therefore you must expect to be down on the ground at Nights.' He stressed that they must keep within their designated teams of ten to stay within the law. He then moved on to the issue of loss of earnings for those on the march: 'Now, are you willing for those that can earn 10 shillings per week to give five shillings of that money to his Wife and family while he is away (Cries from all sides Yes, Yes).' Above all, Bagguley emphasized, 'conduct yourselves peaceably and show an example to the Police Fiends... We do nothing to be afraid of. We come out in the open air. We have nothing to say, but so that every one may hear.' He ended his speech triumphantly, ''Tis Liberty we will have.'[8]

When the meeting resumed after an adjournment, a Mr Pilkington objected to the plans that had been agreed earlier, pointing out the obvious difficulties arising from the weather conditions, while doubting that sustenance and shelter for thousands of men could be guaranteed over the entire 150-mile journey. But he was shouted down with cries of 'off with him!' Livesey believed the speaker made himself unpopular by presenting the undertaking in 'too black a character'.[9] William Benbow then stood up and said that 'if every man came forward to the Public meeting on Monday next, with the same true English Heart as he had, he was bold enough to say, they would be free in another month, for he was determined to be free or lose his life in the attempt'. This was followed by three loud hurrahs.[10]

Bagguley spoke next, to cries of 'Baguley [sic] for ever'![11] He declared that he was a reformer, a republican and leveller,* and that he would 'never give it up till we have establish'd a Republican Government'.[12] At this declaration the other speakers, fearing

---

* At the time of the Civil War, the Levellers had demanded social reform, religious freedom and the abolition of the monarchy.

accusations of sedition, attempted to check him. In response, Bagguley 'turn'd the Oration', saying that he wanted his rights and his liberty 'and on these grounds he called himself a Republican & Leveller'.[13]

Bagguley went on to describe spies – some of which were present in the room – 'in the blackest terms'. He then turned his fire on the corruption 'of those infernal diabolical fiends of Hell', meaning the government, including Lord Castlereagh, whom he termed the 'Murderer', a reference to the brutal quelling of the Irish rising of 1798. He exhorted the gathering to be firm, and echoed Benbow's phrase, 'I am determined to be free or die in the attempt.' However, should the leaders be arrested during the march, he asked those present to 'come forward and rescue us'. This was greeted with more loud cheers: 'we will, we will!'[14]

By 6 March the resolution to keep the peace seems to have weakened. Johnston, Bagguley and another of their comrades, Joseph Mitchell from Liverpool, were once again holding a programme of meetings at Bibby's Rooms to garner support. John Livesey was in the audience. Johnston stood up and commenced his address: 'Gentlemen if you set off from Manchester in the way proposed you will not get 3 Miles without an attempt to stop you.' Surrounded by the police and perhaps soldiers, the marchers would be easy prey, – 'if', that is, 'you have nothing but your open hands [long and significant pause] you may rest assured it will be the Case so look for nothing else.' The implication, in Livesey's recollection at least, was that the marchers should come armed.[15]

John Bagguley, the star speaker, then rose to his feet: 'Gentlemen I think it necessary to say something to our observers, Police Hirelings who are come here to pick up any thing they can – I would not have them to tell no lies – there were two of them kept an eye on me & my Friend to day & seem'd to pursue us.'

Bagguley proceeded to describe how he and his companion outran the 'hirelings' because 'our Legs was longer than theirs!'[16] Laughter followed. Bagguley then underlined the need for the march to be conducted in an orderly fashion, and for the marchers to organize themselves in groups of ten: 'I wish you to be ruled by Constitutional Laws or I will not go a yard with you.' He appealed to the men to 'bear each others Burden as well as you can by Keeping one regular mode of Conduct & be like the Egyptians in the Wilderness and their noble Leader: I mean Moses – who was determined to hazard all hardship that might befall them.' (This analogy of the Old Testament prophet leading the Israelites out of slavery was typical of the biblical references with which Bagguley and Drummond scattered their speeches.) Would they turn back if there was a 'Hail Storm or Rain'? Once again there came cries of 'no We will not!' Bagguley assured them, 'I will go with you & stick while a drop of Blood will circulate in these Veins.' As he said this he stretched out one arm theatrically, to wild cheering and applause.[17] Bagguley reminded the thousands gathered that the scriptures state 'do not kill – Remember this and also do not steal.' Finally, 'When you have got your liberty be not so ready to applaud for you must keep Equality in your minds and consider yourselves equal to any one – The King is but a Man and you are Men.'[18]

On the evening of the 8 March, two days prior to the great event, another meeting was held at Bibby's Rooms, with the local spinner from Houldsworth mill, Elijah Dixon, in the chair.[19] Around two thousand people were recorded as being present, all gathered, as on the previous occasions, after a long day's labour. Bagguley, the popular hero, spoke again, offering a few last pieces of advice for the marchers. Given the weather, he advised that they should come in their warmest clothes. If anyone had two pairs of shoes, he might consider lending one pair to a fellow marcher who had none, or 'if any one hath 2 Coats he will let his Friends have one'. This is a poignant indication of the poverty of many of the participants. Bagguley reminded them that they were to gather in groups of ten, each of which would carry a petition signed by twenty neighbours: 'you must wrap it up in a piece of Brown Paper and tie it round your right arm with a bow of white tape and come with your things on your back with your 10th man being the chosen man with the Petition on his right arm.' Finally, 'You must shew great Fortitude and I exhort you to be steady & quiet.'[20]

A man from the crowd then advanced towards the front of the room, saying he was from Middleton and that many of his neighbours and fellow townsfolk would be joining the march on Monday. He then said in a hostile manner, 'England expects every Man to do his Duty.'* Immediately the chairman stood up and told the gathering, 'I do not know what the man means by saying England expects every man to do his Duty – it appears to me that there is some fighting meaning in this.' The crowd shouted in response, 'No, No. No!'[21]

The spies and informants standing among the crowd, of course, relayed everything to local magistrates, including the Reverend Charles Ethelston. Anxious at what they reported, Manchester's stipendiary magistrate, William Evans, wrote by express to warn Lord Sidmouth of 'a very serious & general Rising of disaffected Persons' either on Sunday evening or, more likely, Monday morning. Evans believed that 'there is sufficient Material to support a judicial charge against several of the Persons, with whose names your Lordship is already familiar, of high treason, with conspiring

---

* This alludes to Lord Nelson's famous signal to his men before the battle of Trafalgar.

to levy War, not the least of the very high Misdemeanours, to promote sedition.' Evans and his fellow magistrates requested that someone be sent from London, of Lord Sidmouth's choosing, to direct proceedings, 'as they consider the importance of the occasion to be much greater than they are individually competent to provide for'. The magistrates were to meet at the Manchester barracks at 7 p.m. on Sunday, with all the depositions, including Livesey's, outlining the arrangements for the proposed gathering on St Peter's Field and the march to London. At the direction of his fellow magistrates, William Evans had also written to General Byng, requesting his personal attendance along with 'the assistance of [as] large a Military Force as can be conveniently supplied, & applications are also made for the assistance of the Cheshire Yeomanry'. Evans concludes his message to Lord Sidmouth by naming the 'Persons' he had earlier referred to as Benbow, Mitchell, Johnston and Knight.[22]

According to Samuel Bamford, the night before the march, some 'friends' in Middleton asked him to attend a meeting and give his opinion on the planned march to London. He offered many reasons why he considered the march to be extremely ill-advised, not least the fact that, with only blankets to protect them, the cold and wet 'would kill a number of you, who perhaps have not had any thing like a belly full of meat these many weeks... you would be frozen still directly'.[23] There was also the risk of infiltration by enemies of reform, 'who may be hired to bring the cause into disgrace and you to destruction'.[24] Once the marchers were denounced as robbers and rebels, the military would inevitably be sent in 'to cut them down or take them prisoners'. Above all, Bamford repeated his belief that the individuals leading this march could not be depended upon: 'their blind zeal over-ran every reasonable consideration'.[25] Years later, Samuel Bamford declared proudly that no one from his home town had attended the march, a statement that calls into question the story of the unnamed individual at Bibby's Rooms who claimed to be one of many Middleton men keen to join it and 'do his duty'.

It is clear that Bamford's opinion was sought on the eve of the march because he was considered a leader among the Middleton reformers, but the purpose is less clear. The discussion may have been an honest one, but it might also have been a contrivance designed to trap him into making compromising statements – or even a final attempt to persuade him to join the marchers, with the inevitable consequence of arrest and imprisonment. But, despite the provocation, Bamford remained resolutely aloof from the entire enterprise. Given his reputation as a leading local radical, however, it remained to be seen whether this would save him from any repercussions.

6

COLD BATH FIELDS

'Our Noble and virtuous undertaking'

The day of the Blanket March arrived, 10 March 1817. 'At an early hour this morning,' the Reverend William Hay recalled, 'large parties were seen flocking towards St Peter's Church – the place of meeting – and soon after ten a very large concourse of people (as I have heard it estimated about 12,000) had assembled. Some very numerous parties marched two a breast regularly, & many of them with knapsacks bags &c. The Ground was occupied much earlier than usual.' Sir John Byng and the boroughreeve, with the King's Dragoons and the Cheshire Yeomanry, were on standby, while the magistrates, as Hay later recorded, 'were in a Gentleman's house close at hand, where we had a full tho' distant view of what passed'. Samuel Drummond and John Bagguley arrived 'in a Hand Coach' pulled by their fellow workers 'amongst loud cheers'. At about a quarter to ten 'the orator proceeded to harangue the mob from a Cart'.[1] According to Bamford, William Benbow, who had been a prominent advocate of the project, was absent.[2]

Samuel Drummond spoke first: 'Gentlemen it is with the deepest satisfaction that I meet you here.' Looking heavenward he continued, 'it seems the sun will shine upon us for that God who looks down upon all things look[s] down upon us.' He rallied the resolve of the assembled marchers: 'our designs &

intentions are good the whole of our Enemies shall see and so shall our [Illustrious?] Prince. We will let them see it is not riot and disturbance we want it is bread we want and we will apply to our Noble Prince as a Child would to its Father for Bread.' He promised fervently that even 'if the whole Hosts of Hell come against me I will not sli[d]e an inch'.

John Bagguley then took the stage on the hustings cart:

Gentlemen when I opened my Eyes this morning & the Sun beam'd through the Window I thought it was a glorious sight to behold such a blessing[,] it elevated my spirits to see the Almighty thus favour our Noble and virtuous undertaking – Gentlemen I feel myself delighted this is one of the hap[p]iest moments of my life to see you all ready to go so virtuous and so ap[p]laudable a Journey; there never was such a thing done before[,] if you look through all the annals of History you will not see any like this [–] in the reign of Richard the second about 40000 men went to London to demand their rights of the King and he granted them their rights and they went home again. But they only came a little way from London they did not go from Manchester.

Like the reformers' earlier invocations of Magna Carta, the Civil Wars and Glorious Revolution, the allusion to the Peasants' Revolt of 1381 gave historical precedent to the present actions of Manchester's working men, harnessing a popular vision of the nation's constitutional history. The people gathered in St Peter's Field were simply emulating, indeed surpassing, the brave deeds of past Englishmen in addressing social ills and grievances. Surely the peaceable presence of thousands of the afflicted on the streets of Westminster could not be ignored.

Bagguley warned the crowd that Joseph Nadin and his constables were waiting for him. He cried that the marchers should not be deterred if he was arrested: 'they cannot take you all'. He assured his audience that their rights were God-given: they would 'not be thus tamely wronged of... rights and privileges given to you by he who is the Father of all'.[3]

As Bagguley suspected, warrants had been issued for his arrest and that of Samuel Drummond. Joseph Nadin and his constables, with the support of the military, now surrounded the cart 'by a very ready and neat movement' and arrested them both, along with the cart's owner. The crowd was told to disperse, 'but with no visible effect'. The King's Dragoons, who then cleared the field, arrested another twenty people and found that two of them had dangerous instruments concealed in their knapsacks. 'After a certain time', Hay continues, 'part of the mob was observed to move off in regular march... They took a direction as for Stockport.' They were followed and hundreds more were detained and imprisoned.[4]

A few of the marchers managed to avoid arrest and even continued on their journey to London. Jonathan Hulton from Stand in Pilkington, near Manchester, for example, got as far as Ashbourne in Derbyshire by Tuesday 11 March. He wrote to his parents to say that 'a grate Many have gone back agen... we see very plane they are determined to stop us... a great many of us 'as been put in prison in nearly all the towns we have Come threw'. The soldiers' 'sordes gliter round our heads but the thing is as it is.' He signs off: 'tell all the men that I am in good Spirits as ever tho' I do not know but I may be in prison in ten minutes from now I am a trew Reformer yet and I do not Care who knows it.'[5] Samuel Bamford asked one of the marchers, 'What would you really have done... supposing you had got to London?' 'Done?' the man replied, surprised at the question; 'why iv wee'd nobbo gett'n to Lunnun, we sud ha' tan th' nation, an' sattl't o'th dett [why if we'd only got to London, we should have have taken the nation and settled the debt].' 'Such,' Bamford reflected, 'and about as rational, were some of the incoherent dreams which at this time began to find favour in the eyes of the gross multitude.'[6] Legend has it that one lone weaver actually made it all the way to the Metropolis, and even deposited his petition with Lord Sidmouth.*

Samuel Bamford also recalled an episode which had even graver consequences. The evening after the failed march, his friend Dr Joseph Healey had brought a stranger to Middleton. His name was Samuel Priestly and he had been asking for Bamford in Manchester, hoping to recruit the Middleton reformers for a scheme to set fire to Manchester – as Priestly phrased it, to make 'a Moscow of Manchester', a reference to the burning of the Russian city by its inhabitants in 1812 – as a reprisal for the treatment of the Blanketeers. The conflagration would draw out the military from their barracks, allowing the conspirators to seize ammunition and arms. They would storm the New Bailey (in an echo of the taking of the Bastille in Paris in 1789), release the prisoners and particularly the Blanketeers, including Bagguley and Drummond, and plunder the houses of public figures. In front of witnesses, including Dr Healey, Bamford declared that he 'would have nothing to do with the scheme; that it was unlawful, inhuman, and cowardly'. He sent Priestly on his way, believing him to be a 'decoy' or, as we might now put it, an unwitting *agent provocateur* acting 'under the influence of spies from the police', attempting to lure the Middleton reformers into violent, unlawful acts.[7]

---

* He is variously named as Jonathan Cowgill or Abel Couldwell.

These were troubled times indeed. Bamford believed those with private vendettas, or simply of a different political persuasion, were using the current environment to pass on false information to the police. Men were torn from their families and taken away in chains. Bagguley, Drummond and Johnston were transferred to prisons in London. Bamford had been warned that he too would soon be arrested, despite his protestations that he had nothing to do with the march, while 'John Knight had disappeared'.[8] Knight had already been detained.

William Cobbett, the great leader and inspirer of the reform movement among the labouring class, fled secretly to America. He did so, as his biographer Robert Huish explains, to escape crippling debts caused by the suppression of his publications.[9] Furthermore, every writer who opposed the government, Cobbett believed, 'must now feel, that he sits down to write with a halter about his neck'.[10] It was a simple choice of liberty and survival in America, or imprisonment and ruin in England. While awaiting his ship at Liverpool, Cobbett penned a heartfelt farewell to his countrymen, dated 28 March but published only after he was safely at sea. Seven weeks later, writing from his temporary residence near New York, he produced a long description of his recent journey from London to Lancashire, tinged with the wistful yearning and regret of the exile. In Warwickshire he beheld,

> beautiful white-thorn hedges and rows of ash and elm dividing the fields; the fields so neatly kept; the soil so rich; the herds and flocks of fine fat cattle and sheep on every side; the beautiful home-steads and numerous stacks of wheat! Every object seemed to say: here are resources! Here is wealth! Here are all the means of national power, and of individual plenty and happiness![11]

Yet in the city of Coventry, which he then passed through, there were eight thousand paupers, out of a population of twenty thousand. The local Member of Parliament, he recalled, had supported all the government's repressive legislation. Continuing through Staffordshire and Cheshire, in the warm daylight he noted the same indications of wealth and sources of power – political and industrial – that he had seen in the countryside around Coventry; by moonlight he saw 'those more sublime signs, which issued from the furnaces on the hills'. He saw the canals winding gently through the valleys and the water craft carrying coal, lime, stone and merchandise, while fat cattle and sheep dotted the hills and pastures. All 'seemed to pronounce an eulogium on the industry, the skill, and perseverance of the people'.

Why, Cobbett then asks, are the people themselves, whose toil produces this great bounty, 'in a state of such misery and degradation?' The answer is evident: 'The farmer, instead of giving to his labourer a sufficient share of what is produced, is compelled to give it to the tax-gatherer', who then passes it to the legions of sinecurists and placemen who consume not only the taxes, but the food and goods on which the taxes are levied. The same, he observes, is true of the manufacturer. The working man is left with little to allow him and his dependants to survive, let alone thrive.

And this stands in contrast with the circumstances Cobbett has observed in his short time in America. For here, he writes from an inn thirteen miles from New York, there is 'no appearance of *great* riches amongst the farmers, and not the smallest appearance of want amongst the labourers', whose wages are 'about *two shillings and three pence* (our money) a day', bed and board included, consisting 'of plenty of excellent meat and fish of all sorts, the best of bread, butter, cheese, and eggs'. All this, Cobbett concludes, 'is the effect of good government; of just and mild government, which takes so little from the people in taxes, that they have the means of happiness fully left in their hands.' Cobbett signs off by declaring that the right to resist oppression remains, despite the recent efforts of the British government to repress it, which has 'placed every man at the absolute mercy of any one of the Secretaries of State.' He advocates another respectful petition to the Prince Regent. Should it be rejected, 'it will remain for us to consider what path our just rights and our duty to our king and country call upon us to pursue'.[12] Cobbett suspended his *Weekly Register* between April and June, but recommended publication in July, providing regular support, advice and critical commentary from the other side of the Atlantic.

On hearing of Cobbett's departure, Henry Hunt declared himself 'thunderstruck'. He was bewildered by his friend's abandonment of the cause, as he saw it, and, on a personal level, of himself.[13] All in all, Bamford later wrote with great sadness, it 'seemed as if the sun of freedom were gone down, and a rayless expanse of oppression had finally closed over us'.[14] Healey and Bamford, in the wake of the 'harum scarum' plot to set fire to Manchester, were under threat of arrest themselves. Eventually, weary of this threat hanging over them, they left Middleton together, intending to lie low for a few days. They journeyed north, across Bagslate Moor, west of Rochdale, towards the farmhouse known as Lark's Hole, where Healey's aged uncle Richard lived. Which is how the two friends found themselves standing on Knowe Hill, looking towards the distant speck of their home town, six miles to the south, feeling cut off and outcast.[15]

But eventually they returned home to Middleton. On 29 March Bamford was awoken from his sleep by a request to join Dr Healey at his house. Here he found the doctor discussing with a neighbour the arrests made at a Hampden Club meeting at Ardwick Bridge the night before, which both had attended; they asked Bamford what they should do. Bamford was incredulous, given the prevailing climate, that they had attended such a meeting at all. He advised them, 'Escape for thy life; look not behind thee, neither stay thou in all the plain, escape to the mountain, lest thou be consumed... the cloud which has so long hung over us, is broken, and if we mind not, we shall be swept away with the deluge that will follow.' Healey made immediately for his brother's house beyond Kersal Moor. Bamford had resolved to try to get passage to America, failing which he would stay and offer no resistance to his inevitable arrest.[16] But before he could even leave Middleton for Liverpool, he was taken into custody by Joseph Nadin and half a dozen constables, 'all well armed with staves, pistols, and blunderbusses'.[17] As the handcuffed Bamford was being led through the town in front of a crowd, 'there was a shout, and a piece of brick passed near the head of Mr. Nadin, who, probably apprehensive, and not without reason, of a volley, snatched a blunderbuss from one of the men, and facing about, swore dreadfully that he would fire amongst the crowd if another stone was thrown'.[18] Bamford was bundled into a coach with a dragoon escort and the whole cavalcade set off for Manchester, with the coach stopping occasionally so the constables could search for other suspects. To reach the New Bailey in Salford, they had to cross a bridge: 'Venice hath her "Bridge of Sighs"; Manchester its "Bridge of Tears",' remarked Bamford in his *Passages in the Life of a Radical*.[19] At the New Bailey he came before the magistrates, the Reverend William Hay and James Norris, to be told that he had been arrested, under the warrant of the Home Secretary, on suspicion of high treason and that he would be sent to London for examination by Lord Sidmouth himself.[20]

While in his cell, waiting to journey south, Bamford heard a disturbance in the courtyard outside. 'Getting up to the iron bars of the window, I was astonished and concerned on beholding there my neighbour, the doctor, stalking, or rather staggering along the flags below, with all the dignity he could assume.' With 'his hands resting upon his hips, his legs extended to a straddle, and an air of authority, he shouted to some persons who were laughing at him – "Bring me that bundle I say; I am a reformer, and such will I live and die. My name is Doctor Healey, and I will never flinch, so help me God! I say, bring hither that bundle."' Despite his current troubles, Bamford recalls, 'I could not contain any longer; flinging myself on one of the beds I gave way to a hearty burst of laughter, and soon afterwards heard them conduct his majesty into one of the lock-ups.'[21]

The two men eventually arrived in London and were taken to the Home Office on Whitehall. As he was escorted along a dark passage, Bamford admitted to some trepidation, as it 'brought to my recollection some matter which I had read when a boy, about the inquisition in Spain'. He was led into a room with two large windows dressed with rich curtains, a marble chimney piece and a table covered in books. At the table 'several persons sat there assiduously writing, whilst others fixed attentive looks upon me. I was motioned to advance to the bottom of the table, and did so.'[22] Lord Sidmouth sat at the head of the table: 'a tall, square, and bony figure, upwards of fifty years of age, I should suppose; and with thin, and rather grey hair: his forehead was broad and prominent, and from their cavernous orbits looked mild and intelligent eyes. His manner was affable, and much more encouraging to freedom of speech than I had expected.'[23] To Sidmouth's right sat a good-looking man in a plum-coloured coat, who occasionally leaned his head against his left hand 'as he eyed me over'. 'This', Bamford informs us, 'was Lord Castlereagh.'

Bamford asked whether he could be given fresh linen until his own could be brought from home, and if he might write to his wife. Sidmouth responded that he should have whatever was necessary, but with one caveat: 'I trust you will see the necessity of confining yourself to matters of a domestic nature.' Bamford was also assured that petitions to Parliament would be permitted.

It was then Dr Healey's turn to be examined. When he was asked to spell his surname, he replied 'in broad Lancashire; "haitch, hay, haa, l, hay, y"', which no one present could grasp. He was asked to write it down. Healey apparently could not write very well, so he pulled from a notebook one of his prescription labels, which stated the following: 'JOSEPH HEALEY, SURGEON, MIDDLETON. PLASE [sic] TAKE —— TABLE SPOONFULS OF THIS MIXTURE EACH —— HOURS.' Both blanks had been filled in by hand with the number '2', but someone had added two zeros to the first, so it read that '200' tablespoons should be taken every two hours. Apparently this not only raised a smile from Lord Sidmouth, but was also a cause of some mirth on the part of the assembled privy counsellors: 'the doctor stood quite delighted at finding them such a set of merry gentlemen.'[24]

This moment of high comedy was a temporary distraction from the seriousness of their situation. The Habeas Corpus Act had been suspended. Therefore they could remain imprisoned, without prospect of a trial, until the Home Secretary saw fit to try them or release them. This could be months. The prisoners were all moved to Cold Bath Fields House of Correction in Clerkenwell, where Samuel Drummond and John Bagguley were also being held, the former 'seemingly in good health and spirits'. Having eaten a fine dinner of beef and bread, washed down with eight pots of porter, they were escorted to a room which, Bamford recalls, if it had not been for the bars at the window, could have been mistaken for a comfortable barracks. They stirred the fire, pulled their seats up around it and talked together of their home, friends and loved ones. Before retiring to bed, the group sang the reformers' Union Hymn, written by Bamford a few months before:

Ye Bards of Britain, strike the lyre,
And sing the happy Union;
In strains of patriotic fire,
O sing the happy Union.
Not distant is the welcome day,
When woe, and want, and tyranny,
Shall from our Isle be swept away,
The grand epoch of Liberty,
Awaits a faithful Union.

Then Britain's Prince shall truly reign,
His subjects will defend him;
And free from loath'd corruption's train,
Bright honour shall attend him.
Whilst foreign despots ever more,
Shall venerate our Albion's shore,
And woe, and war, and blood, and gore,
Forgotten and for ever o'er,
Shall crown a Nation's Union.[25]

'Thus,' Bamford recalled, 'we made the very walls of our prison to vibrate with the shout of liberty.'[26]

While at Cold Bath Fields, Bamford wrote to his wife Jemima, or Mima (his pet name for her). In later life, he would remember her as a 'young woman, of short stature, fair, round, and fresh as Hebe; with light brown hair escaping in ringlets from the sides of her clean cap, and with a thoughtful and meditative look'.[27] As directed by Sidmouth, he restricted the note, in the main, to domestic issues: 'I am well in health... I am not permitted to write much to you... Send my trousers my other hat, white handkerchief &c &c as I wish to be decent.' He also wrote some words of reassurance: 'I have the satisfaction to inform you you have nothing to regret on my account – Save my absence, give not way to ungrounded fears... A Reformers Wife ought to be an heroine, comfort yourself and my dear child & my father.' He signed the letter: 'I am yours very affectionately Sam.l Bamford.'[28]

After several further examinations, on 29 April Bamford faced the Privy Council once more. 'Mr. Bamford, I hope you are now before me for the last time,' Lord Sidmouth told him. 'You will be discharged... I assure you I feel great pleasure in thus restoring you to your family... We are not adverse to the subject petitioning for a redress of grievances; it is the manner in which that right has been exercised which we condemn.' Sidmouth wished to impress three things upon Bamford: 'that the present distress of the country arises from unavoidable circumstances... that his majesty's ministers will do all they can to alleviate such distress', and finally that 'no violence, of whatever description, will be tolerated, but it will be put down with a very strong hand'.[29] Thus lectured and then dismissed, Bamford was free. Catching the coach from outside the Peacock Inn in Islington on 30 April, he arrived home in Middleton on 2 May.[30] He immediately returned to work, 'my wife weaving beside me, and my little girl, now doubly dear, attending school or going short errands for her mother'.[31]

Despite his recent experiences, Bamford continued to hope for a better future 'for every person'. His spell in prison had not humbled him. Rather 'in the ardour also, and levity of youth, and impelled by a sincere and disinterested wish to deserve the gratitude of my working fellow-countrymen... with a strong, though discreetly tempered zeal, I determined to go forward in the cause of parliamentary reform'.[32]

7

DEWSBURY

'First to tempt and then to destroy'

O ver a month on from Samuel Bamford's release, on 14 June 1817, the editor of the *Leeds Mercury*, Edward Baines, reported on a sequence of curious events connected to a rumoured insurrection in the surrounding district in Yorkshire, and the arrest of ten persons near Dewsbury on charges of treasonable practices. The planned insurrection was allegedly a response to the arrests and imprisonments after the Blanketeers' failed march. The report referred to a Mr Oliver inveigling his way into the confidence of 'the most violent members' of the Political Union societies in the area, telling them that the people of London wanted a change of government, and that a plan was in place for a general rising the night before the trial of John Bagguley and his fellow prisoners:

all the public offices were to be taken possession of, all the constituted authorities seized, and the state prisoners released; and that a plan had also been arranged for securing all the military, by which means a change in the government would be effected, without any effusion of blood. It was further represented to them, that in order to carry into effect this bloodless revolution, it was absolutely necessary that the same plan should be simultaneously acted upon in all parts of the country; that it was therefore necessary, that on the night agreed upon, namely, on Sunday the 8th inst. all the military in every district of the kingdom should be secured in their quarters, their arms seized, and that the magistrates and other civil officers should be arrested and placed in a state of restraint, not merely that no opposition might be made to the designs of the insurgents, but that they might serve as hostages for the safety of such of their own party as might fall into the hands of government.

'This absurd and wicked project', as Edward Baines described it, 'is said to have been entertained, and in some degree acted upon, by a number of individuals in different parts of this district; and a participation in this plot is alleged against the persons who were apprehended yesterday se'nnight, at Thornhill Lees.' Among the magistrates present at the examination of these prisoners was the Reverend William Hay.

The second edition of the paper contained an update. Since the first edition had been printed, 'the highly important fact has been communicated to us, from a respectable quarter... the plot referred to in the above statement, has been got up under the instigation of an agent from London, and that the principal offender has been suffered to escape with impunity.'[1] Edward Baines and his young son, also Edward, who was a junior reporter on the paper, had travelled to Dewsbury on a tip-off and discovered something extraordinary. Mr Willams, a local bookseller, told them that 'about two months ago, a person of the name of Oliver, called upon him, and introduced himself as a Parliamentary Reformer, sent from London, to ascertain the dispositions of the people in the country'. This Oliver he described as 'of genteel appearance and good address, nearly six feet high, of erect figure, light hair, red and rather large whiskers, and a full face, a little pitted with small-pox'.

'Mr. Oliver', Williams continued, had called upon him several times, during which he declared that, as it was evident that the government were ignoring the petitions of the people, 'it had now become necessary that they should be compelled to attend to their demands'. Williams informed Oliver that he would not get involved in any action 'that implied the use of force, or the shedding of human blood'. Despite this, Oliver continued to attempt to persuade Williams to attend the meeting at Thornhill Lees, 'telling him at the same time, that *his friends in London "were almost heart-broken that the people in the country were so quiet"*'. At the meeting, the conspirators, including Oliver, were arrested under escort of a detachment of cavalry and imprisoned at Wakefield, 'all except Mr. Oliver, who had the *good fortune* to be liberated.'[2]

After his release, Oliver was seen by Williams's acquaintance, John Dickinson, being approached by a servant in Dewsbury. When Dickinson asked this servant how he knew Oliver, he replied that he had seen him at his master's house. When asked who his master was, the servant replied, 'General Byng.' 'Why,' Baines queried,

such a wretch, the main spring and master-piece of the conspiracy, by which the country has been thrown into its present state of alarm and agitation, was suffered to escape, while the poor unfortunate victims of his machination are held in confinement, is more than we can say; but the subject requires deep and grave investigation, and we call upon the magistrates of this riding, now that we have given them the clue, to go to the bottom of this nefarious transaction.

He ended the report with a heartfelt plea to the magistrates:

We ask this boon from them in support of their own character – we ask it from a regard to the character of the country – we ask it from a regard to the Government – we ask it in justice to the advocates of Parliamentary Reform – and above all, we conjure them to enter into this inquiry, from a regard to the families and the lives of the men at present in confinement, on the information of this prototype of Lucifer, whose distinguishing characteristic it is, first to tempt and then to destroy.[3]

Oliver, whose real name was W. J. Richards, was at some time a carpenter and builder or surveyor and had spent a period in the Fleet Prison for debt in 1816.[4] He may have committed bigamy, among other crimes. By chance Richards had met Joseph Mitchell, the leading radical who had been at the meetings at Bibby's Rooms and who had apparently fled Manchester after the Blanket March debacle. On hearing, from Mitchell, of the activities of the reform movement in the north of England, Richards decided to use his talents for subterfuge and double dealing to act as a spy and *agent provocateur* on behalf of the Home Office. He managed to arrange a meeting with Lord Sidmouth on 28 March 1817 and was taken on, under the Home Secretary's direct authority. Richards, as 'Oliver', and Mitchell then toured the Midlands and North of England together, encouraging insurrection, though it is unclear whether Mitchell was aware or not of Oliver's actual identity and aims.

Oliver told his 'fellow' reformers that he had been delegated by Sir Francis Burdett, Lord Cochrane and Major Cartwright, among others, to inform their friends in the North 'that they were heart-broken at the lukewarmness of the people' – echoing the words he had used to Willams. He also swore that 150,000 men could be raised in London 'at an hour's notice'.[5]

'In this manner', reported Baines,

they exasperated the bold by tales of tyranny and woe, encouraged the timid by expectations of instant and undoubted success, decided the wavering by presentations of national unanimity, laid the scruples of the conscientious by using the names of honourable and patriotic men, communicated to others the infectious spirit of enthusiasm which they themselves displayed, and gave to the cause of insurrection the appearance of organization and of system; – thus collecting together all the embers of disaffection, adding to them whatever was inflammable, and fanning the whole into a flame, that must inevitably destroy the poor and suffering, the ignorant and deluded victims of their infernal machinations.[6]

Oliver came to the notice of the Sheffield magistrates, who, in all innocence, wrote to Lord Sidmouth stating that this man was 'organising sedition, and exciting the people to acts of treason',[7] only to be informed by the Home Secretary himself that '_O_' was a government agent 'employed by me' and should be allowed to proceed.[8] This was damning indeed. It was usual for spies and informants to glean intelligence of such activity, but not to encourage it themselves as _agents provocateurs_. Yet Sidmouth was acknowledging that this was exactly what Oliver was doing, and, rather than taking measures to curb his behaviour, was urging that it be allowed to continue. With the testimony of his servant, even the upright war hero General Sir John Byng was implicated. Oliver therefore continued his activities throughout Lancashire, Yorkshire, Derbyshire and Nottinghamshire unchecked.

As Baines makes clear, Oliver was kindling and then fuelling, rather than creating, the impulse to resort to physical force. In some quarters it was considered a hallowed ancient custom for members of the labouring class to take direct action in response to injustice, should modern peaceful means appear ineffectual or simply too protracted. Rather than Oliver, the real leaders of this sequence of insurrections included Jeremiah Brandreth, an unemployed framework knitter from Sutton in Ashfield, whom Oliver had first met in Wakefield on 5 May and now revisited. Baines's characterization of Brandreth and his fellows as 'ignorant' and 'deluded' victims of Oliver's manipulation falls wide of the mark.* In fact discussions concerning an escalation to some form of insurrection had been in train for months. Even around the time of the Hampden Club convention in January, William Benbow and Joseph Mitchell had been party to such talks. Samuel Bamford recalled that shortly after his release from prison, he met Thomas Bacon of Pentrich, Derbyshire, another Hampden Club delegate, in Middleton accompanied by a young man, William Turner. Bacon informed Bamford of the imminent rising in Yorkshire. Bamford begged him not to get involved, but Bacon responded that he was 'too old a politician to be counselled by one so young'.[9] So Oliver was in many ways pushing at an open door. But his information did encourage the idea that this planned unrest was part of a much greater nationwide insurrection.

In the event three isolated risings occurred, including one in Huddersfield. The most significant, however, was Brandreth's mobilization of the villagers of Pentrich (old spelling 'Pentridge') and the surrounding area of Derbyshire to march on Nottingham. On 9 June one hundred men arrived in the town, bedraggled and soaked through by rainstorms, only to be greeted by troops of

---

* E. P. Thompson in *The Making of the English Working Class* considers Brandreth a heroic figure, a working-class activist who led 'one of the first attempts in history to mount a wholly proletarian insurrection, without any middle-class support'.

hussars. The authorities had been lying in wait for several days. Brandreth escaped but failed to board a ship bound for America via Bristol and returned home to Nottinghamshire, where he was arrested.[10]

It was Edward Baines' investigative journalism which gradually and painfully revealed, between June and July in the pages of the *Leeds Mercury*, that there was one individual connected to all of these incidents – Oliver. Baines returned to these events years later in his *History of the Reign of George III*, but despite the passage of time he had lost none of his incredulity and disgust at the behaviour of Oliver and his ilk and the actions of Lord Sidmouth:

> While the manufacturing parts of the country were in the situation of distress and discontent already described, the secretary of state for the home department adopted the fatal policy of sending out emissaries to insinuate themselves into the confidence of the disaffected, for the purpose of revealing their practices to government. The extreme folly, iniquity, and danger of the spy system will be amply illustrated, by a narrative of the actions of that emissary, whose conduct was most fully developed.[11]

Sir Francis Burdett read out lengthy extracts from the *Leeds Mercury* reports in the House of Commons, severely embarrassing and damaging the government, and the case was also championed by his fellow MPs Sir Henry Holland and Henry Grey Bennett. But no one was held to account, and the practice of employing spies continued unabated. Hiley Addington organized a Home Office investigation into the case, which, unsurprisingly, exonerated Oliver from the charge of being an *agent provocateur*. If he had been found guilty, where then would the ministers have been?

Meanwhile John Knight continued to languish in prison. From Salisbury Gaol, on 17 July 1817, he wrote a dignified but somewhat desperate letter to Lord Sidmouth:

the labouring class in the vicinity of Manchester... have seen very few good days since the year 1792; compared with those they experienced before that period; notwithstanding the vast improvements which have, during that time, been made in their Manufactures: and this excites the idea that some way or other their Interest has been overlooked or forgotten – But that, my Lord, which more than any thing else astonished the Public and raised dissatisfaction to its zenith, was; that when the War was o'er and the People expected, as usual, Plenty to have returned w[i]th Peace, their sufferings became greater than ever; and I understand this to have been the case in most other Towns.

It is the opinion 'of most thinking Men', says Knight, 'that at that juncture, the Populace would have fallen upon their Employers or the Dealers in Provisions, or both; but for the views exhibited by the advocates of parliamentary Reform'. In other words, the leaders of the reform movement had, through their advocacy for peaceful, constitutional means, prevented the very violence that Lord Sidmouth feared.

Knight tells Sidmouth that 'I have long and deeply felt for the Labouring Class; and that it was this feeling alone which induced me to assist in promoting Petitions for constitutional Reformation in the representation of the People, in the House of Commons; for believe me my Lord when I say That I fear the distress of the People is too great to be removed by any Power, less than that of Parliament'. On a more personal note, Knight points out how his current situation has affected himself, his wife and his family: he has 'already suffered severely, in being separated from my family (seven in number) nearly nineteen weeks; and having been myself nearly sixteen of them in close, solitary and now dreary and unhealthy confinement; and my pecuniary affairs ruined.'[12] In a footnote he asks Sidmouth to excuse his 'Penmanship' as 'I am not allowed my Pen knife', used to sharpen his quill pen.

While still in prison, Knight drew up petitions to the House of Commons and was supported by fellow reformers including Sir Francis Burdett. One such petition, presented to the House, made the desperate plea *'to be brought to trial, or to be transported out of the country'*. Knight's case was highlighted by Richard Carlile, editor of another radical newspaper, *Sherwin's Weekly Political Register*, on 26 July 1817: 'He has not been charged with any offence, yet it appears that the Ministers treat him as they do other persons who may be so unfortunate as to come within the reach of their malice, – solitary confinement, and no communication with any person except the Gaoler.' *'Why'*, demands Carlile, 'is he not brought to trial? The reason is evident... He has committed no offence: if he had, he would have been brought to trial long ago.'[13]

Six months on, the leaders of the Blanket March, including John Bagguley and Samuel Drummond, were still in prison. From his cell in Tothill Fields gaol near Parliament, Elijah Dixon wrote to his 'Dear Girl', certainly his wife Martha, on 19 September:

I am fully confident, that I shall be able to prove myself completely innocent if ever I should be brought to the test. But as I apprehend, I am detained more from motives of state policy than from any solid evidence that can [be] brought against me in support of high treason, I am sorry that ministers should think it necessary to keep so poor and obscure an individual as I am, either as a terror to others or on account of any weight that I have given to the legal opposition which the people have made to their measures. I will always protest against all violent and unlawful measures both in my family, and amongst all who know me, you and they very well know. If I have been to blame, it is I think in continuing to support the peaceable petitions of the people for parliamentary reform, when as it appears from recent events they were pre-determined not to listen to those petitions.[14]

He was eventually released, without charge, on 17 November.[15]

On 7 November, Jeremiah Brandreth and three others, including the stonemason William Turner, the young man whom Samuel Bamford had met with Thomas Bacon (the latter was transported for life for his involvement), were hanged outside Derby Castle and posthumously beheaded for their part in the June insurrections. Brandreth remained silent up to his execution, probably to protect the secret networks of local protest, and his defence counsel decided not to call 'Oliver' for fear his incriminating evidence would widen the net.[16] Samuel Bamford gave Brandreth a dignified and patriotic voice through the poem 'Brandreth's Soliloquy in Prison':

> I must die, but not like a slave,
> To his tyrant in penitence bending;
> I shall die like an Englishman brave,
> I have liv'd so, and so be my ending.[17]

Henry Hunt had tried to intervene on the men's behalf: he wrote to Thomas Cleary, secretary of the London Hampden Club, to call upon the club to join with him in attempting to assist them, but no one was willing to get involved. Undaunted, Hunt travelled to Derby, only to be informed by the defence lawyer, Thomas Denman, that 'there was no chance of saving them'.[18]

Oliver himself slipped silently back into the shadows and very soon emigrated to the Cape Colony in southern Africa, under the name William Oliver Jones.* Although he was never officially held to account, much less his masters in the Home Office, the events highlighted both the strength of public demand for reform and the depths the government had plumbed in their response to it. In the opinion of a very wide section of the populace, as Edward Baines articulated, it was seen as wholly alien to the spirit of English law and an outrage to free-born Englishmen.[19] Henry Hunt declared, following the widespread tendency to depict the labouring class as naïve dupes, 'O, it was a horrible plot, to entrap a few distressed, poor creatures to commit some acts of violence and riot, in order that the Government might hang a few of them for high treason!'[20]

This unsavoury episode was eclipsed on 6 November 1817 when Princess Charlotte, the 'nation's brightest hope', died in childbirth, along with her infant son. Three of her royal uncles promptly abandoned their mistresses and bachelor lifestyles, and married: this desperate rush to produce an heir eventually resulted in the birth of the future Queen Victoria.† Charlotte's widower, Prince Leopold, had had £50,000 per year settled on him for life, as Henry Hunt observed, 'in case the Princess should *pop off*'.[21] All right and

---

* He probably died in Cape Town in August 1827; see Malcolm Chase, 'W. J. Richards', *ODNB*, article 57111, 2004/2008.

† Christened Alexandrina Victoria; her father was Prince Edward Augustus, Duke of Kent (1767–1820), George III's fourth son.

proper, within the parameters of the current system at least, but, as Hunt went on to suggest, yet another burden on the public purse and, in turn, on the nation's impoverished, disenfranchised workers.

Jeremiah Brandreth… Beheaded for High Treason at Derby,
by Samuel John Neele after W. Pegg, 1817.
(Alamy Stock Photo)

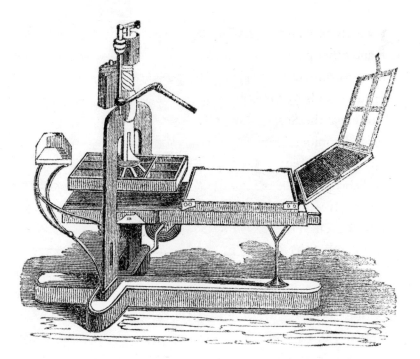

8

COVENT GARDEN

'Hunt and Liberty'

B y early 1818 John Bagguley, Samuel Drummond, John Knight and other political prisoners had been released, an indication of the government's confidence that the repressive measures had been successful. At the same time, Lord Sidmouth introduced a bill to repeal the Suspension of Habeas Corpus Act, as well as a Bill of Indemnity intended to protect ministers from scrutiny once the act was restored.

In February 1818, Richard Carlile published an article in *Sherwin's Weekly Political Register* under the headline 'DIS-CLOSURE OF THE GOVERNMENT-PLOTS AGAINST THE PEOPLE OF MANCHESTER', reporting on a petition to the House of Commons from the inhabitants of that town regarding 'the Meetings of the People and the machinations of Government spies'. It is not, says Carlile, 'what even the Ministry will be hardy enough to call a Petition from the ignorant or disaffected'; it contains 'a clear exposure of the falsehoods that have been trumpeted forth by the hireling press, and it sufficiently explains the motives of the Government in not proceeding with the trials of the "Blanketeers"'. The only conspiracy, Carlile concludes, which has ever existed in Manchester or any other part of the country 'is a conspiracy on the part of the Government to goad the distressed labourers and manufacturers to the commission of acts and outrage, that the former might have an opportunity and excuse for slaughtering the latter through the medium of their soldiers. The Ministers would willingly have butchered one part of the People to have enslaved the other.'[1] The Habeas Corpus Act was restored on 10 March 1818.

The new year of 1818 also saw the first issue of a new publication, the *Manchester Observer, Or Literary, Commercial and Political Register*. While providing the usual material expected of a local newspaper – articles and stories of regional interest as well as reprinting others from around the country, alongside advertisements for local businesses, situations vacant and required – under James Wroe as editor, and his colleagues John Thacker Saxton and John Knight, the paper swiftly became the organ for radical reform in Manchester and the surrounding district. The paper presented 'To the Public' its manifesto in its first edition, declaring itself, 'Free from all party attachments – uninfluenced by names and factions':

> we feel the strongest security for the independency of our political opinions. Others may devote their time and talents to prop the falling fortunes of their favourite party, whether Whig, or Tory; we, however cannot be limited in our support of any portion of our countrymen; our cause is that of the People – our interests are those of the Nation. Happy would it be for our common country, if Britons would for ever abjure all party spirit, and unite in redressing the wrongs which they suffer. If those abuses were removed, which have been gradually introduced into our excellent institutions, neither the people nor the government should have anything to fear; the former would be sured from the encroachments of power, and the latter from the turbulence of anarchy.[2]

James Wroe was born in Manchester in 1789, that auspicious year, and had established himself as a bookseller in Port Street. By 1818 he had a shop in Great Ancoats Street.[3] James Weatherly, a fellow bookseller, recalled in his autobiography that 'Radical Wroe' sold 'Pamphlets and Periodicals' and that 'his stock of old Books was of low Priced articles'.[4] The role of newspaper editor was a departure from the focus of Wroe's business to date, but his new publication gave a voice and a champion to the reformers of Manchester and beyond. John Saxton seems to have had a chequered professional history, but one that brought the necessary practical experience to their new venture. In November 1800, on the announcement in the *Derby Mercury* of his marriage to Susannah, daughter of Mr Hoole of Walton 'in this county', Saxton is described as a 'printer, of Chesterfield'.[5] In 1804 he was named on a list of bankrupts as a 'printer, bookseller, and stationer'.[6] He appears on another list of insolvent debtors in 1816, in the *Leeds Intelligencer*, described as 'late of Sheffield, Printer'.[7] In 1818, no doubt seeking a fresh start, he and his wife, Susannah, had moved to Manchester.[8]

The *Manchester Observer* was based at 18 Market Street, a locality later described in *The Times* as '"Sedition corner"... perpetually beset with poor misled creatures, whose appetite for seditious ribaldry, created at first by distress, is whetted by every species of stimulating novelty'. In the same article *The Times* witheringly dismissed other radical publications, including *Black Dwarf*, *The Medusa* and *The Gorgon*, and those who read them: 'all the monstrous progeny begotten by disaffection upon ignorance, are heaped on the table or in the windows, with hideous profusion, and the money which should be expended in buying bread for their famishing families is often squandered in the purchase of such pestilent publications.'[9] Nevertheless, the *Manchester Observer* soon established itself as the leading challenge to the authorities and

Representation of the election of Members of Parliament for Westminster, by Robert Havell II after George Scharf, 1818. (Bridgeman Images)

the loyalist press, notably the *Manchester Mercury* and *Manchester Courier*. Samuel Bamford not only read the *Manchester Observer* in the privacy of his own house, but also, as recalled by an attendee, Willam Elson, shared reports from the paper at reform meetings.[10]

A significant shift in the dynamics of the Home Office had begun with the appointment of Henry Hobhouse as Permanent Under Secretary in 1817, replacing John Beckett. Educated at Eton College and then Oxford University, and a former barrister at Middle Temple, Hobhouse had been Treasury Solicitor since 1812, through the period of the Luddite Revolt.[11] He filled the void as Lord Sidmouth gradually retired from day-to-day involvement in the department's activities, a change brought on by the death of his brother, Hiley, in June 1818, as well as Sidmouth's own declining health.[12] It was Hobhouse who kept up regular correspondence with the magistrates of Lancashire, Cheshire and beyond, passing on to them the opinion of Lord Sidmouth on all proceedings. As a lawyer, he gave measured instructions or, more accurately, advice. He left much of the decision-making to the judgement of local magistrates – albeit based on principles established by the Home Office – thereby ensuring his department would not be directly culpable for any mistakes they made.

The general election of 1818 publicly highlighted the splits that had formed within the reform movement, which had been evident from the Hampden Club convention the previous year. The election ran from 17 June to 18 July. Only 120 of the nation's 380 seats were contested, one of these being Westminster, lately represented by Sir Francis Burdett and Lord Cochrane. Henry Hunt, with the encouragement of William Cobbett (from his refuge in America), now decided to stand for election there, as he considered that Burdett had effectively abandoned the cause of radical reform, while Cochrane had made it known he would not be standing again. In the initial stages, Major Cartwright was also in the running. Richard Carlile and William Sherwin supported Hunt, with Carlile providing Hunt's colours, 'a scarlet flag, with UNIVERSAL SUFFRAGE as a motto, surmounted by a Cap of liberty, surrounded with the inscription of Hunt and Liberty'.[13] This eye-catching standard was proudly displayed on the hustings at Covent Garden – here a substantial wooden structure, with a raised gallery, located in front of St Paul's Church in the main square or piazza.

Over the period of the Westminster election campaign, Hunt was attacked in the press and, when on the hustings, by partisan individuals in the crowd. The secretary of the London Hampden Club, Thomas Cleary (now Major Cartwright's election agent), the same man who had rejected Hunt's plea for the club to assist Jeremiah Brandreth and his companions – attempted to ruin his candidacy by dirty tricks including crude references to Hunt's companion, Mrs Vince, and even challenged him to a duel. Eventually, after an ill-tempered contest which was divisive for the reform movement, Burdett and Sir Samuel Romilly were elected (the latter a Whig supporter of parliamentary reform). Burdett, however, came second to Romilly (5,238 and 5,339 votes respectively), with Hunt receiving only eighty-four votes.[14] Hunt had been the popular choice among the crowds who gathered to hear his rousing speeches delivered from the hustings, but not among the local householders, who, unfortunately for him, made up the limited electorate.[*]

Hunt, however, was unbowed: he clearly felt the event deserved celebration and remembrance. He would later recall, with justifiable pride, that:

---

[*] Westminster had 12,000 voters from a population of 158,210.

at the general election in June 1818, for the first time in England, a gentleman offered himself as a candidate, upon the avowed principles of 'Annual Parliaments, Universal Suffrage, and Vote by Ballot;' that at this election, which lasted fifteen days, the Cap of Liberty, surmounting the colours with that motto, was hoisted and carried through the streets morning and evening, preceding my carriage to and from the hustings in the city of Westminster; and that these were the only colours that were suffered by the people to remain upon the hustings.

If anyone attempted to remove the banner, the cry would rise up: 'Protect Hunt's flag, my lads; touch it if you dare!'[15] For his pains, the election organizers sent Hunt an exorbitant bill for £250, representing a third of the construction costs for the hustings.[16] He had commenced the journey to reform as a man of means, but his dedication to the cause was chipping away relentlessly at his resources.

Meanwhile John Bagguley, after his release from prison, was teaching at a working men's school in Stockport. Far from being chastened by his experiences, he had returned to prominence as a radical speaker, along with Samuel Drummond and John Johnston. The slump in trade throughout 1818 had further reduced workers' weekly wages, not just in the textile industry but in the coal mines and elsewhere. Strikes were now escalating throughout the region.[17] Capturing the general mood, Bagguley and his friends were reported to be using ever more violent language during political meetings. 'Liberty or Death!' was their refrain, which they encouraged the crowds to chant.

William Boulter described being present at a meeting of three to four thousand people at Sandy Brow on 1 September 1818, at which Bagguley, Drummond and Johnston spoke, alongside the

Reverend Joseph Harrison of Stockport, a well-known radical and now something of a mentor to the three men. Bagguley apparently rebuked the assembled crowd for their apathy, asking whether the 'immortal' Thomas Paine would have acted with such 'cool indifference'. He declaimed, 'If you want a leader, I will lead you, and sword in hand I'll lose the last drop of my blood in the glorious cause of freedom.' He also declared that this would be the last occasion for discussion, for 'they had talked long enough, they must now act: the next time they met would be in the glorious struggle of death or liberty.'[18] According to John Livesey, still busy on behalf of the authorities, Bagguley also encouraged the workers to continue their months-long strike action, 'for it is your Labour that supports everything'.[19] John Johnston then arrived and was pulled up onto the hustings. He declared, so said the informants, 'Oh that I had a sword in my hand to cut off the heads of all tyrants!' Of Lords Sidmouth and Castlereagh he said: 'I am regardless of consequences, and say coolly and fearlessly, I will shoot them whenever I can, I would sooner do it than have a dinner and bottle of wine; I say again, I will blow out their brains whenever I have an opportunity; and if I do not live to do it, I hope some of these women will have the opportunity of tearing them limb from limb.' He hoped that every mother present would put a poker, a knife or a pistol in her son's hand 'and send him forth to meet the death of Hampden,* in the cause of liberty'.[20] Livesey reported that Samuel Drummond called on the people to arm themselves to regain their ancient rights and their lost liberty, and promised them: 'For my part, I will stick to you till the last drop of my Blood is expended.' Finally, 'as loud as his lungs wou'd

---

* John Hampden had died in battle in 1643 commanding cavalry in the Parliamentarian army.

admit', he urged them to 'get all Armed – for nothing but sword in hand will do at all – Oh! Liberty thou sweet liberty is what I will gain or die in the attempt. Liberty or death!' He sat down to great cheers.[21]

The following day, 2 September, Bagguley, Johnston and Drummond gathered their supporters together and marched to Manchester, where they joined thousands of fellow strikers. Despite the anxiety this provoked in the local magistrates, James Norris most notably, the event passed off quietly enough. But Bagguley, Johnston and Drummond were now marked men, with fresh warrants issued against them.[22] They 'got out of the way' of the pursuing constables, at which John Lloyd, secretary of the Stockport magistrates, who was co-ordinating the response from the authorities, declared sarcastically in a letter to Henry Hobhouse that 'I hope they are not to be overtaken & that the "true land of Liberty – America!" may be their destination'.[23] The three men did not make it as far as the promised land across the sea. They were accosted at Liverpool docks by Joseph Nadin, clapped in irons and taken to Chester Castle on charges of sedition. Writing to the Reverend Joseph Harrison from his cell at the end of September, Bagguley said he believed that revenge was the motive behind his arrest. He quoted Nadin as saying he had now twice had the honour of seeing Bagguley escorted to prison. There followed a tirade against 'the celebrated Nadin', 'this wretch – a stranger to Religion, a savage to Humanity, a Child in virtue, a boy in Honour, a Cipher in Love, but a man in cunning, a Giant in Hypocrisy a monster in Collective vice and a Devil in human form'. Bagguley described how Nadin's eyes rolled in his 'Bullhead' as he enjoyed the moment of putting his prisoner in irons. 'Oh for another Shakespear [sic] to draw in nature this uncommon savage "Oran Outang".' He concludes by asking Harrison how bail might be arranged.[24] In fact bail was set so high that there was no hope of releasing them before trial.

The immediate result of the imprisonment of the three reform activists was a cessation of strikes and demonstrations and the reopening of the factories, mills and coal mines. John Lloyd was congratulated for dealing with the situation in a timely and rigorous manner: something the Home Secretary hoped to see demonstrated elsewhere in the region, should the situation arise.[25]

HONI SOIT QUI MAL Y PENSE

9

THE SPREAD EAGLE

'May the thrones of Tyrants tremble'

At the beginning of 1819, John Knight, James Wroe, Joseph Johnson, a local brush-maker, and James Moorhouse (of Stockport) established the Manchester Patriotic Union Society, whose primary objective was parliamentary reform. Under this banner, they called a meeting for 18 January. Henry Hunt, champion of the working man and now something of a hero in the northwest, was invited to chair this large public gathering on St Peter's Field. The reformers had not yet begun to plan the fateful meeting which would take place in August that year, yet this January event – in its form, content and style – can nonetheless be seen as a dress rehearsal for it. Indeed, Hunt saw it as the first of many such mass demonstrations across the country, increasing in strength and scale until they culminated in one great 'monster' meeting in the capital.

In preparation for the January meeting, James Wroe had ventured to London in December 1818 to meet Richard Carlile at his Fleet Street offices. Carlile gave Wroe a large red flag emblazoned with the words 'Hunt and Liberty', fixed to a staff surmounted with a Cap of Liberty. It was the very banner, treasured and protected by the crowds, that had been displayed on the Westminster hustings six months earlier.[1] This was now proudly exhibited on the makeshift hustings in Manchester, where Henry Hunt stood ready to address the crowd, calculated as a modest, but encouraging, eight to ten thousand people.² He was accompanied by John Knight, John Thacker Saxton, James Wroe and William Fitton. The principal purpose of the meeting was to call for the repeal of the Corn Laws, or, as Hunt christened them, the 'Starvation' Laws, 'passed at the point of the bayonet by the late hard-hearted parliament'.³ Hunt assured the cheering people that their cause 'was too pure ever to be subdued'.

John Knight announced during his speech that a requisition for the present meeting had been submitted to the boroughreeve and constables, but that they had refused permission for it to take place, in another instance of the local authorities' opposition to the interests of Manchester's labouring class. In terms which everyone could understand, Knight explained that the Corn Laws 'take out of the pockets of the inhabitants of Manchester, two-fifths of what they lay out in food; i.e. if persons consume five shillings worth of food a week, these Corn Bills take two shillings of the five from them on an average; or £5 4s. a year', amounting to £520,000 from Manchester's population of one hundred thousand. The local authorities were refusing to allow the people to protest against the pernicious Corn Laws, while the reformers sought to alleviate their suffering. But if, Knight said,

> any individual possessing, a little better understanding, or more fellow-feeling than themselves, has at any time attempted to represent to the inhabitants of this town and neighbourhood, the enormous burthens imposed thereon by the government, or taken any steps to prevent the imposition of new, or remove any old, burthens; they have uniformly vilified and calumniated them in the most scandalous and shameful manner: and not content with this, they have, as is well known, caused great

numbers to be thrown into prison, and there endure every species of suffering their malignity could procure them. I myself, gentlemen, have had the distinguished honour of being TWICE the object of their malignant vengeance.[4]

Knight then proposed, seconded by William Fitton, that the meeting should vote on whether to petition the House of Commons for the repeal of the Corn Laws. This was universally rejected. The next proposal was to 'remonstrance' or forcefully appeal to the Prince Regent, and to issue a 'declaration', for which measure 'the votes were universal'.[5] It was Henry Hunt who had encouraged the Manchester radicals to move beyond mere petitioning, as advocated by Major Cartwright, and adopt the more direct tactics of 'remonstrance' and 'declaration': effectively final and public warnings from the people to the Prince Regent, which Hunt had first instigated at an open meeting in Palace Yard, adjoining Westminster Hall, the previous September. Both documents had been rejected on that occasion, but it was a change of approach which may be seen as marking the commencement of the great radical mobilization of 1819.[6]

The remonstrance was lengthy (as was the declaration, both brought by Hunt from London), but one stirring passage contained the essence of the reformers' demands:

the impeachment, and if found guilty, the condign [appropriate] punishment of the present ministers. – A change of measure, and an immediate abolition of the odious and accursed Boroughmongering-system. – A radical, and such a complete Reform, as will secure to the People the exercise of that great and incontrovertible principle, that every human being is entitled to, an equal participation in the sacred blessings of political freedom; and every industrious labourer, manufacturer, and mechanic, has a right to reap the ample and substantial fruits of his virtuous and USEFUL TOIL.[7]

The declaration was then read out by James Wroe 'with great energy and effect'.[8] Among the many points raised were some familiar ones, alongside some very strident statements, each no doubt accompanied by a loud and enthusiastic cheer of agreement:

> That the only source of all legitimate power, is in the People, the whole people, and nothing but the people... That all Governments, not immediately derived from, and strictly accountable to the People, are usurpations, and ought to be resisted or destroyed... That all Men are born free, equal and independent of each other... That Taxation without Representation is illegal, and ought to be abolished... That Annual Parliaments and Universal Suffrage, were formerly, and ought *now*, to be the Law of the Land.

One statement that should have given the Prince Regent pause for reflection was this: 'That the Crown is a sacred trust and inheritance, held only by the free consent, and for the sole welfare and benefit of the People.'

The declaration, like the remonstrance, made direct reference to the events of 1817 and the government's deployment of spies, specifically the controversy over the infamous 'Oliver': 'That the conduct of the present Ministers in employing a vile band of spies and informers, for the purpose of encouraging disturbances throughout the country, and afterwards cruelly punishing the unfortunate victims of their artful snares, was an act of High Treason against the nation, for which they ought to be brought to public justice.'

The final point of the declaration concerned Habeas Corpus:

That the conduct of the late Parliament in passing the suspension of the Habeas Corpus Act, and other restrictions on the
liberty of the subject and in afterwards screening Ministers by
a Bill of Indemnity, from all enquiry or punishment for their
wanton and tyrannical persecutions of the friends of Reform,
was a violation of every principle of justice and humanity,
and will be handed down to posterity with everlasting infamy
and disgrace.[9]

The next to address the crowd was John Thacker Saxton, who
announced that his motto, like that of Bagguley and Drummond
before him, was 'DEATH OR LIBERTY!!!' This brought another
cheer and great applause. He argued that a petition to the House
of Commons – which had already been voted against – was a futile
measure, since that institution, as it was presently organized, 'can
never be looked upon as the rational, fair, and full representation
of the Commons of Great Britain'. Therefore the people had a
duty to impress upon the Prince Regent that it was to 'this corrupt
House of Commons, (the majority of which is under the direct
influence of the Aristocracy) to the base servility of a pensioned
House of Lords, and the unbounded profligacy and extravagance
of the Regent himself, we may justly attribute our present national
calamities, and cannot but anticipate an increase of evils already
too great to be borne'.[10] Saxton believed these burdens, and the
Corn Laws most of all, to be 'certain precursors of speedy and
inevitable ruin – a ruin equally fatal to the existence of both Prince
and People'.[11]

Saxton moved towards the close of his speech by honouring
the immortal memory of the 'great THOMAS PAINE', and then

congratulated the people of Manchester for welcoming Henry Hunt to their town and for the presence of such a significant national figure in their midst. Hunt's example of friendship, sympathy and political fellow-feeling, said Saxton, and his demeanour and rectitude as witnessed at the meeting, gave the lie to the poison propagated about him by the press. Saxton exhorted them all to follow Hunt's 'bright example, and pursue the fair and constitutional path that leads to our deliverance – carry this principle to your homes – those who have wives, teach them the inestimable blessings of liberty – and let the infant imbibe this noble spirit with his mother's milk'.[12]

As chairman, Hunt spoke once more to close the meeting. He reiterated the points that the various speakers had made, and drew attention to the fact that they were gathered on 'the same spot, where the brave blanketeers were so illegally treated... to prove to our enemies, that when men are actuated by honest principles, no persecution can put them down'. The leaders of that ill-fated march less than two years ago were now back in prison awaiting trial. Hunt declared to the people of Manchester, with passionate humility, that he had not entered on this path for personal interest, that he willingly and cheerfully devoted half his income to the service of the people and the recovery of their rights. 'If I desert the principles which I have hitherto professed,' he announced dramatically, pointing to Carlile's blood-red standard, 'may that colour... be my winding sheet.' In evoking his own shroud, Hunt was offering a more poetic rendering of the cry 'Liberty or Death'. A cheer and loud applause followed this statement and the meeting was duly closed.

Apart from the hustings partially collapsing under the pressure of the large crowd and having to be hastily rebuilt, Hunt's time in Manchester appeared to pass off with little trouble. He was abused by officers of the 7th Hussars during a visit to the Theatre Royal a few days later, and when he attempted to return the following evening, he found the theatre completely shut and disgruntled audience members gathered outside. Yet during his sojourn in Manchester no incidents of violence or wanton destruction – as darkly predicted by the informers' regular reports to the Home Office – came to pass. Hunt had consistently requested calm throughout the meeting itself and his subsequent carriage parade. He was relying, he told his audience, on their integrity, good sense and peaceable demeanour. He was not disappointed, and his ability to maintain control of so large a crowd augured well for any future gathering.

At five o'clock, immediately after the meeting on 18 January, a dinner was held in Henry Hunt's honour at the Spread Eagle Inn on Hanging Ditch, attended by two hundred people.[13] Each of them had paid five shillings for a ticket, purchased either at the bar of the inn or through James Wroe.[14] Among the toasts raised that evening, each followed presumably by a swig from a regularly topped-up rummer, were the following: 'The source of all legitimate power, the *People*'; 'the Rights of Man, and may the thrones of Tyrants tremble'; 'May the sword aimed at the breast of liberty be buried in the heart of despotism'; 'Our Chairman, Henry Hunt'; 'the immortal memory of Tom Paine'; 'the venerable father of reform, Major Cartwright'; 'our banished countryman William Cobbett and may we all witness his speedy return'; 'the beautiful Lancashire Witches'; 'the brave Reformers of Lancashire'; and 'the poor weavers of Lancashire, and may the day soon arrive, when their labours may provide not only sufficient to supply their wants, but to give them the comforts of life'.[15]

One of those at the dinner was Joseph Johnson, secretary of the Manchester Patriotic Union Society and a supporter of the

Manchester Observer. This was Hunt's first meeting with him, for Johnson, Hunt later wrote, 'had not the courage to accompany me upon the hustings'.[16] However, as 'this meeting passed off without any difficulty or danger, Johnson the brush-maker, who was very young in the ranks of Reform, professed a determination to take a more active part at a future opportunity'.[17] Thereafter the two regularly corresponded.

Hunt now left for London, intending to present the Manchester Declaration and Remonstrance to the Prince Regent. At first Lord Sidmouth managed to fend him off, and on 29 May, Henry Hobhouse wrote to Hunt informing him that his lordship declined to present either document to His Royal Highness. Hunt demanded that the Home Secretary return the Declaration and Remonstrance so that, as *Black Dwarf* reported in early June, he could find 'some other means of making the prayers and complaints of the suffering people of Lancashire and Cheshire known to his royal highness the Prince Regent'.[18] However, the rejection served to galvanize the radical campaign in the northwest of England. In response, the call went out that every town and city in the entire country should form a Union Society to disseminate political information and to co-ordinate mass meetings. This was to be a great national union of the people, with Manchester as the focus of the largest regional meeting and the culmination of a summer of agitation, prior to a general gathering in London. The sheer scale and speed of this mobilization caused great excitement among the participants and, in equal measure, fear among the local authorities.[19]

On 3 July 1819 Joseph Johnson, on behalf of the Manchester Patriotic Union Society, invited Henry Hunt to attend this public meeting in Manchester, which was to be held in early August.[20] Hunt's acceptance, sent from his home in Hampshire on the 6th, was intercepted, along with several others, by the Postmaster

General on behalf of the government. The letter is cheerful and friendly, a far cry from the cold, even disparaging recollections in his *Memoirs* of a year later. In his letter, Hunt refers to a local dignitary and parliamentary reformer, Sir Charles Wolseley, who would be in attendance on the day; although 'not the most brilliant Man in the world, nor the boldest perhaps', yet his support, being sincere, 'must be cherished'. Sir Charles's title 'may go a great way with the Multitude & it must be a cursed Eyesore to our aristocratical opponents'. Hunt tells Johnson, 'my good fellow, there is nothing on Earth I would like better [than] to visit the reformers of Manchester again'. He adds that since his last trip, he has been stripped of every shilling of 'ready rino' (cash) by his enemies. Later that month the *Manchester Observer* would carry advertisements for subscriptions on Hunt's behalf.[21]

Hunt goes on to recommend that the meeting must bring together people from all over Lancashire, not just Manchester, and should be advertised well in advance, to encourage as many as possible to attend. He suggests that a formal invitation and response could be published in the *Manchester Observer*, to build up a sense of anticipation and raise public interest: 'I think by management the Largest assemblage may be procured at Manchester... that ever was seen in this Country.' But 'unless the People are prepared to come from almost all Parts within 20 Miles around I think we had better let the matter rest a while. What say you?' His closing words suggest that he suspected that his mail was being intercepted: 'Write, but be careful to say nothing that can by implication [be] taken hold of by the Villains... God bless you.'[22]

Hunt prepared for his journey north, reassured by Joseph Johnson that great numbers could be expected to attend the meeting. In the wake of a successful mass gathering at Smithfield in London on 21 July, a date of 23 August had already been mooted for a 'monster' rally on Kennington Common in London, the climax of the summer's campaign programme.[23] In another intercepted letter to Johnson, written just before he left Hampshire, Hunt shares his hope that the authorities 'will not be able to excite the Reformers to any Act of Violence. We have nothing to do but concentrate public opinion, and if our Enemies will not listen to the voice of a whole People, they will listen to nothing, and may the effects of their Folly and Wickedness be upon their own Heads.'[24]

10

CAMPSMOUNT

'Sir Arthur'

On his appointment as commander of the Northern District, General Sir John Byng set about finding a suitable estate to lease within the region, from which he could breed and train racehorses while farming the land. The general alighted on Campsmount, an elegant house then in the ownership of the Cooke-Yarborough family, with a sizable estate in the southern part of the West Riding of Yorkshire, near the village of Campsall, about eight miles from Doncaster. The house, designed by the leading local architect John Carr, sat atop a steep rise with spectacular views across the surrounding fertile countryside. The general was extremely happy with his new situation, located as it was within easy distance of some of the best horse breeders and racecourses in England. Byng's official headquarters, meanwhile, was at Pontefract. Neither venue, Campsmount or Pontefract, was particularly convenient for the trips across the Pennine Hills to Manchester which would be necessary when the military were called to assist in policing mass meetings. It was a journey which the Reverend William Hay, whose parish was also in this part of Yorkshire, was obliged to make regularly in his role as a magistrate.

Sir John shared his passion for horse racing with many local dignitaries, most notably the Earl of Fitzwilliam. The earl was a prominent Whig politician, Lord Lieutenant of the West Riding of Yorkshire and the owner of the palatial Wentworth Woodhouse near Rotherham. He had inherited this estate from his uncle, a fellow Whig (twice prime minister) and horse breeder, Charles Watson-Wentworth, second Marquess of Rockingham and owner of the legendary champion Whistlejacket, immortalized by George Stubbs in 1762.* Evidence that General Byng was quickly and fully immersed in the county's horse-racing business appears in *The Sporting Magazine or Monthly Calendar* in 1834, in a report on the death of Humphrey Clinker, another famous racehorse that was bred by Lord Fitzwilliam and foaled in the year 1822. 'Sir John Byng', the article says, 'at that period had the management of the late earl's Racing Establishment.'[1]

In 1819 Byng was listed as a steward for the Spring Meeting at York, and then as one of the owners and trainers entering horses at the August Meeting, on Thursday 12th.[2] His horse was the three-year-old colt Sir Arthur, presumably named after the Duke of Wellington, whose proud bloodline was listed as 'by Sorcerer, out of Sheba's Queen'. Among the other runners were Lord Scarbrough's Black Prince, Lord Queensberry's Fitz-Walton, Lord Milton's Palmerin and a Mr Bamlett's colt, forcefully named 'Destruction, by Thunderbolt'.[3]

Sir John had every hope of attending the whole week of the York August Meeting, from Monday 9th to Saturday 14th, but, given the illustrious competition and the presence of the local aristocracy and gentry, he was particularly keen to see his horse run on the Thursday. The occasion also offered some royal glamour, as the Prince Regent's recently widowed son-in-law Prince Leopold

---

* The monumental painting originally hung at Wentworth Woodhouse, but is now in the National Gallery, London.

was expected to be there, escorted by Lord Fitzwilliam and the Archbishop of York.*

The general was therefore greatly dismayed to learn, at a summit with the magistrates held in Manchester on 31 July, that a mass meeting of Manchester's reformers was to take place at St Peter's Field on Monday 9 August and that the magistrates expected him to be in attendance, as he had been in March 1817, co-ordinating the crowd control on St Peter's Field itself and then patrolling the streets in the following days. This meant, obviously, that he would miss the first day's racing. And, given that York was seventy miles away, it was unlikely that he would see Sir Arthur race on the Thursday. On 2 August Sir John wrote from Manchester to Henry Hobhouse, marked 'private': 'I have been exerting myself all day in speaking to the select committee'; his advice to them was that they should not attend the mass meeting themselves. He told Hobhouse he had promised the magistrates that he would 'start at a minutes [sic] notice upon hearing from them', and that he would, of course, be present 'if necessary', but that it would be 'particularly inconvenient, having been long engaged to go with Lord Fitzwilliam to York on that day for the Races'.⁴ It was around this time that Sir John decided to delegate

---

* Leopold arrived in York at 10.30 on the morning of Friday 13th, attended the racing in the afternoon, slept at the Black Swan Hotel and left for Northumberland on Saturday morning. The *Yorkshire Gazette*, on 14 August 1819, reported, 'His Royal Highness was upon the Course in the afternoon during the running of the horses: and afterwards dined with his Grace the Archbishop, at his Palace... we understand [he] proceeds this morning on his road to Alnwick Castle.' The *Leeds Mercury* of 21 August 1819 describes how Lord Fitzwilliam 'introduced Prince Leopold to the Stand, in which were the Archbishop of York and his daughter, and many of the surrounding Nobility and Gentry'.

on-the-spot military command of the Manchester meeting to someone else.

Lieutenant Colonel George Guy Carleton L'Estrange (b. 1776), known to his family as Guy, came from a solidly military family from Moystown, King's County (now County Offaly), in Ireland. His cousin, Edmund, was in the 71st Regiment of Foot and his nephew, George, was in the 31st Regiment. By tradition, young men of the family were educated at the prestigious Westminster School in London. Guy had entered the army in 1798 and had commanded the second battalion of the 31st Foot at the Battle of Albuera on 16 May 1811. Under attack from French cavalry, Major L'Estrange devised a defensive manoeuvre known, from then on, as the 'Albuera square' and, because of his quick thinking, his troops were able to withstand the enemy onslaught.[5] In fact, according to the colonel of the regiment, Lord Mulgrave, L'Estrange and his men had 'arrested the successful progress of the enemy, and turned the tide of battle'.[6] After the battle, Lord Wellington recommended him 'in the strongest manner for promotion in some way or other',[7] and Lord Mulgrave confirmed his immediate promotion to brevet lieutenant colonel. 'Never', Mulgrave wrote to L'Estrange, 'was rank more nobly achieved or more honourably borne. My praises can add nothing to the general applause which the conduct of the 31st and its leader on the glorious 16th of May have excited.'[8]

In 1812 Guy L'Estrange was confirmed in his promotion to lieutenant colonel (that is, given the associated pay) with the 26th Regiment of Foot stationed at Gibraltar. However, unwilling to miss the 'winding up of the war' after Napoleon Bonaparte's first abdication in 1814, he and a friend found some good horses and proceeded to ride across Spain to France, arriving outside Toulouse where his old regiment, now including his nephew, was stationed.

Guy was so popular that on his arrival, as George L'Estrange recalled, he was greeted by 'a loud cheer' and 'the caps of every soldier in the regiment waving in the air over their heads'.[9]

Also present at Toulouse were Major Edwin Griffiths and Lieutenant Colonel Leighton Dalrymple of the 15th Hussars. Major Griffiths recalled the ecstatic celebrations at the abdication of Emperor Napoleon and the restoration of the Bourbon monarchy under Louis XVIII, brother of the executed King Louis XVI: 'Thousands of Country People crowded each side of the road for a League before we reached Toulouse, and absolutely deafened us with acclamation so that we could hardly hear the thunder of Artillery and the Bells of the Churches.' On arrival in the city, 'Triumphal arches, the white & fleur de lys, crossed the streets every twenty paces, and windows and even the house tops were crowded full of ladies, waving handkerchiefs, clapping hands, & calling with all their might "Vive the Roi! Vive les Bourbons!"'[10] George L'Estrange was appointed aide-de-camp to General Sir John Byng, at that time commander of the 31st, who, he recalls, 'was not a man of very many words'.[11]

Guy officially returned to the 31st Regiment of Foot on 6 June 1815, by which date it was stationed in Malta. Sir John, meanwhile, was commanding the 2nd Brigade of Guards near Brussels, with the battle of Waterloo fast approaching. In 1817, Guy married Sarah Rawson of Nidd Hall, Yorkshire. The 31st Foot was recalled from Malta to England in 1818, its core troops stationed initially at Dover. In the summer of 1819, it was among the regiments being gathered for duty in the northwest of England, supporting the civil powers. Given their professional and personal connections, it was therefore natural for the general to turn to Lieutenant Colonel Guy L'Estrange for assistance with his diary conundrum. In fairness to both, L'Estrange, quick-thinking and intelligent even under the stress of battle, was more than capable of commanding professional troops in the established manoeuvres now commonly used to control civilian crowds.[12]

Besides, Sir John's preparations were well advanced. He had gathered troops of cavalry from the 15th Hussars and 6th Dragoon Guards, who were now stationed within Manchester and in the towns around it, including Bolton, Oldham, Ashton, Preston and Blackburn. Infantry companies from the 31st and 88th Regiments were also in Manchester as well as Rochdale, Macclesfield and Warrington. The Cheshire Yeomanry, who had been mobilized during the Blanketeers' march, were stationed at Stockport, Macclesfield, Altrincham and Knutsford. In addition, Sir John had requested from the Duke of Wellington, Master-General of the Ordnance, two six-pounder guns accompanied by a troop from the Royal Horse Artillery, and these had now arrived, commanded by Major Thomas Dyneley. In all there were over a thousand men in Manchester and the vicinity, mainly regulars – that is, professionals – under the direct command of General Byng and, on the ground, his trusted officers.[13]

The 15th Hussars had begun their journey to Manchester as early as 25 May, when the troops under the command of Major Skinner Hancox, Captain William Booth and Captain Frederick Charles Philips marched from Ipswich, and those commanded by Captain William Bellairs marched from Norwich. A further two troops were located at Preston and Blackburn, who were later ordered to Manchester.[14] At Manchester, the regiment was quartered at Hulme Barracks, built in 1803. Just after their completion, Joseph Aston described the barracks as 'built upon an uniform convenient plan... They are intended for dragoons; the stables are on each side of the yard, and over them are the apartments for the soldiers. The quarters of the officers are in an insulated building near the north end of the yard, which is capacious enough for most manoeuvres which are generally used in exercising a squadron of horse.'[15]

The commanding officer of the troops from the 15th who were readying themselves for the mass meeting on St Peter's Field was Lieutenant Colonel Dalrymple. In addition to Major Hancox and Captains Booth, Philips and Bellairs, the officers included Captain John Whiteford, Captain Charles Carpenter, Lieutenant James McAlpine, Lieutenant Frederick Buckley and Lieutenant Charles Rutledge O'Donnell. Of these ten officers, five were proud recipients of the Waterloo Medal (Dalrymple, Hancox, Whiteford, Booth and Bellairs).

Among the junior lieutenants was William Jolliffe. He later recalled that the 15th had been stationed at Hulme Barracks since late June or early July and that it 'was my first acquaintance with a large manufacturing population'.[16] Jolliffe's remark raises the interesting question of the military's attitude to such duties, particularly those seasoned individuals who had known the heat and blood of battle and who now found themselves marshalling civilians, whose grievances they may or may not have understood or sympathized with. The reformers' criticisms of the duration and expense – and even futility – of the Napoleonic Wars may not have endeared them to the men who had fought, been maimed and lost comrades during these two decades of conflict. One veteran corporal of the 15th declared: 'No beings on earth are subjected like the military to the whims and caprices of their countrymen. On ordinary occasions they are looked upon as little better than wastrils [sic], useless, and a burthen to the nation; their room [absence] more acceptable than their company.' However, in 'cases of emergency and dread of civil outrages, they are petted from the soles of their feet upwards; and all ideas of the "invasion of ancient privileges" vanish.'[17]

Rudyard Kipling pinpointed these contradictory attitudes in his 1890 poem 'Tommy':

For it's Tommy this, an' Tommy that, an' Chuck him out, the brute!
But it's 'Saviour of 'is country' when the guns begin to shoot;
An' it's Tommy this, an' Tommy that, an' anything you please;
An' Tommy ain't a bloomin' fool – you bet that Tommy sees![18]

Such writings convey a sense of two separate worlds, regarding each other with mutual suspicion and even animosity, or, at best, weary resignation. What might happen if these civil and military opposites were to collide?

The creation of Hussar regiments in the British army had resulted from the Prince of Wales's association with French royalty and aristocracy in the years leading up to and following the French Revolution. The Marquis de Conflans, the colonel of a Hussar regiment in the French army, seems to have had a particular influence on the young George and, through this suave, dissolute and outlandish individual's example, the future Prince Regent soon acquired a taste for the elaborate regimentals – and wild excesses – which distinguished French Hussar officers.[19] The name comes from ancient Hungarian (or Magyar) tribes of marauding horsemen, whose wild ways their early-nineteenth-century spiritual descendants endeavoured to emulate. British Hussars, formed in the early 1800s out of the Light Dragoon regiments – characterized by their light weaponry and armour – were distinguished by their short dark-blue jackets heavily braided across the front (the 15th Hussars' braiding was silver), the sabretache, a small red-and-gold bag hanging from the sword-belt, the stirrup-hilted curved sabre (1796 pattern) and the tall hat or 'mirliton'. Officers wore a fur-lined pelisse, a short jacket, raffishly hanging from the left shoulder. As well as their exotic finery, the Hussars wore extravagant moustaches, in a period when wigs had become a rarity and gentlemen were invariably short-haired and clean-shaven: this was partly to appear unnervingly strange and ferocious, and partly to look older. Although the Hussar regiments had acquitted themselves well in battle, notably at Waterloo, the highest accolades at that signal victory had gone to the heavy cavalry with their captured imperial eagles and thousands of enemy prisoners. The relative poor showing from the dandy Hussars prompted rebukes in the press from fellow British cavalrymen:

> Shave off those mustachios, let us see the honest countenances, that we may know our friends, and dress them once again in red, that their enemies may dread them. No man, be his rank or pretensions what they may, should be suffered to gratify his capricious fancy by any innovation on national dress... If our mustachio, whiskered, sheep-skins could not beat the other mustachio, whisker, bear-skinned fellows, it is evident these whimsical freaks do not answer.[20]

It would seem that the Hussars needed to prove themselves, in order to counter such criticism: as a matter both of regimental pride and of survival.

11

THE UNION ROOMS

'Witches in politics'

At the dinner following the Manchester Patriotic Union Society's mass meeting in January 1819, one of the toasts had been, somewhat curiously, 'to the beautiful Lancashire Witches'. The infamous Lancashire witch trials of 1612 had left an indelible mark on county folklore and belief. Eight women and two men from the area around Pendle Hill, near the East Lancashire towns of Burnley, Padiham and Clitheroe, had been arrested, interrogated – including under torture – and tried at Lancaster Castle for the murder by witchcraft of ten people. One of the accused, Elizabeth Southernes, 'Old Demdike', aged eighty, died in her cell. The others were hanged at various locations around Lancaster. It was a story that continued to inspire and appal local antiquarians and authors in the early nineteenth century, including James Crossley and William Harrison Ainsworth, the latter nicknamed the English Walter Scott.[*]

A hundred years after these terrible events, the term 'Lancashire Witches' began to take on a different meaning. As Daniel Defoe recounted, during his tour through Great Britain:

---

[*] Ainsworth penned a celebrated novel, *The Lancashire Witches*, serialized in 1848 and then published complete in 1849, inspired by James Crossley's writings.

Lancashire Witches are pleasantly said, and not undeservedly, to allude to the Beauty of the Women in this County; but in the times of Superstition, and even since the Reformation, it had a more serious Relation to the general Belief, that there were such unhappy Creatures, who sold themselves to the Devil, to be enabled to do Mischief for a Time: a Belief that obtained much in this particular County, and for which many a poor old Creature suffered.[1]

Soon afterwards, James Ray, a British army volunteer from Whitehaven during the troubled years of 1745 and 1746, recalled that Lancashire was rife with Jacobite sympathisers. Like Defoe, he commented on the recent use of the term 'Lancashire Witches' to denote beauty, but he warned that this could be employed by those of the Jacobite persuasion to seduce unsuspecting loyalists:

In this County the Women are generally very handsome, by which they have acquired the Name of *Lancashire Witches*... but some of the pretty *Jacobite Witches*, chuse to distinguish themselves by wearing Plaid Breast-knots, Ribbons, and Garters tied above the Knee, which may be remonstranced as dangerous to the Constitution; for that above a Lady's Knee is of so attracting a Quality, it's not only in Danger of drawing his Majesty's good Subjects in the Civil, but Military Gentlemen off their Duty.[2]

John Harland's volume *Ballads and Songs of Lancashire: Chiefly Older than the 19th Century* includes a sprightly song, from a street-ballad sheet entitled 'Lancashire Witches', with the lines:

My charmer's the village delight,
And the pride of the Lancashire witches,

Then hurrah for the Lancashire witches,
Whose smile every bosom enriches.

Only view the dear heavenly belles,
You're soon seized with love's twitches,
Which none could create but the spells,
From the eyes of the Lancashire witches.[3]

In his edition of Thomas Pott's 1613 book *Discovery of Witches in the County of Lancaster*, James Crossley concluded his introduction with the observation: 'In process of time even the term *witchfinder* may lose the stains which have adhered to it… and may be adopted by general usage, as a sort of companion phrase, to signify the fortunate individual, who, by an union with a Lancashire witch, has just asserted his indefeasible title to be considered as the happiest of men.'[4]

A different kind of public attention was drawn to women in the first half of 1819, by a new and, to some, unwelcome development. Women from labouring backgrounds as well as the middling sort were not only supporting the reform movement, but establishing their own Reform Societies.[5] The prevailing opinion of the time derided the notion of women entering the public arena. Yet radical ideas and principles were bringing them into the political sphere alongside wage-earning menfolk. Women were the hub of any household: it was they who gave birth to and nurtured the young, and were their offspring's first teachers. John Saxton had called upon the men at the January 1819 meeting to teach their wives 'the inestimable blessings of liberty' and therefore to transfer the principle, metaphorically at the mother's breast, to the next generation. The involvement of women increased the scale and impact of the reform movement and the mass-meeting forum in particular. By mid-1819, the profusion of these meetings across the country, supported and attended by women, was causing great alarm among the authorities.

As we have seen, after the reinstatement of the Habeas Corpus Act in early 1818, political meetings were organized once more across the northwest. Samuel Bamford recalled one such gathering, at Lydgate in Saddleworth, at which the speakers included John Bagguley and Samuel Drummond. During his own address, Bamford 'insisted on the right, and the propriety also, of females who were present at such assemblages, voting by show of hand, for, or against the resolutions. This was a new idea; and the women, who attended numerously on that bleak ridge, were mightily pleased with it, – and the men being nothing dissentient, – when the resolution was put, the women held up their hands, amid much laughter.' The atmosphere may have been light-hearted, but, as Bamford concludes, it was a momentous occasion, for 'from that time, females voted with the men at the radical meetings... it became the practice'. Further still, 'female political unions were formed, with their chair-women, committees, and other officials; and from us, the practice was soon borrowed, very judiciously no doubt, and applied in a greater or less degree, to the promotion of religions and charitable institutions'.[6]

This galvanizing of women's participation is credited as being the earliest example of organized female activity in British politics. It was, in its early days, very much a northern English – indeed, largely a Lancastrian – phenomenon.[7] Female Reform Societies were established in Lancashire and some in adjoining Yorkshire, for example in Stockport, Blackburn, Leigh, Rochdale, Royton, Leeds and Manchester.[8] The first to form was Blackburn on 18 June 1819, under the leadership of Alice Kitchen. So novel was this concept that it became national news. Following an announcement in the *Manchester Mercury* under the subtitle of 'PUBLIC MEETINGS', on 1 July 1819 the London *Morning Chronicle* reported the arrival of the 'BLACKBURN FEMALE REFORM SOCIETY':

> At Blackburn, near Manchester, a Society has been formed under the above title, from which a circular has been issued to other districts, inviting the wives and daughters of the workmen in the different branches of manufacture to form themselves into similar Societies. They are not only to co-operate with the different classes of workmen in seeking redress of their grievances, but 'to instil into the minds of their children a deep rooted hatred of the Government and Houses of Parliament,' whom they are pleased to call 'our tyrannical rulers.'[9]

This announcement was repeated by the *Leeds Intelligencer* with the observation that the aims of this and 'similar societies' were 'most wicked and vicious'.[10]

On 5 July 1819, members of the Blackburn Female Reform Society paraded to a meeting in their town, chaired by John Knight. According to the report in *Black Dwarf*, more than thirty thousand people were in attendance. In a satirical letter from 'The Black Dwarf' to 'the Yellow Bonne at Japan', the former declares: 'Here the ladies are determined at last to speak for themselves; and they address their brother reformers in a very *manly* language.'[11] How, he ponders, will the law respond? 'They will not sure be so ungallant, as to call the ladies seditious, or threaten them with imprisonment, and whips!'[12] Should, for example, the Attorney General attempt to arrest them for treason, the Black Dwarf believed, 'he would probably find a jury more disposed to favour the *petticoat* than the *gown*. And for the soldiers and police officers, they cannot be arrayed against WOMEN!! That would be despicable in the extreme.'[13]

In his address, John Knight spoke of the necessity of a radical reform of the House of Commons, calling upon William Fitton to read out the particulars of his proposal. At this point, according to *Black Dwarf*, 'a most interesting and enchanting scene here ensued'. The committee of the Blackburn Female Reform Society, with Mrs Kitchen at its head, were desirous of approaching the hustings. The women 'were very neatly dressed for the occasion, and each wore a green favour* in her bonnet or cap'.[14] They were invited to approach and, having ascended the hustings, Mrs Kitchen presented John Knight with a Cap of Liberty, 'made of scarlet silk or satin, lined with green, with a serpentine gold lace, terminating with a rich gold tassel'. She then asked the chairman to accept and read out an address that 'embraces a faint description of our woes, and may apologise for our interference in the politics of our country'. This was greeted by *very great applause*.[15]

Such attention to presentation and detail is not insignificant. The pride with which the elaborate Cap of Liberty was fashioned and publicly displayed was wholly appropriate to an area built largely on the textile industry, in which many of the women were directly employed, or to which they were connected through their menfolk and children. In addition, in wearing 'favours' and presenting tokens to their male 'champions', the women appeared to be evoking ancient chivalric customs with military associations (whether the joust or the battlefield) as well as echoing courtly love and gallantry. There was a decorum and ancient ritual in this gesture, and perhaps a conscious reference to Edmund Burke's

---

* The green favour could have been a ribbon, an early French revolutionary symbol, or, more likely, a laurel sprig signifying peace.

famous declaration of 1790 that 'the age of chivalry is gone', made in reaction to reports of the Women's March on Versailles in early October 1789 and the mob's ensuing rough behaviour towards the imprisoned king and Queen Marie Antoinette:

> little did I dream that I should have lived to see such disasters fallen upon her in a nation of gallant men, in a nation of men of honour and of cavaliers. I thought ten thousand swords must have leaped from their scabbards to avenge even a look that threatened her with insult. – But the age of chivalry is gone. – That of sophisters, œconomists, and calculators, has succeeded; and the glory of Europe is extinguished forever.[16]

It has been argued that Burke was celebrating the civility and ceremony of public life as the crucial bond that holds a complex society together: a bond he considered had been undone by the turmoil of 1789, while predicting its full destruction during the Reign of Terror that followed. The attack on the French queen represented the Revolution's revolt against humanity.[17] Mrs Kitchen's apology 'for our interference in the politics of our country' underlines the unexpected nature of the women's intervention, and thereby reveals how desperate the times had become. The overt gallantry of the leading reformers, in inviting women to join the male speakers – in contrast to the way that they were derided, belittled and denigrated by the opponents of reform – declared that chivalry, or respectful decorum, was far from dead. Rather, it was alive and well in the parliamentary reform movement.

This projection of seemingly conflicting signals for the benefit of the opposition – the embrace of traditional courtesies by radical women agitating for reform – was conscious and highly effective. The presence of women at the Blackburn Reform

Meeting wrong-footed the authorities, while their mobilization brought a new energy to the reform movement, after a period of disappointment and setback.[18]

Having made her appeal, Alice Kitchen handed the women's address to John Knight, who duly read it out to the assembled throng. The address was full of passion, dignity and power. The women argued that 'we can speak with unassuming confidence, that our houses which once bore ample testimony of our industry and cleanliness, and were fit for the reception of a prince, are now alas! robbed of all their ornaments', while their beds, 'that once afforded us cleanliness, health and sweet repose, are now torn away from us by the relentless hand of the unfeeling tax gatherer, to satisfy the greatest monsters of cruelty, the borough-mongering tyrants, who are reposing on beds of down' while they had nothing but 'a sheaf of straw'. And the address drew attention to the suffering of the women's families: 'behold our innocent wretched children! ... how appalling are their cries for bread!' Like an invitation from the Spirit of Christmas Present, the women were offering a challenge to their political masters: 'Come then to our dwellings, ye inhabitants of the den of corruption, behold our misery, and see our rags! We cannot describe our wretchedness, for language cannot paint the feelings of a mother, when she beholds her naked children, and hears their inoffensive cries of hunger and approaching death.'

The address warned that 'we are not without proof in history of women who have led armies to the field, and carried conquest before them', and that were it not for the hope of reform, 'we should long ere this have sallied forth to demand our rights, and in the acquirement of those rights to have obtained that food and raiment for our children, which God and nature have ordained for every living creature, but which our oppressors and tyrannical rulers have withheld from us.' It ended on a grim note: 'We look forward with horror to an approaching winter, when the necessity of food, clothing, and every requisite will increase double-fold.'[19]

In its content, language and tone, the address set the standard for female participation in the reform movement. The women's testimonies sprang from their own personal experiences, which were amplified with biblical, classical and historical references. They emphasized their traditional roles as mothers, wives and sisters, and dwelt on their arena of expertise, the home. They also hinted at historical precedents for women to play other roles – notably female warriors, evoking the mythical Amazon tribe, the Iceni queen Boudicca and Joan of Arc – which they were choosing, for now, not to emulate. Only Parliament, or more precisely the House of Commons, they insisted, could relieve their individual and collective suffering. But to do so, the House of Commons must truly represent the 'Common Man'. At this time there is no obvious suggestion that female suffrage was on the agenda, but if all adult males could vote, at least the family as a unit would also be represented.

Samuel Bamford had emphasized the family unit as integral to the struggle for reform in his 'Lancashire Hymn', composed to be sung, he hoped, to inspire the hearts and souls of his brother and sister reformers at their political meetings:

Have we not heard the infant's cry,
And mark'd the mother's tear?
That look, which told us mournfully
That woe and want were there?
And shall they ever weep again,
And shall their pleadings be in vain?[20]

The content of the Blackburn Female Reform Society address is not dissimilar to Bamford's emotive and evocative vision of want and poverty. Here, of course, women were politely and with due decorum (unlike their French sisters) demanding for themselves the changes they desperately needed in their circumstances and that of their menfolk and offspring.

Although female suffrage was not publicly discussed, the activities of the new Female Reform Societies seem to have drawn attention to the plight of women more broadly: their limited education and opportunities for employment, self-expression and personal fulfilment. John Bagguley, for example, actively encouraged the embryonic Female Reform Society in his adopted town of Stockport. He and his fellow agitators for reform Drummond and Johnston had finally come to trial on 15 April, seven months after their arrest. They had been found guilty of conspiracy and unlawful assembly and sentenced to two years' incarceration.[21]

On 19 June 1819, from his prison cell in Chester Castle, Bagguley wrote: 'It appears to me that the female part of the nation have too long been kept in a kind of slavish inferiority[,] their tyranic [sic] lords say that they are slow in their movements... [and to] convert women into Philosophers they say [would] destroy their natural softness nay it would completely metemorphos [sic] these Enchanting[,] these lovely Daughters of [Venus].'

Bagguley argues that, in truth, women 'can be rational companions to their Husbands':

they can heighten their joys and alleviate their sorrows, By the strength of understanding they may give good council, by their tenderness sooth the heart in the day of trouble and in the hour of anguish can smooth the bed of sickness and alleviate even the forebodings of despair[,] and to crown all a woman can educate her... Children and train them up to virtue, and Honour and Liberty.

He refers to recent leading English intellectuals, including the classicist and translator Elizabeth Carter (1717–1806), the reformer and writer Elizabeth Montagu (1718–1800) and Mary Wollstonecraft (1759–97), the latter reviled and revered in equal measure for her seminal tract *A Vindication of the Rights of Woman* (1792) where she argues for a rational education for womankind.[22] His comments on women being 'rational companions' and educators of children suggest that Bagguley had read, absorbed and been motivated by Wollstonecraft's powerful arguments.

Bagguley goes on to ask whether a woman's soul is 'formed of different materials or derived from a different source than mans [*sic*]'. In answer, 'I say no... away then with this vain disparity, and let us see female Newtons, and female Locks, and female Hampdens.'* He continues, 'I begin to think that the inequality of sexes aught to subside; yes ladies exercise your intelects [*sic*] you have the power, you only want the will to become great[,] do but exercise your wills and you must soon rise.'[23]

The degree to which female political activity was regarded as a threat to the natural order is reflected in the extraordinary odium directed towards women who engaged in it, both in newspapers and via satires and caricatures. On 14 July 1819, *The Public Ledger and Daily Advertiser* published a full transcription of the Blackburn Female Reform Society's address, alongside a letter announcing that a London society was to be established on similar lines. How many Blackburn Female Reformers there were, the author did not know, but 'there cannot be a doubt that London will *out-number* all Lancashire in *Female Reformers*, were we only to form our

---

* English Enlightenment figures: the natural philosopher and mathematician Sir Isaac Newton, the philosopher John Locke and the politician and patron saint of the reform movement, John Hampden.

Much wanted Reform among females!!! by J. Lewis Marks, 1819.
(© The Trustees of the British Museum)

estimate from the display of female reformation which decorates our *streets* every night'. He alludes to the capital's 'society ladies', or prostitutes, and to the areas notorious for streetwalkers and brothels, Drury Lane and Covent Garden, where they 'pour out [in] their hundreds and their thousands, all as well qualified to judge of Universal Suffrage as the Ladies of Blackburn'. Having equated female reformers with London's whores, the writer next compares them with the coarse-mouthed fishwives at Billingsgate market, which is not only 'remarkable for excellence of fish' but also for 'plainness of speech'. Local magistrates, he goes on, had tried to frighten the 'Blackburn Petticoat Reformers' by ordering out the fire engines; 'I remember that this trick was once played in France, at the beginning of its Revolution, which our Reformers are so desirous of imitating.' But for '*Our* Female Reformers', the author says, the engines should be filled with gin, since 'I am not sure that the stoutest of our Female Reformers may not sink under it; but *water* has no terrors for them. It is seldom allowed to injure *their* charms.' These 'London *Sans-culottes*' and 'the *Poissardes* of Lancashire' are only fit for houses of correction or workhouses, 'but let us not for a moment think of calling in the military to quell rioters of a description so despicable', and who, in every sense of the word, are 'not worthy of *powder* and *shot*'. He concludes:

> Among those female Viragoes there are probably few of the reclaimable kind. A woman must have pretty well *unsexed* herself before she could join the gangs of Blackburn Rioters. But if there be among the males any well-meaning, however deluded, characters, let those who are better instructed warn them against the danger of associating with, or listening to, those pests of society who would be the first to save their own lives at the expence of *theirs*. Your's, &c. R.S.[24]

No doubt taking inspiration from such diatribes, in August 1819 the printmaker J. Lewis Marks produced a caricature – of the least subtle variety – entitled 'Much wanted REFORM AMONG FEMALES!!!' It depicts an open-air public meeting with an all-female group on the hustings. The breasts of all the women are exaggerated, their eyes wide and staring and their faces flushed. The Cap of Liberty perched on a tall staff forms an enormous phallic symbol, held strategically between the legs by one woman; another holds her hands in the shape of a vulva, while others grasp rolled addresses in imitation of erections. In the crowd a young man fondles a milkmaid's breast, declaring, 'I feel for your Sex my Dear.' The main female figure points to the prominent red Cap of Liberty and declaims, '(Dear Sisters) I feel great pleasure, in holding this thing "um-bob" in my hand, as we see our Sweethearts, and Husbands, are such fumblers at the main thing, we must of course take the thing, in our own hands.'[25]

This cruel parody – ripe with sexual innuendo, gender-swapping, and the idea that women only take command when their menfolk are inadequate, sexually as well as politically – appears to satirize the speech given by Susannah Saxton, wife of John Thacker Saxton and secretary of the Manchester Female Reform Society (MFRS), delivered at the society's inaugural meeting at the Union Rooms on George Leigh Street, Manchester on 20 July 1819 and published in the *Manchester Observer* eleven days later.[26] Saxton began with the phrase 'Dear Sisters of the Earth'. She declared that soon, under the current system, 'no thing [*sic*] will be found in our unhappy country but luxury, idleness, dissipation, and tyranny, on the one hand; and abject poverty, slavery, wretchedness, misery and death, on the other.' She called upon her audience to 'unite with us as speedily as possible; and to exert your influence with your fathers, your husbands, your sons, your relatives and your friends, to join

the Male Union for constitutionally demanding a Reform in their
own House, viz. The Commons House of Parliament; for we are
now thoroughly convinced, that for want of such timely Reform,
the useful class of society has been reduced to its present degraded
state.' Saxton turned to the late war, which she considered 'unjust'
and 'against the liberties of France', terminating at Waterloo
'where the blood of our fellow-creatures flowed' not for the
betterment of mankind, but simply to return the Bourbon kings
to the throne of France. 'Our enemies', she believed,

> are resolved upon destroying the last vestige of the natural
> Rights of Man, and we are determined to establish it; for as well
> might they attempt to arrest the sun in the region of space, or
> stop the diurnal motion of the earth, as to impede the rapid
> progress of the enlightened friends to Liberty and Truth. The
> beam of angelic light that hath gone forth through the globe
> hath at length reached unto man, and we are proud to say
> that the Female Reformers of Manchester have also caught its
> benign and heavenly influence; it is not possible therefore for
> us to submit to bear the ponderous weight of our chains any
> longer, but to use our endeavour to tear them asunder, and
> dash them in the face of our remorseless oppressors.

'We can no longer bear', she cried, 'to see numbers of our
parents immured in workhouses', where fathers and mothers were
separated,

> in direct contradiction to the laws of God and the laws of man;
> our sons degraded below human nature, our husbands and
> little ones clothed in rags, and pining on the face of the earth! –
> Dear Sisters, how could you bear to see the infant at the breast,

drawing from you the remnant of your last blood, instead of the nourishment which nature requires; the only subsistence for yourselves being a draught of cold water?

'Remember,' she continued, 'that all good men were reformers in every age of the world.' Susannah named Noah, the Prophets and Apostles as reformers, and then 'the great Founder of Christianity, he was the greatest reformer of all'. If Jesus returned now and preached against the current Church and State, 'his life would assuredly be sacrificed by the relentless hand of the Borough-Judases; for corruption, tyranny, and injustice, have reached their summit; and the bitter cup of oppression is now full to the brim.'[27]

The transcript of this compelling speech, rich with biblical allusions, even enlisting Jesus Christ to her cause alongside more recent political theorists – notably Thomas Paine – was followed by a notice that the MFRS committee would sit every Tuesday evening from six until nine o'clock for the purpose of enrolling new members 'and transacting other Business relative to the Establishment'.[28]

In preparation for the mass meeting to be held in August, the MFRS committee designed a banner. This was a large rectangular piece of white fabric, on which was depicted a well-dressed woman in a gown of duck-egg blue, holding the scales of justice and trampling the serpent of corruption. By now other Female Societies, like those of Royton and Stockport, were also preparing their banners or 'colours' for the occasion. Royton's text was 'Let Us Die Like Men and Not Be Sold Like Slaves', while Stockport focused on key tenets of the reform movement, 'Annual Parliament', 'Universal Suffrage' and 'Vote By Ballot'.

The MFRS, meanwhile, were aiming to process in front of Henry Hunt's carriage dressed in white, like Vestals honouring a conquering hero of antiquity. In addition to Susannah Saxton as secretary, the society included the president, Mary Fildes (born Mary Pritchard in Cork, Ireland, 1789; she married William Fildes in Cheshire in 1808), Elizabeth Gaunt and Sarah Hargreaves. Inspired by the Blackburn meeting of 5 July, Mrs Fildes intended to present Hunt with the society's banner and then hand him an address to read out to the vast assembly, in the full expectation of gallantries, respect and cheers as reported by *Black Dwarf* from that earlier meeting. This address would be one of the set pieces of the occasion. It read:

> Sir – Permit the Female Reformers of Manchester, in presenting you with this flag, to state, that they are actuated by no motives of petty vanity. As wives, mothers, daughters, in their social, domestic, moral capacities, they come forward in support of the sacred cause of liberty – a cause in which their husbands, their fathers, and their sons, have embarked the last hope of suffering humanity. Neither ashamed nor afraid of thus aiding you in the glorious struggle for recovering your lost privilege – privileges upon which so much of their own happiness depends; they trust that this tribute to freedom will animate you to a steady per[s]everance in obtaining the object of our common solicitude – a radical reform of the Commons House of Parliament. In discharging what they felt an imperative duty, they hope that they have not 'overstepped the modesty of nature,' and they shall now retire to the bosoms of their families with the cheering and consolatory reflection, that your efforts are on the eve of being crowned with complete success.[29]

The address concluded, 'May our flag never be unfurled but in the cause of peace and reform! and then may a female's curse pursue the coward who deserts the standard!'[30]

The use of the term 'curse' may be a sly reference to the Lancashire Witches, while her threat of pursuing anyone who 'deserts the standard' echoed Henry Hunt's dramatic declaration at St Peter's Field the previous January. Fildes had clearly taken note. Her admiration for Hunt is shown by the name of one of her sons, Henry Hunt Fildes (born 1819). The names of her other boys, Thomas Paine Fildes (1818) and John Cartwright Fildes (1821), stand as further testament to her radical politics.

Three weeks after Mary Fildes and her companions had gathered at the Union Rooms, another mass political meeting was held in the market place at Leigh. One of those present, Mr. Wright, later recounted:

> As soon as Mr. Bamber [a Quaker] was chosen for their Chairman, a parade of the Female Reformers took place, headed by a Committee of 12 young women. The Members of the Female Committee were honoured with places on the carts [hustings]. They were dressed in white with black sashes, and what was most novel, these women planted a standard with an inscription "No Corn Laws, Annual Parliaments, and Universal Suffrage"; as well as another standard, surmounted with the cap of Liberty on the platform. Both the flag and the cap were presents from the <u>Ladies Union</u>!! I was seated by the side of these <u>patriotic ladies</u>, and was informed of their rules and regulations, which I am certain no one of common sense in London, would believe it was capable of bringing women into an organised system of operation.

He closed with a familiar comment: 'These Lancashire women are proverbially witches in politics, (if not in beauty).'[31]

12

SMEDLEY COTTAGE

'The most disagreeable seven days'

The mass meeting scheduled for 9 August in Manchester was widely advertised through the *Manchester Observer* and the prominent display of posters, as Hunt had wished. That the Home Office and local magistrates were fully aware of the reformers' preparations is evident from the flurry of correspondence through early summer to and from Whitehall. The Lord Lieutenant of Lancashire, the Earl of Derby, alongside his fellows in Cheshire and Yorkshire, were told to prepare their local forces. By now Manchester had its own citizen regiment, the Manchester and Salford Yeomanry Cavalry, formed as a direct response to the Blanket March two years earlier.

The Yeomanry Cavalry regiments formed part of the system for maintaining law and order that was directed by the Lords Lieutenant, via the magistrates and constables. By the close of 1815 a sizable element of what was left of the regular army was divided between India and France, the latter as part of the army of occupation. The contingent that remained at home was not considered sufficient to maintain peace across a troubled land. Lord Sidmouth was therefore keen to encourage the formation of citizen regiments to supplement the regular troops which could be sent in to assist the civil powers. Some such regiments already existed in Lancashire and adjoining counties, for example the Cheshire Yeomanry Cavalry – 'the Earl of Chester's Yeomanry Cavalry' – whose colonel in 1818, and for some twenty years prior, was Sir John Fleming Leicester, an intimate of the Prince Regent and owner of Tabley House near Knutsford. Sir John was the proud owner of a very fine art collection – among his works by modern masters were paintings by J. M. W. Turner.* The government provided a little money to equip and arm these citizen regiments, but most of the essential kit, including a horse, horse furniture (or tack) and uniform, was the responsibility of the individual volunteer and/or his aristocratic commander.

In 1817, as Manchester had no such regiment, the magistrates had no local support to command during an emergency. Soon after the Blanketeers' march, Anthony Molyneux, a Manchester manufacturer, wrote to Lord Sidmouth suggesting that this should be rectified.[1] At the end of April 1817, the Reverend William Hay likewise wrote to Sidmouth stating, 'I have the satisfaction to inform you that the Grand Jury has come to an unanimous declaration of their opinion as to the necessity of having a corps of Yeomanry Cavalry in the County; and that they have come to a resolution in which they have appointed a committee of their own body to confer with the Magistrates as to the best mode of carrying this measure into effect.'[2] In June 1817 an announcement appeared in the *Manchester Mercury*, addressed to the boroughreeve and constables of Manchester and Salford: 'It appears to us that a CORPS OF YEOMANRY CAVALRY, for the more effectual security of the Towns and Neighbourhood of Manchester and Salford is highly expedient'. Among the undersigned was Hugh Hornby Birley.[3]

---

* In 1823 Sir John offered his collection to Lord Liverpool as the core element of a new project to establish a National Gallery. This was declined.

By September 1817 the Manchester and Salford Yeomanry Cavalry was established under the command of Thomas Joseph Trafford, a wealthy Roman Catholic, resident at Trafford Hall. The most senior of Trafford's supporting officers was Hugh Hornby Birley, a mill owner, who had at one time been the town's boroughreeve and who had opposed the Corn Laws, not through any concern for his workforce, but because he believed they would raise wages.[4] The recruits that made up the Manchester and Salford Yeomanry troop, which would be supporting the civil powers at St Peter's Field, were, according to contemporary chronicler and reformist Archibald Prentice, 'hot-headed young men who had volunteered into that service from their intense hatred of radicalism'.[5] They were mainly from Manchester itself and were by profession innkeepers, tailors, butchers, cheesemongers and the like. The regiment was not included in General Sir John Byng's list of troops, as it was under the direct authority of the local magistrates.

That the Yeomanry were seen as enemies of reform is evident from the disdainful way in which they were characterized in the *Manchester Observer*. By July 1819, rumours were circulating that working people across Lancashire were preparing for the forthcoming mass meeting with regular military-style drills, equipped with pikes and other such weapons. In mid-July, the paper reported:

The stupid boobies of Yeomanry Cavalry, in the Neighbourhood, have only just made the discovery that the MIND and the MUSCLE of the country are at length united, and the poor dunghills have, during the past week, been foaming and broiling themselves to death, in getting their swords new ground, their pistols examined with the minutest scrutiny, and their bridle reins made impenetrable to the steel of the mere phantom of an improved Pike.

Quoting Thomas Wooler, the article goes on to describe the Yeomanry as 'generally speaking, the fawning dependents, or the supple Slaves of the Great, with a few fools, and a larger proportion of coxcombs, who imagine they acquire considerable importance by wearing Regimentals'. As for being soldiers, 'their ridiculous assumption of being able to put down the PEOPLE, will one day be as dangerous as it is now contemptible'.[6]

This was followed by another tirade in the *Manchester Observer* in early August: 'To the Official Gentlemen of Manchester... Gentry, I pity you, and your *dernier resources*, but,' and here the tone becomes a little threatening, 'whilst the world laughs at your *foiblesse*, I hope Englishmen will not forget to enter you in their Black Book.'[7] Francis Philips, a local loyalist who had been one of the signatories for the creation of the regiment, complained in his *Exposure of the Calumnies circulated by the Enemies of Social Order... Against the Magistrates and the Yeomanry Cavalry of Manchester and Salford*, 'The grossness of the terms lavished on the yeomanry, and on the Magistrates and the Town's officers, just prior to the meeting... not only in the Observer, but in placards upon the walls, exceeded all bounds of decency – they met the eye in every direction.'[8]

It was in this atmosphere that Major Trafford now ordered his men to prepare for the mass meeting. A journeyman cutler called Daniel Kennedy, working for a Mr Richardson on Deansgate, was instructed to make their sabres 'very sharp' and by the week ending 17 July he had prepared sixty such weapons.[9] Francis Philips challenged the interpretation that the sharpening of sabres suggested an exaggerated blood lust:

The simple history of all the tales we have heard of sharpening sabres is briefly this. On the 7th of July Government issued orders to the Cheshire and Manchester Yeomanry Cavalry, through the Lords Lieutenant of those counties, to hold themselves in readiness, and consequently most of the Manchester Cavalry sent their arms to the same cutler, which the corps during the last war had employed, to put them in condition; this was a month *before* the Manchester meeting of reformers had been advertised.[10]

Henry Hunt recalled in his memoirs that the advance publicity for the meeting, including in the London papers, had 'excited a very considerable sensation throughout the country, and particularly in the North of England. As I strongly suspected that my letters to Manchester, about this time, were opened at the post-office, I sent them by other conveyances than by post.'[11] The *Manchester Observer* made its first announcement on 31 July, in which it stated that the purpose of the meeting was 'to take into consideration the most speedy and effectual mode of obtaining Radical Reform in the Common House of Parliament' and 'to consider the propriety of the "Unrepresented Inhabitants of Manchester" electing a Person to represent them in Parliament', as had already been done in Birmingham, where an unauthorized poll had resulted in the 'election' *in absentia* of the reform sympathizer Sir Charles Wolseley. This phenomenon of the populace electing an alternative representative 'without the King's Writ', as Henry Hobhouse informed an increasingly nervous James Norris, had been assessed by the Attorney and Solicitor Generals to be 'a high misdemeanour, and that the Parties engaged and acting therein, may be prosecuted for a conspiracy'. Such a meeting, Hobhouse advised Norris, would be an unlawful assembly and the magistrates should decide whether to disperse it.[12] However, the advertisement in the *Manchester Observer* had stated that the meeting would only 'consider the propriety' of a vote for a mock Member of Parliament, which would not, in itself, be illegal. Yet, Hobhouse continues, unlawful behaviour or resolutions might manifest themselves at any point during the course of the event, therefore the magistrates should be vigilant.[13]

Despite Hobhouse's nuanced advice on the legality of proceedings, the special committee of magistrates, led by the young and relatively inexperienced William Hulton, chairman of the Lancashire and Cheshire magistrates, responded immediately to the *Manchester Observer*'s announcement by printing and circulating – for display in all prominent public spaces – a poster headed, in very large black letters, '*Illegal* MEETING'. The poster warned the public:

Whereas It appears by an Advertisement in the 'Manchester Observer' Paper of this day, that a PUBLIC and *Illegal* MEETING, is convened *FOR MONDAY The* 9th *Day of August NEXT*, To be held on the AREA, Near ST PETER'S CHURCH, in Manchester, WE, the undersigned *Magistrates*, acting for the Counties Palatine of Lancaster and Chester, do hereby Caution all Persons to abstain *At their Peril* from attending such ILLEGAL MEETING.[14]

A few onlookers may have scratched their heads at the idea that they would be in 'peril' should they *not* attend the meeting,* but the message of the poster was clear enough.

On becoming aware of this, Hobhouse wrote again to Norris

---

* Perhaps the most famous grammatical error in British history.

on 3 August, repeating the advice given by the Attorney General, and reiterating that he could not see how the meeting on the 9th could be illegal, provided it adhered to the terms of the original advertisement. He therefore requested of Norris, 'when the Magistrates next meet, you will call their attention to this Subject, with a view to their reconsidering the Resolution to which they came on Saturday, of preventing the assembly'. It was imperative, Hobhouse repeated, that the magistrates should 'act strictly within the Law, because it would give a great advantage to the disaffected to find the Law on their side, & we know there will be many ready to take advantage of any error which may be committed'.[15] The following day, he wrote again to Norris on the same subject. His letter described how, after reflection, Lord Sidmouth had become even more convinced 'of the Inexpediency of attempting forcibly to prevent the Meeting on Monday':

Every Discouragement and obstacle should be thrown in its way, and the Advertisement from the Magistrates will no doubt have a salutary effect in this respect. But his Lordship thinks that it would be imprudent to act up to the Spirit of the Advertisement. He has no doubt that you will make arrangements for obtaining evidence of what passes; that if any thing illegal is done or said, it may be the subject of prosecution. But even if they should utter sedition or proceed to the election of a Representative Lord Sidmouth is of opinion, that it will be the wisest course to abstain from any endeavour to disperse the Mob, unless they should proceed to Acts of Felony or Riot. We have the strongest Reason to believe that Hunt means to preside & to deprecate disorder. I ought to have mentioned that the opinion which I have expressed for Lord Sidmouth, is supported by that of the highest Law Authorities.[16]

In response to the magistrates' declaration of illegality, John Saxton travelled to Liverpool to obtain legal advice on behalf of the *Manchester Observer* and was told, by a Mr Ranecock, that, to remain firmly within the law, advertisements for the meeting should omit any mention of electing members of Parliament.[17] A new announcement was placed in the paper's 7 August edition, declaring that the revised purpose of the meeting was *'To consider the propriety of adopting the most* LEGAL *and* EFFECTUAL *means of obtaining a* REFORM *in the Commons House of Parliament'*.[18] It also contained the important information that the meeting was postponed to Monday 16 August. This gave the organizers an additional week to prepare themselves and attract more attenders – as Sir John Byng wrote to Hobhouse: 'It will give the disaffected more time to muster their forces' – for what promised to be the greatest gathering of people ever seen in the region.[19] In the same letter, Sir John also suggested that to reduce tensions, the authorities and factory owners in the district might meet with deputations of local workers: 'then an opportunity will be afforded to communicate with these men – the folly of the means lately used by them to seek redress, might in plain conciliatory language be pointed out to them, and their real wants might be [inquired] into and it might be seen if any good can be done for them.'[20] There is no evidence that such a move towards meaningful dialogue was ever made.

Henry Hobhouse, having received a letter from James Norris (dated 5 August) which brought news of the rescheduling of the meeting, declared: 'This Postponement His Lordship thinks the Magistrates may look upon as a triumph; & it occurs to his Lordship that they might avail themselves of the opportunity to put forth a monitory & conciliatory Address to the lower classes which might be productive of a very salutary effect.'

He also told Norris, 'The subject of the drilling Parties has met with the most anxious & attentive consideration of Lord Sidmouth & his Colleagues.'[21] In the opinion of the Home Secretary, the intelligence coming from Lancashire that large groups of men were drilling in a military fashion suggested the calculated involvement of a far from peaceable element. The *Manchester Observer* treated such fear-mongering (as they saw it) with disdain, particularly directed against the Manchester and Salford Yeomanry. As William Fitton wrote in a letter published in the paper, 'what they smell danger, do they? They have heard rumours among the poor weavers of pikes have they? And now shrink back! Brave fellows! And well they may; for half a dozen hungry, angry weavers, would eat a whole corps of Yeomanry fellows.'[22] That the editors of the paper were guilty of baiting the authorities is undeniable, if understandable.

As the day of the meeting drew near, Henry Hunt drove himself northwards from his home in Hampshire, in his own gig – pulled by his horse Bob, 'a great favourite and most valuable animal'[23] – and accompanied by his manservant, Henby Andrews. On the journey, Hunt met Sir Charles Wolseley, who had also been invited to the meeting on Monday, 'but some family reasons prevented him from complying.'[24] On Sunday 8 August, at Bullock Smithey near Stockport, about ten miles from Manchester, Hunt was informed that the meeting had been postponed until Monday next. 'The cause', Hunt recalled, 'was that Mr. Johnson and those concerned in calling the meeting had, in their advertisements, stated one of the objects to be, that of electing a representative or legislatorial attorney for Manchester. This foolish proposition... was seized on by the Magistrates of Manchester, and they issued hand-bills, and had placards posted all over town, denouncing the intended meeting as illegal, and', Hunt recalls with scorn, 'cautioning all persons *"to abstain at their peril from attending it".*'[25] Hunt recounts the sequence of events – Saxton's visit to Liverpool, the redrafting of the meeting's purpose, the new date – all arranged, he observes, 'without my having in any way received the slightest intimation of what was going on'.[26]

> I had travelled two hundred miles in my gig for the purpose of presiding, and when I learned that I had been made a fool of, I expressed considerable indignation, and declared my intention of returning into Hampshire immediately. I was, however, at length prevailed upon to proceed to Stockport to sleep that night, as I understood that Mr. Moorhouse had provided a bed for me, and a stall for my horse.[27]

On the road to Stockport, Hunt was met by Joseph Johnson and John Saxton, who explained what had happened and 'expressed a great desire' for Hunt to attend the meeting on the 16th, as they had already advertised that he would be the chairman, 'without my knowledge'. Hunt resisted, but was persuaded to go on to Manchester the following day, and to have dinner there with Johnson and others at Smedley Cottage, Johnson's farmhouse.

Before leaving James Moorhouse's residence on the Monday morning, Hunt received a note from Sir Charles Wolseley saying that he would like to accompany Hunt into the town, and 'after breakfast, we proceeded together in my gig to Manchester, attended by many thousands of the Stockport people. Johnson, the brush-maker, and others, from Manchester, had come to meet us, and they followed in a chaise, and Mr. Moorhouse followed, with a party, in his coach. We were greeted with the utmost enthusiasm by the people of Manchester.'[28] On arrival, Hunt addressed the gathering and then went on to Smedley Cottage with Sir Charles.

In the early twentieth century, Smedley Cottage, near Smedley Lane in the Cheetham Hill district to the north of Ancoats, was described as still 'standing in the midst of fields'. The cottage was 'a pleasant place to live in. In its garden and orchard were fine fruit trees that bore many great crops of apples, pears, plums and cherries. There was also a fountain and fish pond, together with a poultry yard, pig styes, and stables.'[29]

After dining there, Hunt was persuaded to remain at Johnson's house until 16 August to chair the meeting that day – 'still very much against my inclination, and quite in opposition to my own judgment',[30] as he recorded in his *Memoirs*. 'Had Johnson's life depended upon the result, he could not have been more anxious to detain me. He begged, he prayed, he implored me to stay; urging that without my presence the people would not be satisfied; and, in fact, foreboding the most fatal consequences if I departed before the meeting took place.' Hunt recalled, 'I solemnly declare that I never before consented with so much reluctance to any measure of the sort.'[31] Even his manservant, Henby, had been desperate to return south when he realized the original meeting had been cancelled: 'I left a wife and family behind me, besides, I had lost my linen in the way down.'[32] To stay a further week would cause Hunt 'the greatest personal and private inconvenience'. But he finally agreed, in the belief that his presence would 'promote tranquillity and good order, and under the assurance that, if I did quit the place, confusion and bloodshed would, in all probability, be the inevitable consequence'.

None of this, however, endeared Joseph Johnson to Henry Hunt: 'As for Johnson, the brush-maker, he was a composition of vanity, emptiness, and conceit, such as I never before saw concentrated in one person. It was the most ridiculous thing in the world to see him assuming the most pompous and lofty tone, while every one about him did not fail openly to express contempt for his insignificance and folly.' According to Hunt, Johnson was terrified at the prospect of managing the event on the 16th, and others agreed that Hunt 'alone had the power of conducting this great meeting in a peaceable, quiet, and Constitutional manner'. Hunt concludes with the thought that he had only remained to support the people of Manchester and to thwart their 'most base and bloodthirsty opponents'. Understandably, Joseph Johnson would later complain bitterly and publicly about Hunt's description of him and the events leading up to and after 16 August.

The week that Hunt spent under Johnson's roof was an uncomfortable one: 'I can, with great truth, affirm that this was one of the most disagreeable seven days that I ever passed in my life... However, most fortunately for me, Johnson was from home a considerable portion of this time, attending to his brush-making and other business.' This account was put to paper more than a year after the event, but the repeated references to the nature of Johnson's business confirms Hunt's disdain for his host. Johnson's absences, Hunt recalled, 'alone rendered the visit to Smedley tolerable'.[33] Hunt refused to join his host on various local visits, which he later considered fortunate, as the authorities might have attempted to use such activity as evidence of conspiracy.

Holed up in Smedley Cottage, Hunt used his time to good purpose. On Wednesday 11 August, he wrote an address to the good people of Manchester and its environs. It began: 'FELLOW COUNTRYMEN – Our enemies are exulting at the victory they profess to have obtained over us, in consequence of the postponement, for a week, of the public meeting intended to have been held on Monday last.' Hunt's main concern was the behaviour of the crowds and he was keen to set out how he wished the people to behave, relying, once more, on their inherent good-temperedness, their basic faith in and respect for their speaker, and their belief in the cause of parliamentary reform: 'You will meet on Monday next, my friends, and by your steady, firm, and temperate deportment, you will convince all your enemies, you feel that you have an important and an imperious public duty to perform, and that you will not suffer any private consideration on earth to deter you from exerting every nerve to carry your praise-worthy and patriotic intentions into effect.' He reminded his audience that the 'eyes of all England, nay, of all Europe, are fixed upon you; and every friend of real reform and of rational liberty is tremblingly alive to the result of your meeting on Monday next.' There was a danger, he said, that their enemies would 'seek every opportunity by the means of their sanguinary agents to excite a riot, that they may have a pretence for spilling our blood, reckless of the awful and certain retaliation that would ultimately fall on their heads'.

With that in mind, Hunt turned to the issue of whether the people should come armed: 'Come, then, my friends, to the meeting on Monday, armed with no other weapon but that of a self-approving conscience; determined not to suffer yourselves to be irritated or excited, by any means whatsoever, to commit any breach of the public peace.' They must trust in the fact that the meeting on the 16th – unlike that of the 9th – had not been pronounced illegal. In the knowledge that the magistrates and Home Office, as well as reform sympathizers, would be sure to read his words, Hunt stressed that the meeting was lawful and that the gathering had no mischievous or seditious purpose. He drew attention to the oppressive tactics employed by the governmental opponents of reform, and emphasized the enduring strength of the principles that inspired the people in their struggle for change:

Our opponents have not attempted to show that our reasoning is fallacious, or that our conclusions are incorrect, by any other argument but the threat of violence, and to put us down by the force of the sword, the bayonet, and the cannon. They assert that your leaders do nothing but mislead and deceive you, although they well know that the eternal principles of truth and justice are too deeply engraven on your hearts; and that you are at length become (unfortunately for them) too well acquainted with your own rights ever again to suffer any man or any faction to mislead you.

In a bold touch, he invited the boroughreeve or any of the nine 'wise Magistrates' who had proclaimed the illegality of the earlier meeting to join the rescheduled gathering. If the organizers' aims were wrong, it was the authorities' 'duty as men, as magistrates, and as Christians, to endeavour to set us right, by argument, by reason, and by the mild and irresistible precepts of persuasive truth. We promise them an attentive hearing, and to abide by the result of conviction alone. But once for all we repeat, that we despise their threats, and abhor and detest those who direct or control the mind of man by violence or force.'

This address was then printed. Copies were circulated throughout the district and displayed on the walls of public spaces, in taverns and in hostelries, for all to see and read. According to Hunt, two thousand copies were sold at a penny each in a few hours.[34]

Hunt also sent a copy of his address to *The Star* in London, asking them to publish it. *The Times*, having got hold of a version, duly did so, alongside a letter from Hunt addressed to the former paper and dated 12 August, which stated:

At a reform meeting held at Leigh yesterday, it is reported two of the speakers had warrants issued against them by Mr. Fletcher, of Bolton, and they were arrested without opposition. We have our meeting here on Monday next, and the preparations for a riot (to be produced, if any, by the agents of the police) are equal to those made by the Lord Mayor previous to the meeting in Smithfield. I have no doubt but we shall conduct the proceeding with great quietness and order, although I dread any mad attempt, to produce disturbance, as the people here, although disposed to peace, are much more determined to resist any illegal attack made upon them; however, I shall do my duty, and I hope to keep them firm and quiet.[35]

As the week progressed, a number of visitors ventured to Smedley Cottage. One was Samuel Bamford, who arrived on Friday 13 August, apparently while Hunt was having his portrait painted by one 'Tuke', possibly a local artist.[*] Bamford does not seem to have had much faith in the painter's ability, as he watched Mr Tuke amend the portrait, 'which indeed it wanted'. No doubt this is one of the depictions that Bamford considered did not fully capture the nuances – physical and psychological – of the illustrious sitter, though the mention of it adds to the impression of Hunt's vanity.[†]

While this was going on and the two brother reformers were engaged in conversation, Hunt expressed concern that some

---

[*] The identity of 'Tuke' and the whereabouts of the portrait itself are currently unknown.

[†] Bamford, writing in his 1844 autobiography, may be misremembering when the portrait was painted. On 17 April 1819 the *Manchester Observer* carried an advertisement: 'Portrait of H. Hunt, Esq. The Print Portrait of HENRY HUNT, Esq from a Painting by Tuke, and engrav'd by J. Sudlow, being now completed, the Subscribers thereto are respectfully informed, that the above Print is now ready for delivery, at Mr. Chapman's, Observer Office, Market-street, and at Mr. Wroe's, 49, Great Ancots-street [*sic*], Manchester. N.B. A limited number of Proofs are struck off on India paper, at 9s each. Ditto on superfine plate, at 7s. After Impressions, at 4s.6d.'

people might come to the meeting armed. He showed Bamford a copy of the address that he had had printed the day before, and asked him 'to caution those from Middleton' against bringing weapons. Bamford found this advice 'unpalatable':

I had not the most remote wish to attack either person or property, but I had always supposed, that Englishmen, whether individually or in bodies, were justifiable by law in repelling attack when in the King's peace, as I certainly calculated we should be, whilst in attendance at a legally constituted assemblage. My crude notions... led me to opine that we had a right to go to this place; and that consequently, there would not be any protection in law, to those who might choose to interrupt us in our right. I was almost certain there could be no harm whatever in taking a score of two of cudgels, just to keep the specials [constables] at a respectful distance from our line. But this was not permitted.[36]

Bamford continued to argue: 'I scarcely liked the idea of walking my neighbours into a crowd, both personally and politically adverse to us; and without means to awe them, or to defend ourselves?' Was it not the case, he enquired of Hunt, that many men who had been sworn in as special constables would be armed, and that weapons had been liberally distributed throughout the town? Had the sabres of the Yeomanry Cavalry not been sharpened? What, he asked, 'could we do, if attacked by those men, with nothing to defend ourselves?' Hunt responded that the laws of the land would protect them, since the magistrates were sworn to uphold them. Would the magistrates interfere with a peaceable and legal assembly? If 'we were in the right,' said Hunt, 'were they not our guardians?' Bamford recalled that Hunt summed up with the reassurance that 'whilst we respected the law, all would be well on our side'.[37] Bamford left Smedley Cottage far from reassured, but, apparently, willing to go along with Hunt's request.

Another visitor was a friend of Hunt's called Edward Grundy, who warned him that a rumour was circulating around Manchester that 'it was the intention of the Magistrates to have me apprehended, under a plea of having committed some political offence, in order to interrupt the proceedings of the meeting'. Grundy had confirmed that he would stand bail for Hunt, should this be the case. But Hunt was determined to confront the magistrates. On Saturday 14 August he drove to the New Bailey to ask them 'if there was any charge against me? – if there was, I begged to know what was the nature of it, as I was then ready to surrender myself and to meet it'. None of those present, including Constable Joseph Nadin, seemed to know anything about the matter. And, according to Hunt, they showed him 'all the polite attention that they were capable of showing'. Hunt left the courthouse with the assurance that there was no charge against him. He had, he believed, deprived the magistrates of any excuse to interfere with the meeting on Monday.[38]

In fact the magistrates had been in contact with the Home Office concerning the possibility of arresting Hunt. In response to a letter from James Norris on 9 August on that subject, Henry Hobhouse observed, on behalf of Lord Sidmouth,

if you find good ground for issuing a warrant it will be adviseable [sic] not to forbear from doing so in the expectation of his giving you a better opportunity unless some other reason for your Forbearance presents itself. We know that all the Demagogues feel extremely sore on the subject of criminal Prosecutions, and that Hunt in particular observes extreme caution for the sake of avoiding them. It is therefore very desirable to take the earliest opportunity of proceeding against him.

Hobhouse also noted that Lord Sidmouth was extremely happy to know that the Reverend William Hay would be assisting the other local magistrates up to and including the meeting on Monday.[39] The Home Office had little confidence in the Reverend Charles Ethelston and some of his fellow magistrates, but were relying on Hay and, to an extent, Norris – the two magistrates with formal legal training – for a sensible and measured response.

On Wednesday 11 August, Sir John Byng wrote to Hobhouse, enclosing a letter from Hay, and expressing some irritation at the to-ing and fro-ing in Manchester and the frequent and increasingly hysterical missives from the local magistrates. Sir John was commander of the entire Northern District, of which Manchester was a small part. Having originally handed over command of the troops to Lieutenant Colonel L'Estrange for the 9 August meeting, he had no intention of resuming that role at the rescheduled gathering. After receiving another letter requesting his presence in the town, Sir John was evidently exasperated. Given, he writes from York, 'the extensive commerce I have, & business to attend to, they were not very considerate in requiring my presence so hastily'. L'Estrange had sent a message by express 'to tell me there was no necessity for my coming'.[40] 11 August was, of course, the day before Sir John's horse Sir Arthur was due to race.

The enclosed letter from William Hay was very apologetic, excusing their last correspondence as written in the heat of the moment, when it had seemed that only Sir John's presence could allay the magistrates' collective fears. 'I am happy', Hay wrote, 'to say that that aspect has been materially altered from the reports which we have since received and in such a degree as to do away with the propriety of applying to you in any further instance.'[41] Sir John was thus released from any sense of duty to attend Monday's meeting in person.

On Sunday 15 August, Henry Hunt received an unexpected visitor at Smedley Cottage. Richard Carlile, who had maintained contact with James Wroe, had received an invitation from John Knight to attend the August meeting and, after arriving at the Star Inn on Deansgate, immediately set off again for Smedley Cottage three miles away. Despite the invitation, Carlile wanted to have Hunt's express permission to attend the gathering and to join him on the hustings. Carlile carried several impressions, or copies, of a pamphlet entitled 'Address to the People of Great Britain to the People of Ireland', which was, in substance, the address made by Hunt at the mass meeting at Smithfield in London, less than four weeks before. Its purpose was to unite the reformers of England and Ireland under the single banner of 'Universal Civil and Religious Liberty.' Hunt saw no need to distribute these pamphlets straight away, since he was intending to focus on the subject of Universal Suffrage at the meeting the following day, but he thought they might be left on the tables at the dinner which was to be held in his honour, as had happened in January, directly after the close of proceedings on St Peter's Field.

Around the same time, Hunt received reports of a troubling incident involving James Murray, 'a sort of spy of the police'.[42] Murray had been watching groups of men marching and drilling on the moors around White Moss, near Middleton, and had been attacked and badly beaten by some of them. Samuel Bamford heard of the incident the same day from his neighbours, who told him that Murray 'had been conveyed in a shocking condition to a house in Middleton, and from thence in a coach to Manchester;

and… was not expected to recover'. Later, in his autobiography, Bamford quoted from Murray's own testimony, given a week after the event in the presence of the Bolton magistrate Colonel Ralph Fletcher – suggesting that Murray was one of Fletcher's spies.[43] He is identified as a confectioner from Withy Grove, Manchester, known as 'Gingerbread' Murray, and said he had been watching between fourteen and fifteen hundred men, 'the greatest number of whom were formed in two bodies, in the form of solid squares; the remainder were in small parties of between twenty and thirty each: there were about thirty such parties, each under the direction of a person acting as a drill serjeant, and were going through military movements.' Murray and some companions were walking amongst the marching men when one of the 'drill serjeants', on noticing him, told him to fall in. Murray made an excuse but, as he turned away, someone shouted, 'Spies'! Others then cried, 'Mill them', 'Murder them'. Murray and his confederates fled for their lives across the fields, pursued by about a hundred men throwing clods of earth at them. When they eventually caught up with Murray, he begged them not to kill him. The men began beating him anyway but then, on reflection, relented.

Bamford deeply regretted the violence of the incident in itself, but he also feared that it would play into the hands of the magistrates, as proof of the inherently violent nature of the crowds marching to Manchester, despite Hunt's pleas and claims to the contrary. 'It was however past, and so far irremediable, and all we could do was to exhibit the greater coolness and steadiness in whatever situation we might be placed. It was certainly a misfortune.'[44] Bamford's narrative of events includes the telling detail that Murray and his companions received a visit from the authorities on their arrival in Manchester, and that a special meeting of the magistrates was convened the same afternoon. Bamford believed that at this meeting it was resolved 'to return a full measure of severity to us on the following day, should any circumstance arise to sanction such a proceeding'.[45]

Hunt shared Bamford's regret at the assault on James Murray. Like his colleague, he feared that the authorities would use the incident to frighten the respectable citizens of Manchester with the spectre of violent unrest. His *Memoirs* capture his concern the day before the meeting: 'I, therefore, passed the Sunday with that degree of anxiety which every person not wholly devoid of sensibility must have naturally felt for the result of the coming day.'[46]

Certain of the magistrates were in a similar state of trepidation. At 11 p.m. on Sunday 15 August, the eve of the meeting, James Norris wrote to Lord Sidmouth:

My Lord,

The Magistrates, the military, and civil authorities of Manchester have been occupied nearly the whole of this day in concerting the necessary arrangements for the preservation of the peace to-morrow, and for the safety of the town, in case riot should ensue. We have been much occupied in taking depositions from various parts of the country; and although the Magistrates, as at present advised, do not think of preventing the meeting, yet all the accounts tend to shew, that the worst possible spirit pervades the country; and that considerable numbers have been drilling to-day, at distances of four, six, and ten miles from Manchester; and that considerable numbers are expected to attend the meeting. I hope the peace may be preserved; but under all circumstances, it is scarcely possible to expect it; and in short, in this respect, we are in a state of painful uncertainty.[47]

13

MIDDLETON

'The greatest hilarity and good humour'

For some weeks now, in the villages and towns of Lancashire and the West Riding of Yorkshire, people had been preparing for their march to the great mass meeting in Manchester. That preparation included the mending and cleaning of best clothing, the crafting of festive decorations, floral and foliage buttonholes and favours, and the making of banners. Far more sinister, from the authorities' point of view, were the reports – gleaned from James Murray among many others – of drilling and marching practice, which smacked of military discipline. What, local magistrates and constables asked themselves, was their purpose? Local people were keenly aware of such activities occurring on the moors beyond their towns and dwellings; they would acknowledge that they had watched from a distance, out of curiosity, but few were prepared to admit to participating.

More worrying still were reports coming to the magistrates' attention that these bands of men were being drilled by British army veterans. William Morris, a weaver from White Moss, recognized a John Whitworth 'who was a private in the 6th regiment of foot; he was drilling the men… John Hayward, who was a private in the 16th dragoons, was doing the same'.[1] Morris was a veteran himself, having been a non-commissioned officer in the 104th Regiment and a recruiting officer, serving in Ireland. 'I know what marching is,' was his trenchant observation.[2]

To some, including the magistrates, these could not be preparations for a peaceful political meeting – their militaristic overtones suggestive of imminent revolution, from which violence and bloodshed must surely ensue. As early as 2 March, Henry Hobhouse had sent a private letter to Colonel Fletcher, acknowledging receipt of updates from the Bolton magistrate and his informant William Chippindale which confirmed 'the opinion long since formed by his Lordship that your Country [region] will not be tranquillized [sic], until Blood shall have been shed either by the Law or the sword. Lord Sidmouth will not fail to be prepared for either alternative, and is confident that he will be adequately supported by the Magistracy of Lancashire.'[3]

Seen from another, less jaundiced point of view, the organizing and drilling of participants could be interpreted as a way of instilling discipline, thereby ensuring that the vast crowds gathered on 16 August would be anything but an unruly, riotous mob bent on destruction and revolution. If the crowds could maintain peaceable order both *en route* to St Peter's Field and on the ground itself, then, it was hoped, there would be no excuse for the authorities to break up the meeting. Besides which, as argued by Bamford, the people maintained the right to do what they could to defend themselves against unprovoked attacks.

But no matter how many times Hunt and his fellow organizers requested that the people arrive unarmed and conduct themselves peacefully, no one could guarantee that everyone present was of the same mind. The authorities had been known to hire individuals who actively incited violence, which suggested that the so-called 'peace makers', the magistrates and constables, could not be fully trusted either.

On the day, the crowds would march in formation, accompanied by music and banners or 'colours'. Dr Joseph Healey later explained (in court) that in Lancashire 'military habits are almost interwoven with the people' who 'walk in procession with music and flags'.[4] His point was that the practice of orderly marching was rooted in local tradition and culture.[5] James Dyson, a Middleton weaver, observed that 'it is customary at our *wakes* and *rush-carts* in Lancashire to have banners and music; the rush carts are held of a Saturday, and on the following Monday the men walk in procession', although, he adds, 'they do not keep the step'.[6] Samuel Bamford elaborated on this description: 'it is an annual custom to have a cart on which rushes are neatly placed; this cart is drawn by young men decorated with ribbons, and preceded by young women, music, &c.'[7]

Healey, Dyson and Bamford present the marching not as an overture to bloodshed and unrest, but as an extension of these community parades and as a means to preserve public order.[8] William Morris adds another dimension: 'I have seen many processions with music at Middleton, of the Orangemen, and Odd Fellows; they had flags and inscriptions.'[9] John Eaton, a plumber and glazier from Middleton, also observed that the 'procession of the Orangemen and Odd Fellows (one of whom I am) often move in regular order... Our flag is called the Union, but it has no inscription. I don't know Mr. Fletcher, the Magistrate, but that he is in our lodge.'[10] In other words, there was a cultural link between the parading of the magistrates in their loyalist fraternities* and the marches being planned by those drilling on the moors in support of parliamentary reform.

Writing in the 1870s, the folklorists John Harland and Thomas Wilkinson observed that in Lancashire 'formerly almost every

---

* 'Orangemen' refers to members of the Orange Order, a Protestant fraternity originally formed in support of William III (of Orange). The Oddfellows were a benevolent society akin to the Freemasons in structure.

parish had its rush-carts and rush-bearing festival'.[11] These customs were also current in the West Riding of Yorkshire.[12] Some of these rush-carts were extraordinary structures: 'On a fixed day in every year – in Rochdale on the 19th August – a kind of obtuse pyramid of rushes, erected on a cart, is highly ornamented in front, and surmounted by a splendid garland. To the vehicle so laden, from thirty to forty young men, wearing white jackets and ornamented with ribbons and flowers, are harnessed in pairs.' On arrival at the parish church, 'the rushes were spread on the clay floor under the benches used as seats by the congregation, to serve as a winter carpet; while the garlands were hung up in the chancel and over the pews of the families by whom they had been presented, where they remained till their beauty faded.'[13]

In a description of the procession from 1825, the author recalls that these 'carts are sometimes drawn by horses gaily caparisoned, but more frequently by young men, to the number of twenty or thirty couple, profusely adorned with ribands [sic], tinsel, &c. They were generally preceded by men with horse-bells about them, grotesquely jumping from side to side, and jingling the bells.'[14]

Music was a key communal activity and a core element of the parades. And it was to be an integral part of the march to Manchester. Firstly, it helped the marchers keep to the pace; secondly, it indicated local affiliation and pride; thirdly, it provided a rallying point on the field itself; and lastly – and just as important – it helped to keep the folk entertained on the journey to and from Manchester. Music was also integral to Christian services, whether Methodist or Church of England. Singing was particularly important in Methodism, the great Wesleyan hymns forming part of a large body of religious songs which supported the act of communal worship. In 1815 Jonathan Crowther observed, 'Singing makes a more considerable part of the worship of the Methodists than perhaps of that of any other denomination of Christians; hardly any exercise, so powerfully affects and raises the soul to heavenly things, as that of singing psalms, hymns, and spiritual songs. The hymns used, by the Methodists not only breathe a spirit of piety, but are beautifully poetic.'[15] One of the most popular, now as then, was Charles Wesley's 'Rejoice the Lord is King', later set to music by the great eighteenth-century composer, and naturalized Briton, George Frideric Handel:

> Rejoice, the Lord is King,
> Your Lord and King adore;
> Mortals give thanks and sing,
> And triumph evermore:
> Lift up your heart, lift up your voice;
> Rejoice, again I say, rejoice![16]

In Anglican services the congregation and choir were supported by 'Gallery Minstrels' of varying levels of accomplishment. In 1831 John La Trobe, giving advice to harassed vicars, believed that very bad musical habits had developed over the previous decades, particularly in rural parishes: 'In the place of the boisterous anthems and fugues, as they are impudently termed, which so generally obtain in country churches, he would seek to substitute simpler and more sober compositions... adhering to the genuine church tune, specimens of which are still extant in the very worst orchestras.' La Trobe favoured tunes such as the staple known as 'Old Hundredth', to which Psalm 100, 'All people that on earth do dwell', was set. Next, he draws the vicar's attention to 'the instruments, badly-sorted and worse played'. Bassoons, he declares, should be dispensed with immediately. Finally:

When he is able to devote an hour to his singers, he will find ample employment. The evils that require a reforming hand are chiefly these, – singing out of tune, frequently too flat, with a nasal twang, – straining the voice to an unnatural pitch, as though it were a contest of physical strength, – introducing awkward drawls, and tasteless ornaments. To remedy these defects, time, care, patience, and perseverance would be required, – but the reward would be ample.[17]

For the local rush-cart celebrations, Samuel Bamford recalled, 'Musicians were also secured in good time; a fiddler for the chamber dancing always, and never less than a couple of fifers and a drummer to play before the cart.' 'But,' he continues, 'if the funds would allow, and especially in later times, a band of instrumentalists would be engaged, often a sorry affair certainly, but still "a band" to swear to, and that would be a great thing for the ears of the multitude.'[18] All in all, local musicians seem to have been famed more for their enthusiasm and gusto than for their musicianship.

These parades traditionally occurred in the late summer – precisely the time of year when the meeting at St Peter's Field was to be held: 'The practice is general in the months of July, August, and September. Those held round this place are at Ashworth, Littlebro, Minbrow [Milnrow?], Shaw, Oldham, Royton, Middleton, Heywood, and Whitworth; the customs at each place being much alike.'[19] The Rochdale parade occurred every year on the same day, 19 August. Spectators too were an important part of the festivities: 'A band of music is always in attendance, which strikes up on the cart moving on, and thousands of spectators, attracted from a distance of ten or even twenty miles around, hail with repeated cheers the showy pageant.'[20]

In his autobiography, Bamford provides a detailed description of the annual rush bearing at Middleton, as he calls it, 'the great feast of the year'.[21] This usually occurred on the third Saturday in August, so in 1819 it was due to occur five days after the meeting at St Peter's Field. The rush-cart processions, like the reformers' march, required preparation and organization well in advance. In both cases, Middleton and Rochdale, the preparations for these two separate events would have been combined.

Bamford describes the evolution of the rush-cart ceremony, from a simple means of keeping parishioners' feet warm during winter church services, to a much more elaborate event, through a natural individual and then collective competitive spirit; 'thus the present quaint and graceful "rush-cart" would be in time produced. Music, dancing, and personal finery would accompany and keep pace with the increasing display; the feast would become a spectacle for all the surrounding districts, and the little wood-shadowed village, would annually become a scene of a joyous gathering and a hospital festivity.'[22] The young women 'would all be employed at over-hours getting their own finery and that of their brothers or sweethearts ready for the great even[t]'.[23]

The overall effect of the parades was of colour, movement, noise, gaiety and pageant, not least because of the participants' banners or 'colours', as described in 1825. Following the men with 'horse-bells', already quoted,

> is a band of music, and sometimes a set of morris dancers (but without the ancient appendage of bells), followed by young women bearing garlands; then comes the banner made of silk of various colors [sic], joined by narrow riband [sic] fretted, the whole profusely covered on both sides with roses, stars, &c., of tinsel (which in this part is called horse gold), and which, being viewed when the sun shines upon it, dazzles the eye.

The banners are generally from four to five yards broad, and six to eight yards long, having on either side in the centre a painting of Britannia, the king's arms, or some other device.[24]

The colours on 16 August would not only show the pride of the local people, emblazoned with messages behind which all could happily march, but would also, like the band, create a rallying point for anyone who lost their way in what was expected to be an enormous crowd.

A committee of Middleton residents met at Langley Dingle, 'a pleasant and retired spot', to discuss the upcoming march. After his unsatisfactory meeting with Henry Hunt, and bearing in mind the confrontation with James Murray at White Moss, Samuel Bamford was fearful of what the authorities might do. He attempted to persuade his fellow townsmen that some of their contingent should be armed, ready to defend themselves, their loved ones and, as important in his eyes, their banners, the protection of which he saw as a matter of local and personal honour: 'I, now more than ever, impressed with the belief that we should meet with opposition of some sort, proposed that a party of men with stout cudgels should be appointed to take care of the colours, in order, that at all events, they might be preserved. This was discussed at some length, but the more confiding [ie trusting] views of my neighbours, together with Mr. Hunt's admonition prevailing, my suggestion was overruled, and we shortly after separated.'[25]

On the Monday, Middleton was abuzz by eight o'clock in the morning.[26] Some were gathering for the march, while others waited around to see this extraordinary mass of local people set off. The crowd came together on open ground at Barrowfields. The Middleton weaver James Dyson was among the throng. He recalled that between nine and ten o'clock there were six or seven hundred people, men, women and children present.[27] Although parades were common, nothing on this scale had taken place in the town before and the excitement must have been palpable. All those present, according to Bamford, were prepared to show a collective strength, a unity of aim and spirit, but in a manner that was peaceful and joyous.

In forming the parade, Samuel Bamford noted, twelve of the most 'comely and decent-looking youths' were placed at the front in two rows of six, each holding a laurel branch 'as a token of amity and peace'. They were followed by men from the various districts that had gathered at Middleton, in rows of five. The band came next, 'an excellent one', followed by the colours. The first was a silk square in a rich Prussian blue with elegant gold inscriptions, likely to stir the heart and soul: 'Unity and Strength', the date '1819' at the lower edge, and on the reverse, 'Liberty and Fraternity'. The next was green silk, again with gold inscriptions: 'Parliaments Annual', 'Suffrage Universal' – the core demands, indeed rights, of the freeborn Englishman. Between these two, on a tall staff, was a red velvet Cap of Liberty, 'tastefully braided with the word, LIBERTAS'.[28] The remainder of the men, from the districts of Back-o'th'-Brow, Heatons and Blackley, followed on, again in rows of five abreast. Each group had a leader, wearing a sprig of laurel, who followed the directions from a man at the head of a column – Bamford called these latter individuals 'principal conductors' – who were all tasked with maintaining orderliness and, more broadly, keeping this large group of people together. A bugle sounded, a silence descended on those gathered, and Samuel Bamford prepared to address them with a mixture of pride, hope and caution.

Dyson recalled that Bamford climbed onto a chair and commenced with the greeting, 'Friends and neighbours.'[29] Bamford himself, many years later, summarized his speech:

I reminded them, that they were going to attend the most important meeting that had ever been held for Parliamentary Reform, and I hoped their conduct would be marked by a steadiness and seriousness befitting the occasion, and such as would cast shame upon their enemies, who had always represented the reformers as a mob-like rabble: but they would see they were not so that day. I requested they would not leave their ranks, nor shew carelessness, not inattention to the order of their leaders; but that they would walk comfortably and agreeably together. Not to offer any insult or provocation by word or deed; nor to notice any persons who might do the same by them, but to keep such persons as quiet as possible; for if they begun to retaliate, the least disturbance might serve as a pretext for dispersing the meeting. If the peace officers should come to arrest myself or any other person, they were not to offer any resistance, but suffer them to execute their office peaceably. When at the meeting, they were to keep themselves as select as possible, with their banners in the centre, so that if individuals straggled, or got away from the main body, they would know where to find them again by seeing their banners; and when the meeting was dissolved, they were to get close around their banners and leave the town as soon as possible, lest, should they stay drinking, or loitering about the streets, their enemies should take advantage, and send some of them to the New Bailey.

Bamford also announced the resolution of the committee that 'no sticks, nor weapons of any description, would be allowed to be carried in the ranks; and those who had such, were requested to put them aside, or leave them with some friend until their return'. As a result, he recalls, many sticks were left behind 'and a few only, of the oldest and most infirm amongst us, were allowed to carry their walking staves'. He concludes, 'I may say with truth, that we presented a most respectable assemblage of labouring men; all were decently, though humbly attired; and I noticed not even one, who did not exhibit a white Sundays' shirt, a neck-cloth, and other apparel in the same clean, though homely condition.'[30]

James Dyson remembered that Bamford's address was met with hearty cheers.[31] Then the column was formed, and the band struck up a lively tune as the silk banners waved and flashed in the bright sunlight. Dyson recalled:

We had music on that day; we had a drum; they do not use it in church music unless at oratorios. We have sacred music sometimes in church, at Middleton; we also have bassoons and clarionets, &c. occasionally on [Sundays]. The bassoon, in our party, belonged to the man who played it; the drum belonged to a man who keeps a farm... Thomas Ogden, a musician; he did play in church... I know [Thomas] Fitton: he and Ogden played with our party.[32]

The Rochdale party then joined that of Middleton and Bamford writes that another shout, this time from a several thousand-strong assembly, 'startled the echoes of the woods and dingles. Then all was quiet save the breath of music; and with intent seriousness, we went on.'[33] James Dyson says that, 'There were men by the side to keep order, and when the step was lost it was recovered again by their calling out, "Left – Right."'[34]

The combined group was now led by a few hundred women, mainly the young wives ('mine own', Bamford later recalled, 'was amongst them') and 'our handsomest girls, – sweethearts to the lads who were with us'. Mary Yates, a mother of six, was walking within this group and recalled, 'I saw Bamford's wife on the way. We walked arm-and-arm together.'[35] They danced to the music, or sang along to the popular airs. A few of the children were sent back, but some continued with the main party. Among the young women was Elizabeth Sheppard, fourteen years old and the daughter of a Middleton publican.[36] On that bright, hopeful morning, as Bamford recounted, 'we went in the greatest hilarity and good humour, preceded by a band of music, which played several loyal and national airs ; and that our fathers, our mothers, our wives, our children, and our sweethearts were with us.'[37] 'And thus,' he continued, 'we went slowly towards Manchester.'[38]

Mima Bamford recollected that, 'I was determined to go to the meeting, and should have followed, even if my husband had refused his consent to my going with the procession.' She had heard 'that if the country people went with their caps of liberty, and their banners, and music, the soldiers would be brought to them'. As a result, she says, 'I was uneasy, and felt persuaded, in my mind, that something would be the matter, and I had best go with my husband, and be near him; and if I only saw him I should be more content than in staying at home.' Having left her little daughter, Ann, with a kindly neighbour, Mima 'joined some of the married females at the head of the procession'. However, she continued to worry and, when glancing across at her husband, 'an ominous impression smote my heart. He looked very serious, I thought, and I felt a foreboding of something evil to befall us that day.' Clearly Mima, knowing Samuel as well as she did, sensed his inner concerns, which his cheerful and encouraging demeanour belied. She continues, 'I was dressed plainly as a countrywoman, in my second best attire. My companions were also neatly dressed as the wives of working men; I had seen Mr. Hunt before that time; they had not, and some of them were quite eager to obtain good places, that they might see and hear one of whom so much had been reported.'[39]

William Elson, a farmer, had joined the procession, accompanied by three of his children: his daughter, aged seventeen, and two sons aged fourteen and thirteen. All three had begged their parents to allow them to participate. Even so, 'I should not have allowed my children to go to the meeting,' Elson said later, 'had I apprehended any disturbance or riot; nor would I have gone myself, had I entertained such a fear... I had no other motive but curiosity in going to the meeting.'[40]

Mary Lees, a mother of five, married to a plumber and glazier from Middleton, stood at the door of her house with her children to watch the procession pass through the town. 'They all seemed quiet and cheerful,' she recalled, noting a great number of women among the Rochdale party. The women, she said, 'were persons of good character'. Mrs Lees remembered that several toasts were made, 'among the rest "God save the King," which though not a common toast, is made use of by the country people.' She also heard the cry 'Hunt for ever!'[41]

14

ST PETER'S FIELD

'A beautiful morning'

On Monday 16 August, as the sun rose over St Peter's Field, all was quiet. The Quaker Meeting House, with its high-walled burial ground, lay to the north on Dickinson Street, while the distinctive Grecian exterior of St Peter's Church could be seen, set a little back from the field itself, to the northeast. The walled garden and terraced houses on Mount Street enclosed the eastern side of the ground and Windmill Street ran at a diagonal along the south. Watson Street formed the short western edge of the field, connecting at its northern point with Peter Street. The latter traversed the field from St Peter's Church in the east, eventually meeting Deansgate to the west, the town's main north–south thoroughfare. Beyond the buildings, the skyline was punctuated by factory chimneys, the towering modern obelisks that had amazed the Swiss visitor, Hans Escher five years before. On this morning, however, many of the clattering machines within these factories would fall silent, and then, unusually, no smoke would be seen belching forth into Manchester's stricken air.

One of the first to arrive at St Peter's Field was Thomas Worrall, assistant surveyor of Manchester. Prior to the abandoned meeting on 9 August, he and his men had cleared stones, sticks and 'every thing which could be used in an offensive manner'[1] from the field itself and adjoining streets. Returning a week later, by eight o'clock they had removed a further quarter cartload of stones, but now, he later recalled, the field remained clear of such debris.

John Tyas, a reporter from *The Times* newspaper in London, had arrived in Manchester the week before. While in the town he 'had heard much conversation about the meeting on 16th' and on that Monday, he left his lodgings early to see the people gathering on the field and to witness the preparations for Henry Hunt's arrival. 'I was on the alert,' he recollected, as his paper was 'always giving the most voluminous accounts of things of this kind'.[2] When he arrived at eight o'clock, just as Mr Worrall and his men were completing their task, Tyas noted 'very few people'[3] on the field, and even after two and a half hours had passed, there were but '250 idle individuals' gathered.[4]

Meanwhile William Hulton and nine fellow magistrates from the counties of Lancashire and Cheshire – including the Reverend William Hay, the Reverend Charles Ethelston, Colonel Ralph Fletcher and James Norris – convened at the Star Inn on Deansgate, a hostelry often used by those magistrates such as Hay who lived further afield.[5] They breakfasted and then, between ten and eleven o'clock, made their way to Mr Buxton's house at the lower end of Mount Street. This house overlooked the field, providing an excellent position from which to monitor events. The magistrates established themselves in the front room on the first floor and waited. Between half past eleven and midday, as crowds were beginning to congregate on the field, they received 'information on oath, relative to the approach of large bodies of people'.[6] These expressions of concern from local people, alarmed at what they had heard about the nature of the meeting and the possible behaviour of its participants, would inevitably influence the magistrates' decision-making. The meeting was not in itself illegal, as William Hulton had confirmed, and they had judged it best, interpreting the advice from the Home Office, to allow it to take place.[7] But if seditious language was used, if the crowd was incited to violence and riot, then they could and would act. Hulton, by his own admission, spent most of his time at Mr Buxton's house writing instructions, in his capacity as chairman of the bench of magistrates for the two counties and therefore of this special meeting, 'but,' he later recalled, 'I frequently looked out of the window, and saw large bodies of men approach.' He describes them arriving with banners and to the sound of bands, and apparently organized into divisions, with people walking beside them bellowing commands. In his testimony, Hulton repeatedly emphasized the regularity with which the groups marched. To better see what was happening, he had a 'glass to look through',[8] which could have been a small telescope or spyglass, or, as some historians have interpreted it – given his cultivated manners and dandified appearance – opera glasses.[9]

During this time, as William Hulton recalled, the hustings from which Henry Hunt would address the crowd – on this occasion constructed from two carts lashed together, with planks on top creating a stage – was placed, at the insistence of the magistrates, so as to allow a double line of constables to reach from the platform to Mr Buxton's front door.[10] Between three and four hundred special constables had volunteered to police the event, many recruited within the previous forty-eight hours. According to one Chief Constable present, Jonathan Andrew, 'the persons selected were householders, and as respectable as they could get them',[11] with himself, Joseph Nadin and John Moore in overall command. Among these special constables were Richard Holt, a dyer from Manchester, Robert Hughes, a builder and innkeeper, and John Barlow, a merchant.[12] Barlow had not intended to go to the meeting 'in an official capacity', but while attending to business

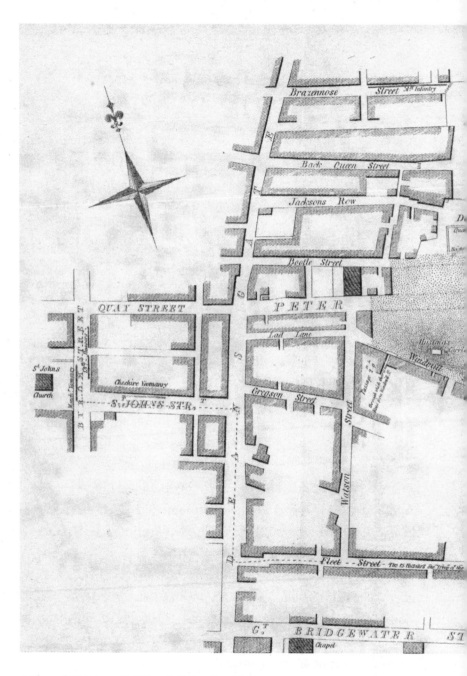

A Plan of St Peter's Field by C. Wheeler, 1823.
(The John Rylands Library, Manchester)

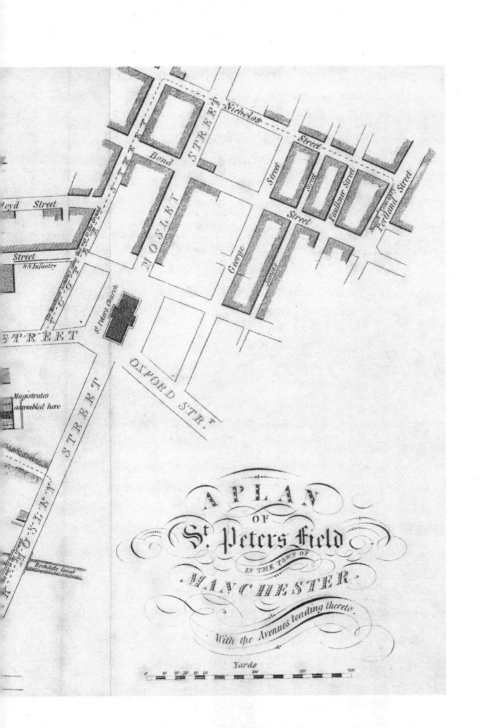

Nicholas Street

Bond Street

MOSLEY STREET

Loyd Street

Street

&8 Infantry

Street

George Street

Thomas Street

Faulkner Street

Mount Newington Street

Portland Street

STREET

St Peters Church

OXFORD STRt

Magistrates
assembled here

STREET

Rochdale Canal

A PLAN
OF
St. Peters Field
IN THE TOWN OF
MANCHESTER.
With the Avenues leading thereto.

Yards
0 10 20 30 40 50   100   150   200

at the Exchange, he saw men carrying what he believed were large bludgeons and hedge stakes, which 'created alarm in his mind' and 'changed his intention'. He recalls that it was 'his duty to give every assistance to preserve the public peace: He did so, on account of the alarm which the appearance of the people had created.'[13] Some residents had closed and even boarded up their shops in anticipation of trouble breaking out. Jeremiah Smith, headmaster of Manchester Grammar School, considered it prudent, for the safety of his scholars, to close the school for the entire day.[14]

The constables formed their lines as directed and Nadin began to patrol up and down the narrow avenue they had created through the crowd.[15] According to his account, he was barracked as he passed. Some called out, 'That's Joseph… he is great guts, he has more meat in his belly than we have'; others dubbed the constables 'the black mob' and declared, 'They have very good coats on their backs – better coats than we have', or shouted encouragement to 'knock him down, and keep him down'.[16] Nadin also observed that certain strangers in the crowd were heckled with the term 'spy'.[17] If Nadin's account is accurate, these expressions show the resentment that Manchester's poor felt towards those who could wield the full force of severe laws against them. Even Nadin himself later observed, regarding the appearance of those that were shouting at him, 'I don't know [if] the people were fed; Some of their coats were very bad.'[18]

Just after the lines of constables were formed, both Nadin and Hulton (the latter here quoted) noticed that 'a number of men had rushed in, locked their arms together, and surrounded the hustings'.[19] Other witnesses believed that this was done to prevent the hustings from being disturbed but, in Nadin and Hulton's opinion, the clear aim was to prevent the avenue of constables from reaching the platform. Jonathan Andrew stated that after the constables had formed up, the platform was purposely moved further away from Mr Buxton's house and the resulting gap immediately filled by a large group of men. Andrew was convinced that the intention was to cut off the lines of communication between the magistrates, the constables and those on the hustings.[20] Whatever the reality – the differing recollections hint at both the confusion of the moment and the subsequent desire to lay blame elsewhere – there was a palpable mood of suspicion and mistrust, and tensions were already mounting.

At around this time, the Reverend Edward Stanley, Rector of Alderley in Cheshire, had arrived in Manchester and was riding along Oxford Road and Mosley Street towards Deansgate, where he had an appointment to meet Mr Buxton at about one o'clock. On the way, he passed the Manchester and Salford Yeomanry Cavalry gathered in Pickford's yard on Portland Street. A little later, he encountered several parties of people, including the large Ashton contingent arm in arm, some carrying banners, and with bands playing. As the morning progressed some of these banners would be placed around the vacant hustings, alongside a wooden sign on a stick with the words 'Order! Order!' painted on it, in preparation for Henry Hunt's arrival.[21] Discovering Mr Buxton was not at his Deansgate shop, Stanley made his way across St Peter's Field to Buxton's house, where the magistrates had gathered. He had hoped to avoid the crowds and the mass meeting, but, in the event, he found himself by chance in the thick of the action. Unfamiliar with Manchester, he simply had to wait until the meeting was over and the streets were passable once more. He would also be, again by accident, one of the most important witnesses to the coming events. Stanley was of the same social and professional class as the magistrates, and knew one of them, Thomas William Tatton, very well; he might be expected to have had a natural loyalty and like-mindedness to them. Yet, crucially, he was one of the most disinterested and therefore reliable individuals present.[22] And, as he was one of the few people on that day to have a similar view of the field to the magistrates, Stanley's evidence forms a critical commentary on their recollections of what they saw and heard.

Stanley's account begins: 'I saw no symptoms of riot or disturbances before the meeting; the impression on my mind was that the people were sullenly peaceful.'[23] He was curious and somewhat excited about the extraordinary spectacle before him. From his first-floor window he could see, to the west, the hustings located midway along Windmill Street. He also observed the men forming a barrier around the hustings, who he assumed were special constables, and the double line of constables extending to the front door of the house, a distance, he calculated, of about one hundred yards. The corridor created by these lines, two or three men deep as Stanley perceived them and about two hundred strong, was established partly, as Jonathan Andrew confirmed, 'in order that they might hear the Orators, convey it to the Magistrates, and keep up the communication'.[24] It would also allow swift access if an arrest were necessary – something that the men obstructing the hustings must have realized.

Behind the hustings, making up the western half of Windmill Street, was a row of dwellings among which stood the Windmill public house, just ten yards from the platform. Along the eastern length of the street was a raised area of rough ground. Here a large group of people, mainly women, had a good view of the field and the approaches to it. At this moment, Edward Stanley describes the 'mob' on the field as a 'vast concourse of people in a close and compact mass' which 'surrounded the hustings and constables, pressing upon each other apparently with view to be as near the speakers as possible'.[25] From his vantage point, Stanley considered that despite the size of the central crowd people were still able to make their way around the area without too much hindrance. His observations indicate that there was a dense concentration of people immediately around the hustings, thinning towards the outer edges of the field and not too constrained. But this may not have been the experience of those within the crowd itself.

Before midday, John Smith, editor of the *Liverpool Mercury*, was standing near the hustings watching with great interest the various parties arriving on the field. He had been invited by John Knight and the committee to join them on the day but had declined, as he did not 'like to take part in the politics of another town, in a public capacity'.[26] As an independent reporter, albeit one with deep sympathies for the reform movement, he recalled observing the people and being 'struck with the orderly manner in which they advanced'.[27] He overheard the conversations of those standing around him and declared to them that he presumed they 'were all friendly to Parliamentary reform. They all said, yes.' Smith asked, 'peaceably so, I hope', to which they responded, 'Nothing but peace and freedom do we seek.' Between midday and one o'clock, he noted, the crowd increased considerably. At over six feet in height, Smith had a good view over the heads of those around him. He observed 'a great many women and children' among the crowd, as well as 'many old people' with walking sticks. He remarked that the crowd in general 'appeared many of them respectable, and clean dressed, as if they came to a holiday feast'. In contrast to John Barlow's recollections of public disquiet, Smith stated, 'I saw no alarm in the respectable persons of the town who had attended the meeting, either expressed in their countenances or conduct'. He took many of them to be 'inhabitants of Manchester from their dress and conversation'.[28]

Archibald Prentice spent some time that morning walking around the edge of the field, mingling with the groups who were standing there, chatting and laughing, before he returned to his house in Salford. As he passed by, he asked some women whether they were afraid, to which they replied, 'What have we to be afraid of?'[29]

Looking past the central mass and the less densely peopled area just beyond it, Stanley could see yet more crowds standing in a greater concentration around the edges of the field, whom he believed to be spectators, as distinct from participants. Of the participants, he says, the 'radical banners and caps of liberty were conspicuous in different parts of the concentrated mob, stationed according to the order in which the respective bands to which they belonged had entered the ground, and taken up their positions'.[30] The array of brightly coloured banners, fluttering above the hustings and being flourished throughout the crowd, lent the proceedings an almost heraldic dash. All were emblazoned with words of inspiration or challenge; they also had a military or regimental aspect embodied in the term 'colours', as Samuel Bamford described those from Middleton. These were civilian legions then, rather than a mob, marching and assembling under the colours of Liberty, Equality and Brotherhood.

Some of the banners, however, with their slogans such as 'Liberty or Death' and surmounted by the distinctive red Caps of Liberty – viewed by many as the symbol of violent revolution rather than freedom – were more provocative and disturbing. They were blamed by some observers for raising fears that violence would break out against citizens and property. Already thousands of people had arrived in Manchester from all directions, many of them strangers to the town, over a relatively short space of time – according to John Tyas and John Smith the main body converged on the field within two hours – creating an inevitable tension and unease among some of the town's residents. A key purpose, after all, of these mass meetings was a powerful display of numerical strength and significant collective will, in order to overawe the authorities. There were those on each side who hoped the other would be the first to move beyond the bounds – transgressing the constitution – and thus forfeit public support.

William Hay considered 'the assemblage of such a large number of people to be a breach of the peace, according to the rules of common sense and the best law authorities'. As he watched the columns of people carrying 'dreadful emblems and flags, he could not help considering it dangerous to the public peace; even singly these things denoted a bad purpose, but taken altogether, no man in common sense could think otherwise'.[31] In reality, very few of the banners bore inscriptions beyond the basic demands of the reform movement, 'Universal Suffrage', 'No Corn Laws', 'Parliaments Annual' and so on: none of which could have come as a surprise, nor be judged particularly aggressive or threatening. Even the banner declaring 'Equal Representation or Death' was not an omen of bloody revolution, as one contemporary reasoned. Rather, interpreted in a patriotic light, it meant that lack of fair representation brought political death; alternatively, it expressed the desire to die rather than be subject to despotism. 'What Englishman', this author concludes, 'but would join in the wish, or the expression!'[32]

The Middleton and Rochdale party, initially six thousand strong, had been joined by others as they walked through towns, including Blackley, on the journey to Manchester. At Harpurhey some among them were refreshed 'with a cup of prime ale from Sam Ogden's tap'.[33] On the sound of a bugle, they formed up again and continued on their way. William Elson said there 'was nothing on the road that induced me to think there would be any disturbance; every thing was peaceable and orderly.'[34]

As they neared Manchester, their leader, Samuel Bamford, was convinced that they would be stopped on the order of magistrates, that the Riot Act would be read and the party instructed to disperse, but the roads ahead were clear. Bamford 'began to think that I had over-estimated the forethought of the authorities; and I felt somewhat assured that we should be allowed to enter the town quietly'.[35] On the road to Collyhurst, a messenger arrived from Henry Hunt, requesting that the party meet him at Smedley Cottage and lead him into Manchester. Bamford attempted to ignore this, mainly, he later tells us, for practical reasons, but eventually he was persuaded to comply and therefore pander, in his opinion, 'to the vanity of our "great leader"' by heading Hunt's triumphant procession from Smedley Cottage.[36]

On the outskirts of Manchester, as they moved towards Smedley Cottage, they met a group of poor Irish weavers, with a banner 'whose colour was their national one, and the emblem of their green island home'.[37] The Middleton band struck up 'Saint Patrick's day in the morning' in their honour, and their new companions, as Bamford describes them, whooped and laughed as they danced along. When they eventually arrived in Oldham Street, one of the town's main arteries, which would take them near their destination, the Middleton and Rochdale party were 'frequently hailed... by the cheers of the townspeople'. Here they learned that several parties had already passed by and were congregating on the field, including the Lees and Saddleworth Union led by Bamford's friend Dr Healey, 'walking before a pitch-black flag, with staring white letters, forming the words, "Equal Representation or death." – "Love," – two hands joined, and a heart; all in white paint'. As Bamford observed, Healey's banner was 'one of the most sepulchral looking objects that could be contrived'.[38] Its dismal appearance and tone were noted by several witnesses, who failed to recall that 'Love' also featured.[39] At this moment Bamford realized, with secret pleasure, that they had somehow missed and therefore lost Hunt's procession: 'I was of opinion that we had rendered homage quite sufficient to the mere vanity of self-exhibition; too much of which I now thought, was apparent.'

Some of the Middleton party had, however, gathered around Smedley Cottage, including Lucy Morville, a widow from the town. She walked along holding hands with her youngest son, aged nine, until they came near to the cottage, where she met up with her elder son, aged twelve. She held his hand too, 'stopping with both till Mr. Hunt came from the cottage. I then went to St Peter's-field, a nearer road than the procession, with my two boys.'[40]

The Waterloo veteran John Lees, now employed in his father's factory, had left his family home in Oldham between eight and nine o'clock in the morning, wearing suitably unworkmanlike clothing, including a corbeau (dark brown) coat.[41] Understandably he had not told his family where he was going. When asked about his son's state of health that morning, Robert Lees considered him 'as hearty as ever he was since he was born'. He met fellow townsman Joseph Wrigley on Oldham Green and they began the eight-mile journey south to Manchester as part of the large local contingent, including marchers from Saddleworth and Lees (among whom was Dr Healey), Mossley and Oldham, all under the overall leadership of John Knight. As elsewhere, posters had been put up in Oldham with a message from Henry Hunt desiring 'the people to go to the meeting peaceably, and without arms'. According to the cotton spinner William Harrison 'they did so', and 'were without sticks or any thing'.[42] Joseph Wrigley recalled that John Lees 'was in good health and spirits'.[43] Jonah Andrew, a cotton spinner from Leeds, caught up with them at Hollingswood and walked with John Lees to Deansgate, where, in the throng, they became temporarily separated. He was then with John on St Peter's Field, about an hour before Henry Hunt's arrival, while the hustings was being set up. At some point John Lees sat or stood on the planks that made up the platform. Joseph Wrigley, too, recalled sitting on the hustings, with his friend now standing nearby: 'We were then both close together, with many women and children among us.' They agreed that they would walk home together later.[44] From their collective descriptions the general ambience appears to have been one of calm anticipation, with people mingling and chatting together while patiently awaiting the famous orator's arrival.

The man of the moment, Henry Hunt, had awoken at Smedley Cottage and, looking out of his bedchamber window, declared it 'a beautiful morning'. Glancing down into the street, he 'beheld the people, men, women, and children, accompanied by flags and bands of music, cheerfully passing along towards the place of meeting'.[45] He later noted: 'Their appearance and manner altogether indicated that they were going to perform an important, a sacred duty to themselves and their country, by offering up a joint and sincere prayer to the Legislature to relieve the poor and needy, by rescuing them from the hands of the agents of the rich and powerful, who had oppressed and persecuted them.'[46] No doubt that is exactly what many present were thinking. For others, though, it was little more than an unusual and welcome break from the relentless rhythm of their working lives.

Richard Carlile had walked the three miles from the Star Inn, where he was staying, to Smedley Cottage to join Hunt's parade.[47] He recalled that a crowd began to congregate around the house at eleven o'clock, and an hour later the hired barouche, a stately open carriage, arrived.[48] Henry Hunt, Joseph Johnson, Richard Carlile and John Knight, who had also now joined them, climbed aboard.[49] Hunt noted, in his *Memoirs*, that the form of the meeting had already been agreed – he was to chair it and a few others would be invited to speak. As they set off they were accompanied by a crowd, buoyed by the festive spirit, which gradually gained in size as the procession weaved its way through central Manchester, all the while a band playing before them. In the distance, Richard Carlile recounted, 'bodies of men were seen… marching in regular and military order, with music and colours. Different flags were fallen in with on the road, with various mottoes' such as 'TAXATION WITHOUT REPRESENTATION IS TYRANNY' and 'WE WILL HAVE LIBERTY', many adorned with Caps of Liberty.[50]

Soon after leaving Smedley Cottage, Hunt and his companions met Mary Fildes, Susannah Saxton and their large group from the Manchester Female Reform Society, 'handsomely dressed in white'.[51] Mrs Fildes was holding the society's magnificent emblematic banner, while Mrs Saxton was carrying the address, on a scroll, to be read out on the hustings and then presented to Henry Hunt with due ceremony. This party now followed the barouche two by two, while Mary Fildes, at Hunt's suggestion, 'rode by the side of the coachman, bearing her colours in a most gallant stile [*sic*]'. Hunt noted that 'though rather small, she was a remarkably good figure, and well dressed' and 'it was very justly considered that she added much to the beauty of the scene'.[52] Far from simply being a gallant gesture on Henry Hunt's part, Mary Fildes's prominence within the party, as he says, set the tone of his procession, although later he felt compelled to justify exposing her to public scrutiny and comment. Among many observers, both men and women, her presence would be deemed wholly inappropriate, even wilfully provocative.

Certainly, such confident possession of what was traditional male territory, a public political meeting, inevitably opened the sisterhood up to abuse. The banner slogan chosen by the Royton Female Reform Society, 'Let us die like men, and not be sold like slaves',[53] was also no doubt viewed by many onlookers as an unladylike and provocative sentiment. According to *The Times* reporter John Tyas, who was now watching the procession, members of the Oldham Female Reform Society were mocked in the street by other women: 'They viewed these Female Reformers for some time with a look in which compassion and disgust were equally blended; and at last burst out into an indignant exclamation – "Go home to your families, and leave *sike-like matters as these* to your husbands and sons, who better understand them." The women who thus addressed them were of the lower order in life.'[54] Henry Horton of *The New Times*, another London paper, described Mary Fildes in the 18 August edition as 'a profligate Amazon'. When Horton was asked why he had characterized her in this way, he answered that it was 'because I thought her appearance in the manner and place where I saw her, justified the observation'.[55] In similar vein, the *Manchester Chronicle* later declared that some of the women had 'come to the meeting under such ideal pomp, and with a demeanour the reverse of every thing that man delights to see in woman'.[56]

In his own and Mary Fildes's defence, Henry Hunt later argued that 'as she was a married woman of good character, her appearance in such a situation by no means diminished the respectability of the procession, the whole of which was conducted with the greatest regularity and good order'.[57] Richard Carlile recalled that Mrs Fildes, far from being visibly distressed by any verbal attack, 'continued waving her flag and handkerchief until she reached the hustings'.[58] He also emphasizes the presence of women in the crowd 'from the age of twelve to eighty' who, rather than abusing the female reformers, were seen energetically cheering 'with their caps in their hand, and their hair in consequence, dishevelled'. Indeed, 'the whole scene exceeds the power of description.'[59]

The barouche took the route from Shudehill to Hanging Ditch and Market Place, then along Deansgate towards St Peter's Field.[60] When it passed the Exchange, 'where the people were cheering most loudly, and Hunt and Johnson joining in the cheers',[61] John Tyas, still standing among the crowds on Hunt's processional route, came alongside the barouche. Hunt later described him as 'a gentleman of a most respectable family and connections' who had 'long occupied the station of reporter to the Times Newspaper, a lucrative and responsible situation'.[62] Tyas asked if he might join the party on the hustings, and with Hunt's consent, as the barouche continued on its way through the crowds, he clung gamely to the carriage door.[63] From this position, Tyas observed that as the barouche passed the Star Inn on Deansgate, where the magistrates had earlier gathered, the accompanying crowd hissed and hooted, although he also states that Henry Hunt took no part in this, nor did he encourage such behaviour.[64] James Moorhouse joined Hunt's party soon afterwards and, with the barouche crammed with people and to the cheers of the crowds, they proceeded towards St Peter's Field.

Meanwhile, Samuel Bamford and his party, having passed through Piccadilly and then down Mosley Street, walked along one side of St Peter's Church and then 'wheeled quickly and steadily into Peter-street, and soon approached a wide unbuilt space, occupied by an immense multitude, which opened and received us with loud cheers. We walked into that chasm of human beings, and took our station from the hustings across the causeway of Peter-street; and remained, undistinguishable from without, but still forming an almost unbroken line, with our colours in the centre.'[65] As Bamford recalled, this was half an hour before the barouche appeared. Mima Bamford had been walking alongside her husband but then lost sight of him: 'Mrs. Yates, who had hold of my arm, would keep hurrying forward to get a good place, and when the crowd opened for the Middleton procession, Mrs. Yates and myself, and some others of the women, went close to the hustings, quite glad that we had obtained such a situation for seeing and hearing all.'[66] Samuel Bamford says, 'My wife I had not seen for some time; but when last I caught a glimpse of her, she was with some decent married females; and thinking the party quite safe in their own discretion, I felt not much uneasiness on their account, and so had greater liberty in attending to the business of the meeting.'[67]

The Reverend Edward Stanley was on the first floor of Mr Buxton's house, awaiting Henry Hunt's arrival, when 'a murmur running through the crowd prepared us for his approach'.[68] At this point, Stanley left the magistrates – he does not comment on their reaction to either Hunt's appearance or the scale of the gathering – and, climbing the stairs to the second floor, he positioned himself at the front window. He recalled that he was now 'commanding a bird's-eye view of the whole area, in which every movement and every object was distinctly visible'.[69] As he watched, he noted that the arrival of Hunt's carriage was signalled by 'a tremendous shout' from the crowd. Directly below, William Hulton heard an 'extraordinary noise' which made him get up from his paperwork and walk to the window to look out over the now densely populated field. Like Stanley, Hulton confirmed that from this window 'I had a view over almost the whole of St. Peter's area'.[70] The noise greeting Hunt was, he said, like nothing he had ever heard before, and he hoped he would never experience such a thing again.[71]

The barouche, with Mary Fildes still perched prominently on the driver's seat, slowly made its way across the crowded ground towards the hustings. William Harrison was watching the procession and particularly recalled the figure sitting atop the carriage, whom he describes as the 'most beautiful woman I ever saw in all my life... all in white, and had on a straw bonnet'.[72] Samuel Bamford also noted the single 'universal shout from probably eighty thousand persons'[73] (the numbers are now thought to have been between sixty and eighty thousand) as the carriage entered the field, along with the 'neatly dressed female' seated at the front. Such comments confirm how unusual it was to see a woman so prominent within a political gathering, confirming Hunt's instinct for the well-timed gesture. Bamford goes on to relate that once on the field, Henry Hunt, wearing his distinctive white hat, 'stood up in the carriage to accept the cheers of the crowd'.[74] Compare this triumphant cavalcade, accompanied by the enthusiastic shouts of thousands of working people, to the descriptions of the Prince Regent in his golden coach and among his military escort, with little but the abuse and disdain of his father's subjects ringing in his ears.

Musicians had been playing throughout the barouche's journey, mixing popular folk songs, hymns and the like. When the carriage entered the field, according to several witnesses, a band mischievously struck up 'See the Conquering Hero Comes' from Handel's *Judas Maccabaeus*, an oratorio composed in celebration of the Duke of Cumberland's crushing of the 1745 Jacobite Rebellion. This militaristic tune, with march-like drumming, was taken up by other musicians and bands across the field. It was followed, according to some witnesses, by spirited renditions of 'Rule Britannia!' and then, in more solemn tones, of what was by now considered the British national anthem, 'God Save Great George Our King' – again an anthem in support of the Hanoverian dynasty, made popular during the '45 rising.[75] John Smith of the *Liverpool Mercury*, standing near the hustings, thought he heard the distinctive drum beat of 'God Save the King', as he calls it, and saw that those nearest the band had uncovered their heads in respect. Someone nearby confirmed it was the national anthem, at which Smith declared, 'I am happy to hear it.'[76] Despite this being a mass meeting in support of radical parliamentary reform, it is clear that loyalty and respect were still being shown towards the Crown.

Samuel Bamford, meanwhile, judged that at this moment Henry Hunt was surveying the vast crowd with a mixture of pleasure and amazement, with the weight of responsibility playing on his mind. Bamford, standing within this sea of people, felt its power 'for good or evil' and considered the sole burden of directing this immense, volatile energy rested on him 'who had called it forth': namely Henry Hunt. 'The task was great, and not without its peril.'[77]

Unlike Bamford, of course, Hunt had addressed large crowds in London and elsewhere, some calculated at over one hundred thousand strong, and had succeeded, despite intimidation from third parties, in maintaining a peaceable assembly while achieving the impact of a mass demonstration. The January meeting here in Manchester had occurred with no disruption, and Hunt can be forgiven for feeling confident that the same would be true on this day, although the current gathering was of a different order of magnitude altogether. As Hunt himself recalled, the impression was astonishing: 'When I entered the field or plain, where the people were assembled, I saw such a sight as I had never before beheld. A space containing, as I am informed, nearly five acres of ground, was literally covered with people, a great portion of whom were crammed together as thick as they could stand.'[78] He had wanted a crowd unprecedented in its size and he had got it. With one eye to posterity, and with no little hyperbole, Hunt asserts in his *Memoirs*: 'Let the reader who was not present picture to his imagination an assemblage of from 180 to 200 thousand English men and women, congregated together to exercise the great constitutional right of laying their complaints and grievances before the throne, and when he has done this, he may form an idea of the scene which met my view.'[79] Some, Samuel Bamford for one, would dismiss such grandiloquence as an example of Hunt's self-serving bluster and vanity. There is undoubtedly bombast – as well as hyperbole – in his pronouncements. But there is also great pride, patriotism and passion, emotion even, in this description. Hunt understood all too well the gravity of the occasion, for all the carnival atmosphere, the responsibility of bringing so many people together, and the great work still to be done to achieve their collective aims. The meeting on St Peter's Field was one important further, rather than final, step on the glorious road to radical parliamentary reform. He also believed, fervently, that right was on his side and that history would prove it.

Henry Hunt noted the striking up, in his honour, of Handel's famous tune by 'ten or twelve bands' and that 'eighteen or twenty flags, most of them surmounted by a Cap of Liberty, were unfurled, and from the multitude burst forth such a shout of welcome as never before hailed the ears of an individual, possessed of no other power, no other influence over the minds of people, except that which he had gained by an honest, straight-forward discharge of public duty.'[80] The barouche made slow progress through the throng, John Tyas still clinging to the side, accompanied by cheers and roars. As they arrived alongside the hustings Henry Hunt, Richard Carlile, Joseph Johnson, James Moorhouse and John Knight stepped out of the carriage, while the crowd opened up to allow them to ascend a ladder onto the platform. At this point Hunt is recorded as querying the position of the hustings, insisting it would have been safer located on the other side of the field. Edward Baines, junior, of the *Leeds Mercury*, who had been present from about midday and on the hustings from about one o'clock, recalled Hunt appeared to be 'out of temper'.[81] In support, John Tyas, who was now also standing on the hustings, observed that the platform was inconveniently positioned, since each speaker would have to attempt to carry his voice across the immense crowd with the wind against him.[82]

With so many people pressing forward around the hustings, it was considered sensible to seat some of the Manchester Female Reform Society committee members in the barouche, including Elizabeth Gaunt, who was feeling unwell, while Mary Fildes and others were helped up onto the platform. Edward Baines observed that a number of young women ascended the hustings 'to avoid the pressure of the crowd, which was very great at the time; one or two women had fainted from the pressure'.[83] Richard Carlile described the meeting at this time as calm and orderly: 'Hilarity', he observed, 'was seen on the countenances of all, whilst the Female Reformers crowned the assemblage with a grace, and excited a feeling particularly interesting.'[84] Carlile's hint that the presence of women helped maintain calm and decorum was echoed by John Smith, who 'looked upon this as a sort of guarantee for the peaceable conduct of the men as to any heated expression; for I consider the presence of the ladies always chastens the company'.[85] Smith later commented that Mary Fildes and her companions did not deserve the term 'profligate Amazons' which had been levelled at them.[86]

John Thacker Saxton had arrived on the hustings only recently, having already been to the *Manchester Observer* offices that morning along with James Wroe. One witness recalled that he was on the platform with a notebook and pencil to report on the proceedings.[87] As the barouche party walked out onto the raised platform, signalling the moment everyone present had been waiting for, the music stopped. Joseph Johnson proposed that Henry Hunt take the chair, which, as Bamford noted, was 'carried by acclamation'. Orator Hunt received another great shout as he walked to the front of the hustings and, removing his hat with appropriate solemnity, prepared to address the vast and expectant crowd spreading out into the distance before him.[88]

Located one hundred or so yards away, the Reverend Edward Stanley heard Hunt begin his address: 'I could distinctly hear his voice, but was too distant to distinguish his words.'[89] Edward Baines, standing a few feet behind Hunt, took down his speech using shorthand and added details from memory a few hours later. According to his notes, Hunt commenced: 'Friends and fellow-countrymen, I must beg your indulgence for a short time, and beg that you will keep silence. I hope you will exercise the all-powerful right of the people in an orderly manner.'[90] Unlike Stanley, John Smith, standing just twenty-five yards to the front of the hustings, appears to have no trouble hearing at all, as his later summary, consistent with that of both Baines and Tyas, confirms. Hunt told his hearers with some satisfaction that the week's delay of the meeting had worked against the magistrates, as it had resulted in a much larger crowd on the day. He asked them all to keep order and to restrain anyone in the crowd who attempted to disturb the peace.[91] This last was directed towards the troublemakers whom Hunt suspected of lurking within the crowd, with the encouragement of the police or authorities.

Stanley was still unable to hear what was being said, but recalled that Hunt 'had not spoken above a minute or two before I heard a report in the room that the cavalry were sent for; the messengers, we were told, might be seen from a back window.' Running swiftly to that window, Stanley 'saw three horsemen ride off'.[92] He then returned to his original station, 'anxiously awaiting the result'.

What had caused the magistrates to request the presence of the cavalry? If Stanley could not hear what was being said on the hustings, then surely nor could William Hulton and his fellow magistrates in the room below. What could Nadin, Andrew and their special constables have reported back to them to create such alarm? Unless Hunt had incited the people to riot, or had used seditious language, there appeared to be no reason to arrest him, no need for the Riot Act to be read and, therefore, no need for the Yeomanry or military to be called upon to disperse the crowd. The magistrates may have been requesting that military forces be drawn closer to the field as a precaution. But Stanley's memory of 'anxiously awaiting the result' suggests that a decision to use those forces, beyond a mere display of might, had already been taken.

William Hulton himself confirms this to be the case. He recalled that over the period prior to Hunt's arrival, he had continued to receive sworn depositions and that 'Many gentlemen stated to me, that they were greatly alarmed'.[93] One declaration was signed, according to Hulton, by sixty people: he was 'acquainted with a great many who signed it; They are men of the highest respectability.'[94] By this time, Hulton says, 'looking to all the circumstances, my opinion was that the town was in great danger.'[95] One circumstance that 'had great influence with me in signing the warrant' was the noise in the crowd on Henry Hunt's arrival, because the contingent accompanying Hunt's procession was 'a great accession of strength to the numbers already collected',[96] and the resulting thunderous roar confirmed the immense scale of the combined crowd which had by now gathered. William Hay later acknowledged the disturbing impression that Hunt's arrival gave, yet he observes that 'long before this, the Magistrates had felt a decided conviction that the whole bore the appearance of insurrection; that the array was such as to terrify all the king's subjects, and was such as no legitimate purpose could justify. In addition to their own sense of the meeting, they had very numerous depositions from the inhabitants, as to their fears for the public safety'.[97] In contrast, inevitably, to the statements of Samuel Bamford and John Smith, William Hulton was convinced that the sticks being carried by members of the crowd were there not for defence, nor to assist the elderly in walking, but for attack, and, he reiterates, they were raised against representatives of the civil and then the military power in an aggressive and intimidating manner.

Hulton noted the last deposition, by a Mr Owen, was received around the time that the barouche arrived alongside the hustings and Henry Hunt and his companions alighted.[98] He also observed that the population of Manchester and Salford combined was (as of 1805) one hundred thousand – the lowest estimate for the numbers gathered on the field is fifty thousand, the figure Hulton himself quotes – and that within this large town were many shops and warehouses, all vulnerable to attack during any public disorder.[99] William Hay considered it to be 'one of the most tumultuous meetings he ever saw... he felt great alarm for the safety of the town; and in that view of the case, he thinks the Magistrates would have betrayed the trust reposed in them if they neglected taking means for the apprehension of the authors of that meeting'.[100]

It was the fear that property might be at risk – amplified by the genuine concerns of the townsfolk, given on oath – added to a deep nervousness at the sheer scale and 'tumultuous' nature of the meeting, that led the assembled magistrates to issue a warrant for the arrest of the 'supposed' leaders: Henry Hunt, Joseph Johnson, John Knight and James Moorhouse. Although William Hulton was unable to produce the warrant at the subsequent trials, a copy – or

at least a document alleging to be a copy – does exist in the Home
Office papers.[101] It reads:

> Lancashire to wit. To the Constables of the Township of
> Manchester in the county of Lancaster, and also to all other
> constables and Peace Officers, within the said County
>
> Whereas Richard Owen hath this day made oath before us, his
> Majesty's Justices of the Peace in and for the said County of
> Lancaster, that Henry Hunt, John Knight, Joseph Johnson and
> — Moorhouse, at this time (from a quarter past one-o-clock)
> have arrived in a car, at the area near St Peter's Church, and
> that an immense mob is collected, and that he considers the
> Town in danger, and the said parties moving thereto. These
> are, therefore, in his Majesty's name, to require you forthwith
> to take and bring before us, or some other of his Majesty's
> Justices of the Peace in and for the said county, the bodies
> of the said Hunt, Knight, Johnson and Moorhouse, to enter
> into recognisances, with sufficient Sureties, as well for their
> personal appearance at the next general Sessions of Assizes to
> be holden in and for the said county... Given under our seals
> the 16th day of August in the year of our Lord one thousand
> eight hundred and nineteen.

This version of the warrant indicates that the original was
signed by all the magistrates present, including William Hulton,
the Reverend William Hay, the Reverend Charles Ethelston, James
Norris and Colonel Ralph Fletcher.

A note at the bottom of the page, in a different hand, reads,
'Examined with the original this 14 day of Nov. 1819. Joseph
Nadin W. Heslop', which, inevitably, raises some questions as to

its authenticity. However, such documentation – whether a true reflection of the reasoning at the time, or a subsequent justification – sets out the motivation for the arrests in accordance with the sworn depositions that the magistrates had received from respected townsmen. It was Hulton's stated opinion that the gathering 'did undoubtedly inspire terror in the minds of the inhabitants'.[102]

This offers an explanation, rather than a justification, for the issuing of the warrant – but not for summoning the Yeomanry Cavalry and military assembled around the area. This decision, according to William Hulton, was taken after the senior constables, including Joseph Nadin and Jonathan Andrew, expressed their fears of the consequences should they attempt to arrest Hunt et al. with only their several hundred assembled constables, without additional support. Andrew later declared that since 'communication with the hustings was, at the time, cut off', with the atmosphere already tense, 'and knowing the state of the country', he 'would not have ventured his life; he should have thought it an act of madness to attempt it; in short, he refused to execute it without military assistance.'[103] According to Nadin, he too declared that from 'all he had seen that morning, he did not deem it practicable to execute the warrant without military aid'.[104] Hulton apparently responded with surprise: 'What! ... not with all those Special Constables?'[105] But Nadin and Andrew were adamant. Clearly now agreeing with them, Hulton sent two notes, one to Major Thomas Trafford, commander of the Manchester and Salford Yeomanry Cavalry, and his second in command, Captain Hugh Hornby Birley, stationed in Portland Street, and the other to Lieutenant Colonel Guy L'Estrange, overall commander of the combined regular military and Cheshire Yeomanry, 'requiring them to come to the house where the magistrates were'. If any delay had occurred between the issuing of these two notes, it can only have been a matter of minutes. Hulton later stated that when he signed the letters he considered 'the lives and properties of the people of Manchester were in the greatest danger; He took it for granted that the meeting in Manchester was part of a great scheme in the district, of the existence of which they had received the most undoubted information some time before.'[106] He insists that he ordered the advance of the Manchester and Salford Yeomanry Cavalry 'to save, and not destroy the lives of his fellow-creatures'.[107]

The loyal newspaper, the *Manchester Chronicle*, summarized the situation in the following manner:

> The rebellious nature of the meeting, its numbers and threatening aspect, the warlike insignia displayed, the order of march and military arrangement, many of the Reformers having *shouldered* large sticks and bludgeons as representative of muskets, coupled with the depositions on oath of very many respectable inhabitants as to the *consequences* that must in their opinion unavoidably flow to lives and property from such an immense meeting, assembled under *such* influences; and the Magistrates' *own view* of the whole of this tremendous scene – rendered it imperative to interfere. To have attempted it by the common means would have been preposterous, and could only have caused the loss of a great number of lives without a chance of completing the object.[108]

Throughout their recollections, the magistrates maintain a distinction between the Manchester and Salford Yeomanry Cavalry, under their direct command, and the 'military'. William Hay stated later that he agreed with Hulton that they should not 'require military aid, if possible', and that 'they had nothing to do with the arrangements of the Military – that they most pointedly left to Colonel L'Estrange, he made all his own arrangements, judging he was the most competent person'.[109] It does not seem to have occurred to anyone present that problems might arise from the fact that the combined troops, amateur and professional, were not under a single overall commander.

Once all the administration had been completed, Joseph Nadin walked back outside to join the special constables, warrant in hand. The plan was that when the cavalry appeared, the lines of special constables would pull back and make way for them to advance to the hustings and then, accompanied by the officers and with the crowd held at bay by cavalrymen, he, Nadin, would make the arrests.

In the usual sequence of events, the Riot Act would have been read out at this point. Its full title was 'An Act for Preventing Tumults and Riotous Assemblies, and for the more speedy and effectual Punishing the Rioters'; once it had been read aloud to an assembly, the people had one hour to leave the area peacefully before the military were sent in to disperse them. William Hay had had the proclamation printed up and circulated to those magistrates attending in advance, and he states that it was read during the 'interval between the Yeomanry coming up and while they were forming'.[110] It fell to Charles Ethelston, with his well-rehearsed and booming baritone, to do the honours; William Hay described him as having 'a remarkably powerful voice'.[111] A powerful voice would indeed be required, as Henry Hunt could testify, if the announcement was to be heard over the crowd. It was usual to read word for word the proclamation as set out in the original act of 1714 – the year the first Hanoverian king, George I, ascended the throne of Great Britain:

Our Sovereign Lord the King chargeth and commandeth all persons, being assembled, immediately to disperse themselves, and peaceably depart to their habitations, or to their lawful business, upon the pains contained in the Act made in the first year of King George, for preventing tumults and riotous assemblies.

GOD SAVE THE KING[112]

Charles Ethelston later asserted that he had attempted several times to read the proclamation out on the ground itself; indeed he had hoped to deliver it on horseback but, in the commotion, his steed had disappeared along with his servant. In any case, 'he found it could not be heard'. He therefore returned to a first-floor window in Mr Buxton's house and tried again from there.[113] William Hay recalled that Ethelston leaned so far out of the window that he 'stood behind him, ready to catch his skirts for fear he might fall over'.[114] It was this scene, ripe with satirical possibilities, that was later ridiculed in a print published by John Saxton.[115] 'When he drew back his head into the room, after having read the proclamation', Hay told him, 'Ethelston, I never heard your voice so powerful.'[116]

Not one witness who was not part of the civil power heard the Riot Act being read. James McKinnel, a salesman from Manchester, who was standing on the steps of the house, declared that 'there was no particular noise to prevent him hearing it read; he heard nothing read from Mr. Buxton's house; The Magistrates were in a room over his head, but he heard no such thing as the Riot Act read.'[117] Edward Stanley, directly above, did not hear it either. William Hay, when asked about this specific point, replied that he 'can't say whether a person standing on the steps of Buxton's house could hear it read, or from the room over that where he was; He cannot account for other persons' organs.'[118] It seems clear that no one present on the field was warned of what was coming.

The 15th Hussars, as Lieutenant William Jolliffe later recounted, had paraded in field-service order at around half past eight that morning. Two squadrons, led by Lieutenant Colonel L'Estrange and Lieutenant Colonel Leighton Dalrymple, had then been marched into Manchester at around ten o'clock.[119] They dismounted in Byrom Street, a wide thoroughfare about a quarter of a mile to the west of St Peter's Field, where they were joined by a squadron each of the Cheshire Yeomanry and the Manchester and Salford Yeomanry (the majority of the latter were still positioned in Portland Street to the east of the field). The cavalry, for speed, would be sent in first, with the infantry, the 88th Foot under Lieutenant Colonel McGregor in Dickinson Street (near the Quaker Meeting House) and the 31st Foot in Brazennose Street (just to the north), brought in if need be. The guns and Royal Horse Artillery under Major Dyneley were located to the southeast, out of sight of those gathered on the field.

Lieutenant Colonel L'Estrange and his assembled cavalrymen remained in Byrom Street for several hours. Throughout that period, while awaiting further orders, Lieutenant Jolliffe observed that 'a solid mass of people continued moving along a street about a hundred yards to our front'. L'Estrange recalled that as Hunt was passing along Deansgate, parallel and just to the east of Byrom Street, he rode with Lieutenant Colonel Townshend, of the Cheshire Yeomanry, to see him: 'When the carriage came up, Hunt, who either rose or was standing before, waved his hat, looked at them, then at the mob, and shouted; they also shouted, he supposed in defiance, from seeing them in uniform.'[120] Given that this incident happened on Deansgate, it is possible that L'Estrange and his fellow officers happened to arrive as the barouche passed the Star Inn and therefore mistakenly took the defiance shown towards the magistrates, as recounted by John Tyas, to be directed at them. After observing the barouche move on, the officers returned to their men stationed in Byrom Street and waited.

In Mount Street, as he watched for the arrival of horsemen, the Reverend Edward Stanley noticed that a 'slight commotion' could be heard from within the large group, consisting mainly of women, standing on the raised ground on Windmill Street, behind the hustings. He believed this signalled the first sighting of the main contingent of the Manchester and Salford Yeomanry Cavalry, commanded by Captain Hugh Birley, numbering about sixty men and horses, arriving at the northeast corner of the field. He describes seeing people in this area, with their clear view across the field, jumping down and hurrying away. Unknown to those watching their arrival, the Yeomanry Cavalry had already claimed their first casualty. As they advanced from Portland Street and then along Cooper Street, eventually turning into Peter Street and onto the field, they had accidentally run down and mortally injured William Fildes – no direct relation to Mary – who was only two years old.[121] Now the alarm was spreading swiftly through parts of the crowd, and Stanley heard cries of 'The soldiers! The soldiers!' All at once, the cavalry appeared 'on a gallop, which they continued till the word was given for halting them, about the middle of the space'.[122] William Elson, the farmer from Middleton, had lost sight of his three teenage children in the crowd* but, he remembered later, 'I was not uneasy about them, as I knew they were acquainted with Manchester. I had no fear... till I saw the Yeomanry coming.'[123] The bookseller James Weatherley, standing near the Quaker Meeting house, watched the troops arrive and

---

* Elson does not go on to explain what happened to his children but, as no 'Elson' is listed amongst the injured and dead, we can assume they survived the event unharmed.

noted that at their head was Edward Meagher, 'an Irishman and Trumpeter... of bad character'.[124] Nathan Broadhurst, an army veteran standing about eight yards from the hustings, described Meagher as 'tall, thin, dark-complexioned' and, distinctively, riding a piebald horse.[125]

The Yeomanry Cavalry moved down Mount Street and paused in front of Mr Buxton's house, where Chief Constable Jonathan Andrew was now standing. He approached their commanding officer, Captain Birley, 'and stated they had a warrant, and desired him to surround the hustings, in order that they might take the parties against whom they had the warrant'.[126] Nadin recalled that on seeing the Yeomanry he 'drew the Special Constables back to the house' as planned, 'to enable the Cavalry to advance'.[127] Andrew, on foot, tried to keep ahead of the Yeomanry for as long as possible, as they moved forward to the hustings, but was prevented by the crowd and then the Yeomanry passed him.[128]

Nadin and Andrew would make no mention in their later testimony of the manner in which the Yeomanry Cavalry arrived on the field, nor how they then moved through the crowd, thereby creating the impression that their approach was orderly and without incident. The *Manchester Chronicle* considered the Yeomanry's advance 'was done in a steady and masterly style; but the Cavalry had not advanced many yards before they were assailed with heavy vollies [*sic*] of stones, shouts of defiance, and the most coarse and insulting language. Till thus assailed, no Yeomanry-man *used* his sword, each man having confined himself to waving it over his head.'[129] This contrasts with most other witness accounts, including, as we shall see, that of William Hulton. Indeed, if the Yeomanry's approach had been conducted in 'a steady and masterly style', how had they managed to knock down and kill William Fildes?

From his position in the crowd, Samuel Bamford watched Henry
Hunt clear his throat. Suspecting there would be nothing new in
the speeches, he started to move away from the field in search
of refreshment, and recalled, as he did so, hearing a 'noise and
strange murmuring' arising from the direction of St Peter's
Church. He stood on tiptoe to find out what was happening,
but rather than seeing, as he expected, more people marching
triumphantly onto the field, he saw a party of cavalry in blue and
white uniforms 'come trotting sword in hand, round the corner
of a garden-wall, and to the front of a row of few houses, where
they reined up in a line'.[130] Bamford turned to a companion and
said, 'The soldiers are here… we must go back and see what this
means.' Someone nearby voiced the opinion that the presence
of the Yeomanry was simply a precaution, in case trouble should
occur on the field; not everyone considered an attack on the
crowd to be inevitable. Bamford, however, was concerned, and
he forced his way back through the throng towards the Middleton
banners, his wife and his party.

Henry Hunt, standing at the front of the hustings, was midway
through his opening salvo, his trademark white hat held in one
hand, his other raised and punching the air in his usual manner.
He was explaining how the postponement of the event had
worked against the magistrates when, in the words of John
Tyas, John Knight 'whispered something into Mr. Hunt's ear,
which caused him to turn round with some degree of asperity to
Knight, and to say, "Sir, I will not be interrupted: when you speak
yourself, you will not like to experience such interruption."'[131] It
is possible that Knight had seen the arrival of the Yeomanry and
was attempting to warn Hunt. But the Orator, feeding off the
intense expectation of the vast multitude, was building himself up

towards his empowering message of hope and justice for all, and was understandably irritated by the disruption to his momentum. Hunt does not mention this incident, but recalls declaring that it was his 'conviction that the orderly conduct of the people would deprive their enemies of all pretence whatever to interrupt their proceedings'. That interruption arrived nonetheless: 'I had scarcely uttered two sentences, urging them to persevere in the same line of conduct, when the Manchester Troop of Yeomanry came galloping into the field.'[132] The Yeomanry formed up in front of Mr Buxton's house, and Hunt observed, 'As soon as the military appeared, the people, (as is always the case under such circumstances) began to disperse and fly from the outskirts.'[133]

James Wroe later reported that at this point Hunt 'broke off suddenly', as the disruption appeared to be spreading, and then attempted to reassure the crowd: 'turning around with a manner that showed him perfect master of the art of managing large assemblies, he explained to his friends, who were at a loss what to shout for, that it was only that "there was a little alarm manifested at the outskirts, and he gave the shout so to inspire confidence – that was all."'[134] According to Henby Andrews, Hunt's servant, his master had encouraged the crowds to cheer the arrival of the military at meetings in Bristol and Spa Fields, and saw this as similar to these occasions.[135] According to Hunt, the cheers 'had the desired effect of restoring the confidence of the people, who did not, indeed, suspect it to be possible that the devil himself would have authorized the Yeomanry to commit any violence upon them.'[136]

After watching the Yeomanry advance about ten yards into the crowd, Edward Baines jumped down from the hustings and made his way through the crowd in the opposite direction to Mr Buxton's house. He turned back to see Hunt 'stretching out his arm' and repeatedly urging the crowd to cheer and to 'be firm'. Baines told Hunt later: 'My impression was, that you merely wished the people to stand, and to prevent danger from their running away.'[137] And he reiterated, 'When you used the words "be firm", you stretched out your arms, with your hands open and the palms down.' At this time, Baines thought, the 'people had not the appearance of disciplined troops, ready to protect Hunt or to fight for him, as occasion offered… My impression was, that the cheers were cheers of conscious innocence, confidently relying on the protection of the laws.'[138]

The chairman of the magistrates, William Hulton, had supposed, with some justification, that the cavalry as a whole – whether Yeomanry or Hussars – would appear on the field at the same time. In the event, it was the Manchester and Salford Yeomanry who arrived first 'at a quick pace' from the Mosley Street end of Mount Street and then formed in a line 'under the wall of the magistrate's house'. According to Hulton the crowd, in response, 'set up a tremendous shout. They groaned and hissed, and those men who had sticks shook them in the air. I saw those sticks lifted up in a menacing manner.'[139] Hulton noticed 'a good many women' among the crowd and 'I heard the women particularly noisy in hissing and hooting the cavalry when they first appeared'.[140] After Hunt encouraged the crowd to shout out, the cavalry brandished their sabres as a response. Bamford also witnessed this: 'On the cavalry drawing up they were received with a shout, of good will, as I understood it. They shouted again, waving their sabres over their heads.'[141] The Yeomanry then advanced, in Hulton's opinion 'at a trot, or rather prancing; the horses were fidgeting in consequence of the noise, and they were not in good order.'[142] In fact, at this moment, as the Yeomanry started to move through the widened avenue between the special constables, one of those volunteers, John Ashworth, was knocked down and, as the *Manchester Chronicle* described it, was 'killed dead on the spot'.[143] This certainly suggests that there was some disarray in the Yeomanry's advance and that they were moving too fast for Ashworth, like the wretchedly trampled William Fildes, to get out of the way.

Hulton, apparently unaware of either casualty, observed what he describes as the difficulties the Yeomanry were having in moving across the field, but added that he distinctly remembered seeing 'stones and brick-bats flying in all directions. I saw what appeared to me to be a general resistance.'[144] He returned to the throwing of stones several times in his evidence, observing it was a 'matter of notoriety; The Field had been, before nine o'clock, cleared of a cart load of stones', which meant that the missiles must have been brought intentionally by participants. This was supported by evidence given by the surveyor Worrall, who found 'a cart load' of such items when he returned to the field at three o'clock that afternoon, the inference being, of course, that they had been 'brought some distance' by members of the crowd.[145] It is fair to say that, in a crowd this size, some troublemakers are inevitable. Casting doubt on Hulton's testimony, however, the Reverend Edward Stanley denied having seen missiles being thrown at the Yeomanry and Constables. Given his commanding viewpoint, he believed, he would surely have noticed something so obvious.

Despite Henry Hunt's attempt to calm the situation, and before he could continue addressing the crowd, the order for the Yeomanry to advance had been given. Hunt looked on with disbelief as 'they charged amongst the people, sabring right and left, in all directions. Sparing neither *age, sex*, nor *rank*.'[146] The Yeomanry forced their way through the crowd towards the hustings, 'riding over and sabring all that could not get out of their way'.[147] John Tyas, still watching from the hustings, stated in his report that, despite extreme provocation, 'Not a brickbat was thrown at them – not a pistol was fired during this period: all was quiet and orderly; as if the cavalry had been the friends of the multitude.'[148] James Weatherley accuses Edward Meagher, leading the Yeomanry, of starting the attack on the crowd, 'he was the first to begin the assault[,] he was four or five yards in advance of the others[,] he kept laying on the People right and left with his sword... he was like most of the others half drunk... he was a hot [tempered] Irishman'.*[149] Richard Carlile, seeing the sudden advance of the Yeomanry, 'appealed to the females on their fear of the approach of the military, and found them the last to display alarm'.[150] John Smith, standing nearby, saw no resistance made to the Yeomanry's advance, no missiles thrown or sticks brandished, but was surprised at the speed with which they moved through so dense a crowd. He recalled that some of the people around him cried, 'What is to be done?' while others judged the advance of the Yeomanry cavalry was merely to hear if any seditious expressions were being used by those on the hustings. They were not, at that point at least, fearful of the Yeomanry.[151] The cotton spinner William Harrison, standing about ten yards from the hustings, confirmed Weatherley's impression that the first of the Yeomanry Cavalry to arrive on the field 'could hardly sit on his horse, he was so drunk; he sat like a monkey.'[152]

Samuel Bamford, in the midst of the crowd, watched the Yeomanry shout and brandish their sabres 'and then, slackening

---

* Weatherley also observes that Meagher 'lived in a room in Queen St Deansgate... he could never get rest in Manchester after this affair.' For his part in the events of 16 August Meagher became known as the 'Peterloo butcher' and 'had to leave Manchester shortly after'.

rein, and striking spur into their steeds, they dashed forward, and began cutting the people'.[153] He shouted for those around him to 'Stand Fast' and a cry repeating the phrase rose up from among them. Bamford noted the Yeomanry were 'in confusion', having great trouble, as he recalled, forcing their way through so great and dense a crowd, who, obviously, had nowhere to run. In terror, frustration or glee – who can say? – the Yeomanry's 'sabres were plied to hew a way through naked held-up hands, and defenceless heads; and then chopped limbs, and wound-gaping skulls were seen; and groans and cries were mingled with the din of that horrid confusion'. Bamford heard shouts of 'For shame! for shame!' and 'Break! break! they are killing them in front, and they cannot get away.' He then describes a strange momentary suspension of action, 'a pause', as if a spell had been cast, or a collective deep breath had been slowly drawn, which was then quickly followed by 'a rush, heavy and resistless as a headlong sea; and a sound like low thunder, with screams, prayers, and imprecations from the crowd-moiled, and sabre-doomed, who could not escape.'[154]

From his position in Mount Street, Edward Stanley too saw that the Yeomanry had halted on the field 'in great disorder'. Those standing with him – Stanley does not say who – attributed the confusion 'to the undisciplined state of their horses, little accustomed to act together, and probably frightened by the shout of the populace, which greeted their arrival'. Henry Hunt, on sighting the Yeomanry, 'pointed towards them and it was clear from his gestures that he was addressing the mob respecting their interference. His words, whatever they were, excited a shout from those immediately around him, which was re-echoed with fearful animation by the rest of the multitude.' As this shout subsided, 'the cavalry, the loyal spectators, and the special constables, cheered loudly in return, and a pause ensued of a minute or two.'[155]

The pause might suggest that neither side really understood the meaning of the cheers directed at them – were they expressions of friendship or aggression? Joseph Wrigley was clear on this matter. Regarding the crowd, 'I thought they meant to show that they regarded them as friends; and I understood the soldiers to return it with the same meaning.'[156] Nathan Broadhurst, the army veteran, similarly believed the crowd cheered in friendship: 'I joined in the cheers, and I know I did it with that feeling.'[157]

Stanley provides this version of events:

> An officer and some few others then advanced rather in front of the troop, formed, as I before said, in much disorder and with scarcely the semblance of line, their sabres glistened in the air, and on they went, direct to the hustings. At first, *i.e.*, for a very few paces, their movement was not rapid, and there was some show of an attempt to follow the officer in regular succession, five or six abreast; but... they soon "increased their speed," and with a zeal and ardour which might naturally be expected from men acting with delegated powers against a foe by whom it is understood they had long been insulted with taunts of cowardice, continued their course, seeming individually to vie with each other which should be first.[158]

Special Constable Robert Hughes claimed that as Hunt pointed towards the Yeomanry, he shouted 'there are your enemies coming' and that he referred to the Yeomanry in insulting terms, as 'blood-suckers' and 'feather-bed soldiers'.[159] Such language was not Henry Hunt's style, however, and several far more objective witnesses had testified to the contrary, so this 'evidence' can be dismissed as an attempt to blame Hunt for inciting the crowd to attack the Yeomanry. Yet others listening, most notably the special constables standing nearby, had already taken Hunt's instruction to the crowd to curb the activities of troublemakers as being directed at themselves and then at the Yeomanry, rather than at *agents provocateurs*.

The Yeomanry pushed and slashed through the crowd, injuring constables as well as demonstrators. They eventually arrived at the hustings where, as Stanley phrases it, 'a scene of dreadful confusion ensued'.[160] Nathan Broadhurst described how, as the cavalry approached, Henry Hunt 'asked them what they wanted', at which one of the cavalrymen answered that he had a warrant against him. This was not strictly true, since it was Joseph Nadin who held the warrant, and the Yeomanry had been called in to assist him. According to Broadhurst, Hunt declared 'he would submit to the civil, but not the military power', at which point Nadin and another constable arrived on the hustings, arrested Hunt 'and pulled Mr. Johnson off the hustings by the legs'.[161] General chaos resulted, during which Broadhurst says he was kicked off the platform.[162]

John Tyas later reported in *The Times*:

the *officer* who commanded the detachment went up to Mr. Hunt, and said, brandishing his sword, 'Sir, I have a warrant against you, and arrest you as my prisoner.' Hunt, after urging the crowd to remain calm, turned round to the officer and said, 'I willingly surrender myself to any civil officer who will show me his warrant.' Mr. Nadin... then came forward and said, 'I will arrest you; I have got informations upon oath against you,' or something to that effect.

The Yeomanry officer then tried to arrest Johnson, who, like Hunt, requested a civil officer. At this point Chief Constable Jonathan Andrew stepped forward. Tyas writes that Johnson and Hunt 'leaped from off the waggon, and surrendered themselves to the civil power. Search was then made for Moorhouse and Knight, against whom warrants had also been issued. In the hurry of this transaction, they had by some means or other contrived to make their escape.'[163] Nadin confirms that neither Knight nor Moorhouse was on the hustings at that point.[164] Both were arrested subsequently, Knight at his own home in Hanover Street and Moorhouse at the Flying Horse Inn.[165]

John Tyas then states that from 'that moment the Manchester Yeomanry Cavalry lost all command of temper'.[166] He describes how John Saxton, still standing on the hustings, was approached by two Yeomanry cavalrymen: 'There', said one of them, 'is that villain Saxton; do you run him through the body.' 'No,' replied the other, 'I had rather not – I leave it to you.' The first then lunged at Saxton and, according to Tyas, it was only because he turned aside quickly that the blow did not kill him. 'As it was, it cut his coat and waistcoat, but fortunately did him no other injury.' Tyas continues, 'A man within five yards of us in another direction had his nose completely taken off by a blow of a sabre; whilst another was laid prostrate, but whether he was dead or had merely thrown himself down to obtain protection we cannot say.' Eventually, realizing that everyone present was now in danger of injury or worse, Tyas offered to give himself up to a cavalryman, declaring that he was only there to report on the proceedings. The cavalryman cried, 'Oh! oh! You then are one of their writers – you must go before the Magistrates,'[167] and Tyas was promptly arrested. James McKinnel, still watching from the steps of Mr Buxton's house, saw the Yeomanry surround the platform 'and immediately after he saw the flags and banners falling from the hustings'.[168] Such items were now trophies to be seized and most destroyed.[169]

In the confusion Samuel Bamford, anticipating the seizure of the banners, had shouted to his companions holding the Middleton colours to break the flag-staves and hide the cloth. The blue banner was quickly hidden – it is the only one to have survived, thanks to Bamford's quick thinking – but Thomas Redford, 'who carried the green banner, held it aloft until the staff was cut in his hand, and his shoulder was divided by the sabre of one of the Manchester yeomanry'.[170]

Nathan Broadhurst also quotes one of the cavalrymen, as the troopers were sabring the crowd, crying, 'Damn you, I'll reform you – You'll come again will you?' and another's grim observation, 'I'll let you know I am a soldier, to-day.'[171] Perhaps the latter was a reference to the articles in the *Manchester Observer* the previous month, ridiculing the 'stupid boobies of yeomanry cavalry in the neighbourhood'.

Despite the pandemonium engulfing the entire field, witnesses perceived that the cavalry's attacks, rather than being random, had a discernible focus. It seemed that women were being targeted, many of whom, like Mary Fildes and Susannah Saxton, were dressed distinctively in white. Mrs Fildes is recorded in one source as having been 'much beat by Constables & leaped off the hustings when Mr Hunt was taken'.[172] Another source describes her as falling from the hustings, her dress catching on a nail; as she tried desperately to free herself, she was cut across her upper body by a member of the Yeomanry Cavalry.[173] Mary Fildes survived this brutal attack, but, according to one source 'was obliged to absent herself a fort night to avoid imprisonment'.[174] Nor did it subdue her determined support for parliamentary reform and the rights of women, deemed so abhorrent by her attacker and his superiors. Richard Carlile, still on the hustings, also saw that women appeared to be 'the particular objects of the fury of the Cavalry Assassins'.[175] He describes a woman standing near him, holding an infant, being sabred over the head, 'her tender offspring

The Peterloo Massacre by George Cruikshank, 1819.
(Manchester Central Library / Bridgeman Images)

DRENCHED IN ITS MOTHER'S BLOOD'. Another woman, he states, was stabbed with the point of a sword in her neck, while others were sabred 'in the breast'.[176] Carlile's famous print of this scene, dedicated to Henry Hunt and the female reformers, depicts a woman located in the barouche falling back into the arms of a companion while a member of the Yeomanry thrusts a sabre's point between her breasts.

Other women were casualties of the general brutality displayed by the Yeomanry Cavalry. Edward Stanley remembered that 'On the commencement of the charge' some stragglers 'fled in all directions; and I presume escaped, with the exception of a woman who had been standing ten or twelve yards in front; as the troops passed her body was left, to all appearance lifeless; and there remained till the close of the business'.[177]

From his high viewpoint, Stanley continued to observe the frenzied scenes around the hustings:

> The orators fell or were forced off the scaffold in quick succession; fortunately for them, the stage being rather elevated, they were in great degree beyond the reach of the many swords which gleamed around them. Hunt fell – or threw himself – among the constables, and was driven or dragged, as fast as possible, down the avenue which communicated with the magistrates' house; his associates were hurried after him in a similar manner. By this time so much dust had arisen that no accurate account can be given of what further took place, at that particular spot.[178]

Henry Hunt later described the undignified manner in which he was seized by Nadin and his men and then forced through the crowd, the clamour of the terrified and injured all about him. He rightly observes that an arrest could have been carried out with far less commotion, and certainly without sending in the Yeomanry. Hunt believed it was done purposely 'to strike terror into the minds of the assembled multitude, and to pull down reform by the sword, regardless of the blood spilt in the enterprise'.[179] Hunt's view was supported in court by Mr Fitzpatrick of *The New Times* in London, who had attended the Smithfield meeting in July 1819, which he described as 'most numerous and peaceable'. One of the speakers, the Reverend Joseph Harrison of Stockport, Fitzpatrick recalled, had been arrested on that occasion, yet 'No obstruction was offered to his arrest on the part of the people'.[180] The dramatic contrast to the current situation was there for all to see.

Hunt also believed, from the brutal way in which he was treated, that 'my life was meant to be a sacrifice'. He was dragged through the avenue of constables, as Stanley observed from his window above, 'amidst the screams of the flying, and the piercing cries and groans of the dying people', while two 'ruffian' cavalrymen, as Hunt recalled, 'made several efforts to cut me down, but each time I guarded myself, by placing Nadin between myself and them as they renewed their charge upon me'.[181] Despite Nadin's struggles to release himself from Hunt's grip and 'leave me to their mercy', Hunt continued to hold fast to the deputy constable, using him as a shield as they forced their way to Buxton's house. As the two reached the building, according to Hunt, the Yeomanry continued to attack him, landing several cuts to his head – piercing his hat – and to his hand, raised up in protection. Even as Nadin and Hunt entered the house, a constable came up from behind and 'levelled a blow at my head with a heavy bludgeon, which would have felled me to the earth, had I not been supported by the constables, who had hold of my arms'.[182] One constable removed Hunt's hat, allowing another to rain further blows upon him, but Nadin himself 'cried shame' at this treatment, placing the battered and bloodied white hat back on Henry Hunt's head with the comment that 'it was too bad!'[183] Hunt, perhaps with a touch of dramatic irony, states that Nadin, of all people, had saved his life. Not everyone was sympathetic, least of all the loyalist press. The *Manchester Chronicle* excoriated Hunt as 'the GREAT Delinquent, the monster in human shape to whom all these evils must be attributed to' and gleefully described how he was dragged to the magistrates 'amidst the execrations and hisses of every good subject'.[184]

In contrast, a witness to this encounter, a Mr Parkins, offered the opinion that Hunt had been 'used… in such an outrageous manner' and that 'I never saw a man behave with more fortitude than Mr. Hunt did on that most trying occasion'.[185] John Tyas considered his treatment 'neither justified by law nor humanity'. Battered, cut and bruised, Hunt was now, at least, safe from physical assault inside Mr Buxton's house, where, he observed with contempt, 'the worthy projectors of the plot', the magistrates, 'were sitting in solemn conclave'.[186] Hunt states that at this moment, having witnessed the full and terrible results of their decision to send for the yeomanry and military, the magistrates 'were dreadfully alarmed at their own deeds'.[187]

Edward Stanley recalled that as the Manchester and Salford Yeomanry were taking possession of the hustings, the Cheshire Yeomanry, led by Lieutenant Colonel Townshend, appeared 'in excellent order, and formed in the rear of the hustings as well as could be expected, considering the crowds who were now pressing in all directions'.[188] Soon after, again according to Stanley, the 15th Hussars also arrived with Lieutenant Colonel L'Estrange. (L'Estrange had in fact led both the Hussars and the Cheshire Yeomanry onto the field.) L'Estrange remembered receiving the summons from Hulton 'about a quarter of an hour' after he had seen Henry Hunt pass in the barouche on Deansgate. He was 'unable to find the letter since: It in substance stated that he [Hulton] required the attendance of the military, as he did not conceive the civil power sufficiently strong for their purposes.'[189]

Having received their orders, as Lieutenant Jolliffe of the 15th Hussars recalled, they moved off at a trot 'which was increased to a canter' and after taking a 'circuitous route', emerged at the southeast corner of St Peter's Field.[190] Lieutenant Colonel L'Estrange explained that they took a detour through Fleet Street in order to avoid moving through 'the mob'.[191] By the time the 15th Hussars and the Cheshire Yeomanry arrived on the field, William Hulton 'conceived the Manchester Yeomanry to be completely beaten', such were the difficulties they had encountered.[192] Their horses 'being raw, unused to the field, they appeared to me to be in a certain degree of confusion', Hulton said.[193] Robert Hughes, standing among the special constables, expected 'that every man would be murdered' and that only the appearance of the 15th Hussars ensured the safety of the beleaguered Yeomanry.[194] L'Estrange recalled that when 'he arrived at the corner he perceived a considerable dust, and he conceived that the Yeomanry were in conflict with the people; Saw missiles in the air in every direction; Was at such a distance from the Yeomanry he could not speak to them'. He feared the Yeomanry would be thrown from their horses.[195]

Lieutenant Colonel L'Estrange, surveying the chaos – we can suppose that this was not the scene he had expected or hoped for – rode over and shouted up to William Hulton, 'What am I to do', to which Hulton replied, 'Good God, Sir, don't you see how they are attacking the Yeomanry? Disperse the mob.'[196] Hulton confirmed later, when giving evidence, that his fellow magistrates were also standing at the window and that he had their full support. Indeed by this time they 'were expressing fear themselves'.[197] Hulton believed, had he not acted as he did, 'he should have been answerable for the lives of the Yeomanry'.[198] Having given L'Estrange his orders, Hulton watched for a few moments and then moved away from the window, preferring 'not [to] see any advance of the military'.[199]

Lieutenant Colonel L'Estrange's recollection differs only a little from Hulton's. He looked up to the window 'and asked for orders; Said "Good God, look at the Yeomanry," or something to that effect; "Save them, disperse the people"; They immediately did so.'[200]

Lieutenant Jolliffe recalls that his troop of the 15th Hussars advanced along Mount Street and, 'without a halt or pause even: the words "Front!" and "Forward!" were given, and the trumpet sounded the charge... When fronted, our line extended quite across the ground, which, in all parts was so filled with people that their hats seemed to touch.'[201] Having registered the general state of the crowd, Lieutenant Jolliffe notes: 'It was then, for the first time, that I saw the Manchester troop of yeomanry.' His impression was that the Manchester and Salford Yeomanry, outnumbered and demonstrably out of their depth, were in imminent danger: 'they were scattered singly, or in small groups, over the greater part of the field, literally hemmed up, and hedged into the mob, so that they were powerless either to make an impression or to escape: in fact, they were in the power of those whom they were designed to overawe; and it required only a glance to discover their helpless position, and the necessity of our being brought to their rescue.'[202] The fact that, years on, Jolliffe continued to use the term 'mob', and his empathy with the 'peace keepers' – whether or not these included inexperienced amateurs, largely responsible, through their incompetence, for the predicament they now found themselves in – explains to a large degree his particular assessment of the situation.

William Hulton saw enough of what happened next to state that the multitude 'fled the moment Lieutenant-Colonel L'Estrange advanced; It was on his advance, certainly, the flight became rapid.'[203] This may be Hulton's way of shifting the blame for the carnage onto the regular military, or it may be simply a statement of fact. The 15th Hussars were ordered to clear the field and, in doing so, to rescue the Yeomanry. And so they rapidly advanced, sweeping the 'mingled mass of human beings' before them; 'people, yeomen, and constables, in their confused attempts to escape, ran one over the other; so that, by the time we had arrived at the end of the field, the fugitives were literally piled up to a considerable elevation above the level of the ground.'[204] Lieutenant Jolliffe also describes how the Hussars used their sabres in clearing the field: they 'drove the people forward with the flats of their swords' as a well-trained, experienced cavalryman – rather than an untrained amateur – would do; yet, as Jolliffe continues, 'sometimes, as is almost inevitably the case when men are placed in such situations, the edge was used'. He argues that, 'believing, though I do, that nine out of ten of the sabre wounds were caused by the hussars, I must still consider that it redounds to the humane forbearance of the men of the 15th that more wounds were not received, when the vast numbers are taken into consideration with whom they were brought into hostile collision.'[205]

Lieutenant Colonel L'Estrange's memory of events is that, in clearing the field, 'they experienced resistance; Can't say considerable resistance; It was partial, as the people were more desperate in some places than in others.' As the Hussars moved through the crowd he had 'his cap struck off by a blow on the head; Supposed that it must have been by a large brick-bat, or stone.'[206] Lieutenant Frederick Buckley in Captain Carpenter's troop remembered that the mass of people was so great that he 'thought it proper to urge his mare as fast as he could; Coming in contact with the people she fell, and he with her... As soon as he disentangled himself from his mare, and raised her, he mounted and galloped to the Peter-street side of the Meeting-house.'[207]

The Hussars had arrived late in a situation that they could exert little control over. If they had reached the field before the Yeomanry, then their experience, superior horsemanship and swordsmanship – not forgetting their horses were also more accustomed to crowds and tumult – would have resulted in fewer casualties. Given how calm and peaceable the crowd had been up to this point, it is likely that the mere appearance of the Hussars would have been enough to encourage an orderly dispersal from the field, even by a gathering of this scale. The panic and confusion created by the Yeomanry charging headlong and randomly into the crowd, not methodically and in an unbroken line as the Hussars were experienced enough to do, was surely the key factor in the violence and bloodshed that ensued.

The Reverend Edward Stanley also describes the Hussars' manoeuvres:

They pressed forward, crossing the avenue of constables, which opened to let them through, and bent their course towards the Manchester yeomanry. The people were now in a state of utter rout and confusion, leaving the ground strewn with hats and shoes, and hundreds were thrown down in the attempt to escape. The cavalry were hurrying about in all directions, completing the work of dispersion, which... was effected in so short a space of time as to appear as if done 'by magic.'

Stanley is here quoting a report in the *Manchester Chronicle* on 21 August 1819: 'The ground was cleared as if by magic.' He also says that he saw the swords go up and then down, but whether they were held with the flat or edge forward 'I cannot pretend to give an opinion.'

In contrast to the account of his fellow special constable, Robert Hughes, that the 15th Hussars saved them from harm, Robert Mutrie, writing to his brother-in-law Archibald Moore, declared that the regular cavalry's late arrival onto the field meant that they 'mistook us constables with our batons for the Reformers with pistols (I suppose) for in one moment upwards of 100 of us are laid on our backs – I was down but got up by laying hold a horses rein without being hurt – I was afterwards, struck on the head with a sabre of the 15th and then by the Cheshire Troop.'[208]

Joseph Wrigley, John Lees's companion from Oldham, saw the cavalry arrive and advance to the hustings. He recalls that Lees received 'a cut on the back of his right arm from a sabre; he was parrying off the blows of one of the military, and another came and cut him; he had his right arm up over his head protecting it with a walking-stick.' (That John, a young man, was carrying a walking stick might suggest that he was suffering from an ongoing debility, as a result of his military service.) When asked if he had assisted his friend, Wrigley answered, 'No, indeed; every one had to look to his own life.'[209] Then a member of the Yeomanry thrust the point of his sword through Joseph's hat. 'I called to him not to murder me, and he struck no more at me.'[210] Joseph Wrigley is yet another witness who says he did not hear the Riot Act read out, nor any magistrate ordering the meeting to disperse.

Robert Cooper, a hatter from Oldham, recalled John Lees saying that while he was on the hustings, the Yeomanry Cavalry 'came cutting and slashing away; he offered to defend himself, as well as he could, with a stick he had in his hand; and while he was defending himself, the cavalry-man, in struggling, fell off his horse, and he jumped off the hustings, and then one of the 15th Hussars came and cut his elbow with a sword'.[211] Jonah Andrew said of Lees, 'I saw the soldiers surround him, and a Yeoman Cavalry-man cutting at him with great vengeance.'[212] According to Andrew, Lees had made for the hustings to get away from the Yeomanry, and had even managed to clamber under the carts, but was then attacked by special constables: 'I saw several constables round him, and beating him with their truncheons severely. One of them picked up a staff of a banner that had been cut with a sword, and said, "Damn your bloody eyes, I'll break your back;" and they struck at him for a considerable time with their truncheons and the staff of the banner.'[213]

A hint only of the 'humane forbearance' Jolliffe attributes to the men of the 15th Hussars can be gleaned from an anecdote, repeated by at least three witnesses, involving an unnamed Hussar officer. Many people were trying to flee the field to the west via Windmill Street, where the narrow junction with Watson Street created a pinch point. Nathan Broadhurst recounted, 'I saw ten or twelve of the Yeomanry Cavalry, and two of the Hussars cutting at the people, who were wedged close together, when an officer of Hussars rode up to his own men, and knocking up their swords said, "D[am]n you what do you mean by this work." He then called out to the Yeomanry, "For shame, gentlemen; what are you about? the people cannot get away."'[214] Another eyewitness, John Jones, a fustian cutter, was watching the event with his wife and children from their parlour window at 14 Windmill Street. He testified that 'people came down in great crowds past my door, and a parcel of them beat down the fence', including the oak stumps and fixing stones. 'The people were so pressed against them in the corner, and the shrieks would astonish you,' yet the cavalry, whom Jones specifically named as the Manchester and Salford Yeomanry, 'were laying on them all the time as hard as they could.' Jones recalled that during this terrible scene, played out on his very doorstep, an officer of the Hussars, possibly the same man and in even the same incident as witnessed by Nathan Broadhurst, 'came up and said, "Gentlemen! gentlemen! for shame! forbear! the people cannot get away.' Just as this happened, 'the rail broke down at my door', collapsing into the basement well in front of Jones's house and toppling 'a whole number of the people into my cellar', a full storey drop; 'at the bottom of my cellar there was a woman took up dead.'[215] According to Jones, people were lying in heaps, 'some of them were as black in the face as they could be, and their eyes nearly starting out of their heads'. He described the noises the injured made, 'just as if they were strangled', and how, while his nephew was attempting to revive a man with water, two members of the Yeomanry whom he identified as Withington and Bowker were 'cutting at the people as hard as ever they could'. Jones's wife Ann, 'a corpulent old lady',[216] managed to drag some people into their house to avoid the relentless sabring and the crush of bodies. She recalled that 'there was a great many people in my house, and all was in great confusion', and that a group of special constables came up to her front door 'in great triumph', shouting, *This is Waterloo for you! This is Waterloo.*'[217]

Lieutenant Jolliffe meanwhile recalled an incident near the Quaker Meeting House on the north side of the field. The 'mob', as he continued to describe them, 'had taken possession of various buildings' including the chapel and walled burial ground. Jolliffe described the people here beginning to fight back, lobbing 'stones and brickbats'. He watched 'a farrier of the 15th ride at a small door in the outer wall, and, to my surprise, his horse struck it with such force that it flew open.' Two or three Hussars then rode into the Meeting House grounds 'and the place was immediately in their possession', a curious description, as if this were an urban English Hougoumont.[218] Lieutenant Frederick Buckley noted 'a greater part of the people were behind the breast-work of a wall', more than five feet high, and that showers of missiles were flying from all sides, with cries of 'pelt them, pelt them'. In the mayhem his mare was injured.[219] One corporal of the 15th who was stationed nearby was later told by his comrades 'that such a vast assembly of the lower orders, with neither character nor property to lose, was truly alarming'.[220]

Samuel Bamford had been carried along by the crowd surging towards the Quaker Meeting House and recalled that some of the people there, Middleton folk included, had started to fight back. He describes how 'a heroine, a young married woman of our party, with her face all bloody, her hair streaming about her, her bonnet hanging by the string, and her apron weighted with stones, kept her assailant at bay until she fell backwards and was near being taken; but she got away covered with severe bruises'. About this time and in this area, one of the Yeomanry, named as John Hulme, was unhorsed 'by a blow from the fragment of a brick… and it was supposed to have been flung by this woman'.[221] While lying on the ground Hulme was trampled by a horse and severely injured.

Private William Rook, of Captain Whiteford's troop, described a man attacking his horse with a gardener's hook. A member of the Yeomanry said to him, 'Dragoon, if you don't take care, your horse's entrails will fall from under you.' Rook looked down 'to see what condition his mare was in, and he saw the blood run… His horse was cut from the end of the saddle-flaps to the flank.'[222] Despite the injury, the horse survived. Several Hussars also testified that a gun was fired by someone in the crowd near the Meeting House.

Lieutenant Jolliffe turned again towards the centre of St Peter's Field and saw what he assumed were 'peace-officers', Hussars and

Yeomanry, around the hustings. Here he met his commanding officer, Lieutenant Colonel Dalrymple, who told him to find a trumpeter to sound the 'rally' and 'retreat'. As Jolliffe later described it, 'The field and the adjacent streets now presented an extraordinary sight: the ground was quite covered with hats, shoes, sticks, musical instruments, and other things. Here and there lay the unfortunates who were too much injured to move away; and this sight was rendered the more distressing by observing some women among the sufferers.'[223]

Around this time, Major Dyneley, stationed to the southeast of the field, 'brought the Guns up at a gallop, but the business was nearly settled by that time, & I had the pleasure of seeing Hunt &c secured & sent off, the Colors [sic] & Cap of liberty in the hands of our troops, the hustings torn to pieces.' However, he goes on, 'I must not say the pleasure of seeing the field of Battle covered with Hats, Sticks, Shoes, Laurel Branches, Drum Heads &c &c in short the field was as complete as I had ever seen one after an action... We remained in full possession of our ground about 1½ hours.' He also observes, with blithe barrack-room insouciance, 'I was very much amused to see the way in which the Volunteer Cavalry knocked the people about during the whole time we remained upon the ground; the Instant they saw 10 or a dozen mobbites together, they rode at them, & leathered them properly.'[224]

Samuel Bamford was surveying the scene before him in horror rather than amusement:

In ten minutes from the commencement of the havock [sic], the field was an open and almost deserted space. The sun looked down through a sultry and motionless air. The curtains and blinds of the windows within view were all closed. A gentleman or two might occasionally be seen looking out from one of the new houses before-mentioned, near the door of which, a group of persons, (special constables) were collected, and apparently in conversation; others were assisting the wounded, or carrying off the dead. The hustings remained, with a few broken and hewed flag-staves erect, and a torn and gashed banner or two dropping; whilst over the whole field, were strewed caps, bonnets, hats, shawls, and shoes, and other parts of male and female dress; trampled, torn, and bloody, The yeomanry had dismounted, – some were easing their horses' girths, others adjusting their accoutrements; and some were wiping their sabres. Several mounds of human beings still remained where they had fallen, crushed down, and smothered. Some of these still groaning, – others with staring eyes, were gasping for breath, and others would never breathe more. All was silent save those low sounds, and the occasional snorting and pawing of steeds. Persons might sometime be noticed peeping from attics and over the tall ridgings of houses, but they quickly withdrew, as if fearful of being observed, or unable to sustain the full gaze, of a scene so hideous and abhorrent.[225]

Lieutenant Jolliffe, meanwhile, watched as carriages arrived 'to convey the wounded to the Manchester Infirmary; and the troop of hussars, which came up with the guns, was marched off to escort to the gaol a number of persons who had been arrested, and among these Mr. Hunt.'[226]

Edward Stanley was still upstairs in Mr Buxton's house, which was now being guarded by a large number of constables in preparation for the reappearance of those who had been arrested. Henry Hunt, John Tyas and Joseph Johnson were being held, Stanley remembers, 'in a small parlour opening into a passage to which I now descended.'[227] Here William Hulton recalled seeing a woman 'in a faint state, and advanced in pregnancy, and blood flowing from her bosom'.[228] Hulton states that he left the house as the military were clearing the field, and just after Hunt had arrived. Tyas also describes being in the house with Hunt and others, along with a woman 'in a fainting condition'.[229] This last may have been Elizabeth Gaunt, who had also been arrested, one of several women mistaken for Mary Fildes.

Stanley had thought, given the circumstances, that Hunt and his companions would be taken to the New Bailey by carriage, but, for some reason not then explained, it was decided that he should walk. Once this decision became known, Stanley heard, 'from all quarters', 'shouts of approbation and "bring him out, let the rebel walk."'[230] The *Manchester Chronicle* records:

The Rev. Mr. Hay came forward: he said he respected the feelings of the good and the loyal, but as Hunt was now a prisoner, and in the hands of the Law, he hoped that no expression would be given which could endanger the man's personal security; but that they would be satisfied to let him pass to the New Bailey Prison with their *silent contempt*. This address was highly applauded, and its purport assented to; but still, when this destroyer of the poor man's comfort was handed out by the Beadles, a *general hiss* could not be repressed. Mr. Hay also said with much manliness, 'I will go down with the prisoner as a protection to him. Shall we put him upon a horse, or place him in a coach?' The general cry was, 'No! damn the brute let him walk!' To this the Magistrate assented.[231]

After some time, Hunt appeared, and Stanley says that, 'notwithstanding the blows he had received in running the gauntlet down the avenue of constables, I thought I could perceive a smile of triumph on his countenance.'[232] The *Manchester Chronicle*, still spitting venom, describes how this 'demi-god' had recovered from 'the surprize of his transition' and now 'stared contemptuously, and braved his fate'.[233] Stanley noticed that Nadin offered his arm to Hunt as a support, but Hunt 'drew himself back, and in a sort of whisper said: "No, no that's rather too good a thing," or words to that effect'.[234] Henry Hunt, injured and shaken but ever the quick-thinking opportunist, was attempting to squeeze every last drop of advantage from this appalling situation. He could not be seen to be cowed or broken by his rough treatment. It certainly seemed as if the authorities had played into the reformers' hands. They had lost their collective nerve and caused a slaughter. Righteousness was on the side of the people. With the civil power condemned and shamed, and the brutality of their actions laid bare, how could the people's suffering and sacrifice – endured in the name of liberty and justice – not provide the momentous final push needed to bring about reform? The horrific events on St Peter's Field, and the treatment meted out towards the meeting's speakers, had been witnessed by several independent journalists: John Tyas, Richard Carlile, John Smith and Edward Baines, alongside John Thacker Saxton of the *Manchester Observer*. Hunt would later describe Tyas's report as 'the most unprejudiced evidence upon the subject'.[235]

Remembering the desperate plight of the woman lying motionless on the ground, Stanley hastily left Buxton's house and 'went towards her. Two men were then in the act of raising her up; whether she was actually dead or not I cannot say, but no symptoms of life were visible.'[236] At this time John Tyas states, in amazement, that as he glanced out of the window he saw that the field had been cleared in ten minutes, except for the cavalry and infantry.[237] And so, less than half an hour since his triumphal carriage ride onto St Peter's Field, Henry Hunt, in the custody of Lieutenant Colonel L'Estrange and escorted by a detachment of the 15th Hussars and the 31st Foot, was marched out of Mr Buxton's house, with the damaged staffs of two banners 'carried in mock procession before him'.[238]

At four o'clock, Major Dyneley was writing his report from Hulme Barracks. Regarding casualties, he observed, 'The number that were rode over must have been very great. I don't know that any of them were killed. I saw several carried very badly wounded to the Hospital. I am sorry to say one of the Manchester Cavalry was shot dead, & two or three of the Constables very badly wounded. One of the 15th Hussars had his arm broken & badly cut on the Head.' Although they had returned to the barracks, 'We are not by any means quiet – a Squadron is this moment ordered down, but I don't know that it is anything more than precautions, and we remain harnessed ready to turn out at a moment's notice.' But, as Major Dyneley proclaims in one of the most extraordinary sentences ever written on the subject, the 'first action of the Battle of Manchester is over, & has I am happy to say ended in the complete discomfiture of the Enemy'.[239]

15

NEW CROSS

'Retreat from the field'

Richard Carlile had been on the hustings at the moment when Henry Hunt was dragged away by Nadin's constables. As the platform was stormed, he recalled, he fell between the two carts, initially getting trapped within the gap, and then landing underneath the gradually disintegrating hustings as it was violently shifted back and forth. He was eventually able to escape and took refuge in a nearby house on Windmill Street, where he remained until six o'clock, when the owner returned home. Carlile feared that being hatless, and therefore inappropriately attired for the street, he would draw attention to himself. He persuaded the owner to buy him a hat so that he could finally venture out. Duly equipped with suitable headgear, he walked the short distance to the Star Inn on Deansgate, only to find cavalrymen celebrating there. He then made his way to James Wroe's house. Wroe encouraged him to travel immediately to London and to publish a full account of what he had seen. Carlile left Manchester at three o'clock on the morning of Tuesday 17 August, in the first mail coach to London. On arrival, he declared his intention of changing the name of his paper from *Sherwin's Weekly Political Register* to *The Republican* and proceeded to publish a graphic account of what he had witnessed.[1]

Battling with overwhelming feelings of horror and disgust at what had occurred, James Wroe, meanwhile, was busy preparing the next issue of the *Manchester Observer*, due to be published on Saturday 21 August. In addition, he had made the decision to print a separate publication specifically dealing with the meeting on St Peter's Field and its aftermath. This would appear as a series of connected issues, the first available on 25 August, building up a multi-layered picture of what had occurred, as the information became available day by day, hour by hour. The first collected edition of 12,400 copies quickly sold out.[2] In the advertisement, dated 23 August, announcing this new pamphlet Wroe called upon his readers, particularly the 'Friends of the *murdered* and *wounded* people', to bring any information they had on events during and after the meeting to the *Manchester Observer*'s offices on Market Street, so that the terrible catalogue of crimes could be published in full. Crucially, the title of the forthcoming work, as advertised, was the first public appearance of the name by which the event would come to be known: 'Peter-Loo Massacre!'[3]

Wroe explained that the title 'was given to the Work from a wish to fall in with the common feeling which the proceedings of the 16th of August elicited, and not on account of its classical elegance. Its quaintness is its only recommendation.'[4] Whatever its origins, the name cleverly melds several related meanings and bitter ironies. It makes a direct connection between the field of Waterloo and St Peter's Field: two events, worlds apart. According to Ann Jones's account, the special constables had already made that link, shouting, 'This is Waterloo for you!' as the people were sabred, crushed and beaten. Within hours, Major Dyneley was describing it as a field of battle. This was made clearer still by a poem entitled '*PETER-LOO*', published in the *Manchester Observer* on 28 August 1819:

This is the field of Peter-Loo.

These are the poor reformers who met, on the state of affairs to debate; in the field of Peter-Loo.

These are the butchers, blood thirsty and bold, who cut, slash'd and maim'd young, defenceless and old, who met, on the state of affairs to debate; in the field of Peter-Loo.

This is Hurly Burly, a blustering knave, and foe to the poor, whom he'd gladly enslave, who led on the butchers, blood-thirsty and bold, who cut, slash'd and maim'd young, defenceless and old, who met, on the state of affairs to debate; in the field of Peter-Loo.

These are the just-asses, gentle and mild, who to keep the peace, broke it, by lucre beguil'd, and sent Hurly-Burly, a blustering knave, a foe of the poor, whom he'd gladly enslave, to lead on the butchers, blood-thirsty and bold, who cut, slash'd and main'd young defenceless and old, who met, on the state of affairs to debate; in the field of Peter-Loo.[5]

The name 'Peterloo' made the point that Waterloo veterans were on both sides but also, more importantly, that British soldiers present at that definitive battle had attacked British civilians, the very people they had been fighting to protect in June 1815. It might also signal that the struggle for parliamentary reform had been turned, by the actions of the authorities, into a war: in Dyneley's terms, the 'first action of the Battle of Manchester' may have been lost by the reformers, but the war for the future of the United Kingdom was still theirs to win.

After witnessing the fighting near the Quaker Meeting House, Samuel Bamford had been able to reach open streets. He describes his 'retreat from the field', continuing the military analogy, via King Street and Market Street, all the while desperately worried about his wife. Happily, he was told that she was safe and on her way home to Middleton. Bamford and a neighbour then walked to Smedley Cottage. On the way they came across a group of the Manchester and Salford Yeomanry Cavalry, one sporting a broad green sash which Bamford recognized as a remnant of one of the Middleton banners: 'the inglorious exhibition of the torn banner, was permitted for the gratification of the vanity of the captor.'[6] At Smedley Cottage he saw Mrs Johnson and Hunt's manservant, the latter just arrived from the tumult to the south. It was here that Bamford was told of the arrest and jailing of Hunt, Johnson, Knight and Moorhouse.

On the road to Middleton, he enquired again about Mima. Receiving no fresh news, he began to walk back to Manchester in mounting fear until, at last, he spotted her in the distance hastening towards him. They met, he recalled, 'and our first emotions were those of thankfulness to God for our preservation'. She had been informed 'first that I was killed, – next, that I was wounded, and in the Infirmary, – next, that I was a prisoner, – and lastly that she would find me on the road home'.[7] With a thousand of their party now gathered, the Middleton folk marched homeward to the sound of a fife and the beat of a drum, the rescued blue banner flying and the Cap of Liberty, found on the outskirts of the field by a young man from Chadderton, raised proudly and defiantly at their head. On arrival, the battered banner, with its mottoes 'Unity and Strength', 'Liberty and Fraternity', was displayed in the window of the Suffield Arms public house. Bamford writes that 'we spent the evening in recapitulating the events of the day, and in brooding over a spirit of vengeance towards the authors of our humiliation, and our wrong'.[8]

In Manchester itself, as Major Dyneley noted, the military were patrolling the streets. A temporary calm had descended throughout most of the town, but soon violence began to flare up in New Cross, near Ancoats, in an area centred on the junction of Tib Street, New Cross (or Swan) Street and Oldham Street. A rumour had circulated that the Female Reformers' banner had been taken on the field and was now on show as a trophy in the shop window of John Tate, a grocer. Although the report was untrue, a crowd had gathered around his shop and proceeded to break the windows and damage the frontage.[9] According to a report in the *Manchester Mercury*, the Riot Act was read and a troop of the 15th Hussars under Captain Booth was sent in to clear the streets. The special constable Robert Mutrie, who was present, later described how the magistrate James Norris was reticent to use the military to disperse the crowd. He also recalled that, once Captain Booth's troop was deployed, 'two people were shot in the first charge'.[10] The *Mercury* report continues, 'The town certainly wears an alarming aspect at the present moment, but we are well supplied with Military protection, and their exertions and resolute conduct are truly praiseworthy and a theme of general eulogium.'[11]

On Tuesday 17 August, Samuel Bamford, disguised as an old man, walked with a neighbour into Manchester. 'All', he recalled, 'seemed in a state of confusion.' He saw the patrols of the military, police and special constables; 'the shops were closed and silent; the warehouses were shut up and padlocked; the Exchange', usually bustling with life, 'was deserted.'[12] He walked from tavern to tavern, listening in on the locals' discussions and overhearing conversations in the streets. The general opinion, he believed, 'was that the authorities were stunned, and at a loss how to proceed; that many of the wealthy class blamed them, as well for the severity with which they had acted, as for the jeopardy in which they had placed the lives and property of the townspeople'. Meanwhile, 'all the working population were athirst for revenge, and only awaited the coming of the country folks to attempt a sweeping havock'.[13] In a similar spirit, when he returned to Middleton, Bamford found young men creating weapons from whatever was to hand. Nothing was organized, however, and these instruments were soon set aside. A few days later he heard that Dr Joseph Healey had been arrested.

On 19 August, in the absence of any report from their own correspondent, *The Times* ran an editorial comment on the events in Manchester, based on the few reports so far published elsewhere – some of which had been sent to London by Archibald Prentice and another local radical, John Edward Taylor. Both had heard of John Tyas's arrest and feared that the magistrates' account, justifying their actions, would be the first to reach the capital.[14] In the editorial, *The Times* considered, in particular, the legality of the actions of the magistrates:

> The Riot Act, and the act against seditious meetings, both limit the magistrate's right of interference, to 'unlawful assembly,' and no other. Was that at Manchester an 'unlawful assembly?' Was the notice of it unlawful? We believe not. Was the subject proposed for discussion (a reform in the House of Commons) an unlawful subject? Assuredly not. Was any thing done at this meeting before the cavalry rode in upon it, either contrary to law or in breach of the peace? No such circumstance is recorded in any statements which have yet reached our hands.

There is a swift dismissal of the *Manchester Courier*'s claims that the meeting was unlawful and therefore the response by the magistrates lawful. *The Times* then turns to due process: 'The Riot Act, some say, was read; some say otherwise – but all are agreed, that before an hour had elapsed from the reading of it, the soldiers attacked, and the people were cut down.' Until further information was available, the paper chose not to make a definitive judgement on what had passed.

However, just before going to press, *The Times* had finally received by express a report from John Tyas, now freed from detention, which offered a dispassionate eyewitness view of the entire event, moment by moment. Archibald Prentice considered that Tyas's report 'corroborated all our statements', i.e. the reports he and Taylor had already sent to London, 'and added details of still greater atrocity'.[15] The result was sensational. After describing the events up to his imprisonment in minute detail, much of it already quoted here, Tyas's story continues beyond his release at midday on Tuesday 17 August. He had walked through the principal streets of Manchester, finding that, at that time, they were 'completely under military disposal. Soldiers were posted at all the commanding positions of the town.' He also noted the desperate living conditions that many of the factory workers were then enduring. This was around the same time that Samuel Bamford, in disguise, was walking through the town. But by three o'clock, the military had 'all of them returned to their quarters, and the town was to all outward appearance once more in a state of tranquillity'.[16] However, on his journey south to London, through Stockport and Macclesfield, Tyas records seeing gangs of men on the streets, universal terror among the unprotected inhabitants – the military, he confirms, were still concentrated in Manchester – and tension breaking out into violence and riot.

The Manchester Infirmary's register for Monday 16 August suggested that the casualties from the events at St Peter's Field had been surprisingly few, with twenty-nine people admitted, of whom two had died. The following day, another thirty-four people were admitted and one of these had since died. This, the magistrates believed, indicated the forbearance demonstrated by their Yeomanry and the military in dispersing so great a mob.[17] In fact the scale of the injuries and deaths would only become clear after a relief fund was set up by concerned local citizens, including John Edward Taylor and Archibald Prentice, to dispense financial aid to the victims. It was publicized in the *Manchester Observer*, and subscriptions poured in from all over the country.[18] For example, at a meeting on 2 September in Palace Yard, Westminster, held in protest at the events of 16 August and chaired by Sir Francis Burdett, subscriptions had been received from, among many others, Sir Francis (£210), Major John Cartwright and friends (£44. 14s. 6d), John Cam Hobhouse (£100), *Black Dwarf* (£1), 'John Hampden' (£1) and twenty-five workmen from Stratford (£1. 5s). Further subscriptions would be taken at thirteen venues around London, including the offices of the *Statesman* and the Crown and Anchor Tavern.[19]

During the Relief Fund Committee's deliberations, they discovered that many of the wounded were afraid to ask for parish relief or medical aid, because admitting the circumstances of their injuries, they believed, might have led to prison or even the scaffold.[20] There was also a general reluctance to go to the Manchester Infirmary, where they would have been 'huffed at and insulted on account of their political principles'.[21] By the time the fund reported on its activities over the six months since the fateful day in August, 420 wounded people had received financial assistance and eleven were recorded as having died, with a further 140 still to be assessed.[22]

Among the victims listed were: John Ainsworth of 2 Duncan Street, Bolton, who suffered 'A severe sabre cut on his right cheek & 2 other cuts' and 'was 3 weeks disabled'; eleven-year-old Samuel Ackerley of 3 Gregson Street, Deansgate, who had a sabre cut on his left leg and was 'knocked down and trampled on'; Ann Bickerstaff

of 63 Cropper Street, Manchester, who 'Was thrown down &
trampled on & so much exhausted as to be carried off the Field for
Dead', possibly the woman mentioned in the Reverend Edward
Stanley's account; likewise Ann Barlow of Coldhurst Lodge,
Oldham: 'This Poor woman who is a Widow with 7 Children
was beat by some of the Constables, thrown down & trampled
on[,] her Breast Bone broke she was in the Infirmary 3 Weeks &
is still very Ill'; Thomas Richardson of 14 Blossom Street, Salford,
who happened to be standing at the door of his father's house in
Jackson's Row (to the west of the Quaker Meeting House), and
'Had his Nose cut down to his face' – John Tyas witnessed such
a mutilation; twenty-two-year-old Peter Welch of 56 Cropper
Street, Oldham Road, who was 'Cut by Meagher... much bruised
3 w[ee]k disabled', an example of a victim naming their assailant;
Ellen Croft of Back Mill Street, Manchester, who was 'crushed
& bruised[,] very infirm, thrown into a Cellar & a good deal
bruised'; Mary O'Neil of Dean Street, Manchester, also 'thrown
into a cellar', as were Elizabeth Ratcliffe of Heaton Norris, James
Kershaw and Joseph Cook both of Greenacres Moor, and Martha
Parkinson of Eccles who 'Was thrown into a Cellar & Killed left
2 Children' – possibly six of the many people who fell into John
Jones's basement well on Windmill Street and were horrifically
crushed; Samuel Allcard of 11 Portugal Street, 'an interesting lad[,]
a plasterer', who was 'saved by one of the 15th who threatened to
cut the yeoman down if he struck him again'; William Cheetham
of Little Bolton, who had a severe cut to the back of the neck,
also delivered by Edward Meagher who 'swore he would cut off
his head'; seventy-six-year-old William Ogden, the printer, 'cut on
the Eye & back of the Head much bruised'; and John Rhodes of
Hopwood, who had a 'Sabre cut on the Head by which he lost
much blood[.] A Woman saw him wandering about bloody & took

him into her House, shaved off the Hair & put on a Plaister. He was dreadfully bruised internally so that he has not since held up his Head & died about the 18th November.'[23]

Archibald Prentice recalled 'Poor old' Thomas Blinstone being interviewed by the committee in Prentice's offices. A pitiful sight with both arms in splinters, Blinstone calmly concluded his tale of misfortune by saying, 'and what is wur than aw [worse than all], mesters, they'v broken my spectacles and aw've ne'er yet been able to get a pair that suits me.'[24] Prentice considered that the overwhelming public response, via subscriptions, to these stories of distress and hardship showed that a 'deep sympathy for the oppressed and injured reformers' now prevailed 'amongst the middle classes', which 'gave the promise of co-operation in the work of reform'. Indeed, deriving some hope from the desperate situation, he sensed 'a marked and favourable change in the current of public opinion'.[25]

Following the arrest of Dr Healey, Samuel Bamford knew that he himself was on borrowed time. At two o'clock in the morning of 26 August, while lying in bed alongside Mima, Samuel was awoken by regular, hasty footsteps in the street outside and then by a loud thump on the front door. It was Joseph Nadin, accompanied by constables, infantry and cavalry troops. 'Well Mr. Nadin,' Bamford said calmly on opening the door, 'and what may be your pleasure with me now?' Nadin informed him 'in his usual dogged way, striving to be civil, that he had a warrant against me for high treason'. The house was searched and Bamford's books and papers, including manuscripts of his poems, were thrown into a pile to be taken away as evidence. Bamford was then chained and, as he was escorted into the street, he cried out in one last act of defiance, 'Hunt and Liberty!' His wife – 'my brave little helpmate' – shouted the same in response. One of the constables, holding a pistol, threatened to blow out her brains if she shouted again. 'Blow away,' she replied, repeating, with greater energy, 'Hunt and liberty... Hunt for ever!'

Bamford was taken to a coach and then, under cavalry escort, they set off for Manchester. He recalled that as they travelled along, Nadin said that this would be their last journey together. Bamford asked why, to which Nadin responded that Bamford would never return from where he was now heading. 'Indeed!' said Bamford. 'Why not?' 'Thou'll be hanged,' came the reply.[26]

—————————— " Great offices will have
Great talents."

16

HMY *ROYAL GEORGE*

'The man in the moon'

On the evening of 16 August the Reverend William Hay wrote his report to Lord Sidmouth. He would soon journey south to London to give a further account in person. Replying to this initial report on the 18th, however, Lord Sidmouth praised the 'deliberate & spirited manner in which the Magistrates discharged their arduous and important duty on that occasion' and told Hay that he had 'had great pleasure in representing their mer[i]torious conduct to His Royal Highness the Prince Regent. I do not fail to appreciate most highly the merits of the two corps of Yeomanry Cavalry, and the other Troops employed on this service.'[1] On the same day, in response to Sir John Byng's letter enclosing Lieutenant Colonel L'Estrange's brief account written on the evening of 16 August,* Lord Sidmouth commended the conduct of the troops, including the Yeomanry, 'no part of which is more eminently deserving of approbation than the Forbearance & moderation with which they sustained the insults unwarrantably directed against them on this trying occasion'.[2]

---

* L'Estrange's account is broadly factual until he states that 'some of the unfortunate People who attended the meeting have suffered, some from Sabre Wounds, and others from the Pressure of the Crowd'.

Light years away from the turmoil and bloodshed on Manchester's streets, the Prince Regent was aboard HMY *Royal George*, termed a yacht but in reality more of a ship, which had been launched in 1817, the year of the failed blanketeers' march. In August 1819 he had been having a perfectly splendid time cruising around the Isle of Wight, giving sumptuous dinners on board, 'served on a new service of china, ornamented with naval emblems, made expressly for use in the yacht', as *The Times* reported. Among the toasts given by His Royal Highness, the first was to 'The King', which, the report continues, was pronounced 'with evident feelings of strong filial affection and attachment'. Given their fraught relationship, this is difficult to imagine. The next was to 'The Duke of Wellington and the Heroes of Waterloo'.

On Saturday 14 August, Commodore Sir George Collier, recently returned from the coast of Africa, had delivered to the yacht 'a fine turtle, weighing about 6 cwt, for his Royal Highness's gracious acceptance'.[3] On the 16th, the yacht had sailed to the Hampshire coast, where the Prince Regent was to dine with Lord Cavan at Eaglehurst that evening. As he and his party disembarked, they were 'saluted by huzzas from the crews of an immense line of yachts and pleasure vessels, and from an innumerable throng of yeomanry and peasantry on the Cliffs, all attracted to witness the landing of the Prince Regent on the New-forest shore'. He had already declared his intention to continue his maritime jaunt for another two weeks. His short visit to Weymouth on 19 August would be followed by a quick excursion to the Channel Islands. In the same column as this report, on 21 August, *The Times* printed word for word the address 'To Henry Hunt, Esq' from the Manchester Female Reform Society, which was 'to have been presented... on Monday last, had not the meeting been so suddenly dispersed by the irruption of the military'.[4] The newspaper had by now, of course, carried the report from John Tyas, detailing the terrible events on St Peter's Field.

In a brief interruption to the Prince Regent's holiday, Lord Sidmouth was commanded to convey His Royal Highness's reactions. Sidmouth duly wrote to the Lords Lieutenant of Lancashire and Cheshire on 21 August, announcing that he had been asked to express to the magistrates 'the great satisfaction derived by His Royal Highness from their prompt, decisive, and efficient measures for the Preservation of the Public Tranquillity', and to 'signify to Major Trafford [and] Lt Col. Townsend His Royal Highness's high Approbation of the support and assistance to the Civil Power afforded upon that occasion by himself and the officers, non commissioned officers, and Privates of the Corps serving under his command'.[5]

In the storm of recriminations which engulfed the magistrates as news of the massacre emerged, William Hulton wrote a desperate letter to the Home Office, requesting permission to publish Lord Sidmouth's letter of 18 August to William Hay, to show the world that they had the Home Secretary's full support. In customary style, having had the time and information to appreciate fully what had happened in Manchester, Henry Hobhouse responded:

As Lord Sidmouth's letters of Saturday last to the Earls of Derby and Stamford conveyed the most gracious appreciation of H.R.H. The Prince Regent, of the conduct of the Magistrates at Manchester, and expressed the great satisfaction which His Royal Highness had derived from their prompt, decisive, and efficient measures to preserve the public Tranquillity, which must be of far greater value than any thing only proceeding from Lord Sidmouth himself; His Lordship presumes that it can no longer appear to the Magistrates to be of any consequence to give Publicity to His letter of the 18th instant; and His Lordship would accordingly prefer that it should not be published. But His Lordship sees no objection to a Publication of His letter of the 21st.[6]

It was thus the Prince Regent's response, delivered by Lord Sidmouth, which was published, rather than the Home Secretary's own opinion. The *Manchester Observer* included it in their edition of 28 August, with an adjacent editorial comment discussing Sidmouth's communication of the Prince Regent's *'satisfaction'* and *'high approbation'* for the 'most wanton effusion of human blood which ever disgraced the English name and nation!' The editor 'must believe' – otherwise how could it be explained – that the Prince Regent was, in reality, ignorant of these 'butcheries' and had been deluded by misinformation 'to protect the Magistracy in unconstitutionally employing a military force without first trying the efficiency of the civil power to disperse the Meeting'. The right of the people to assemble had been clearly set out by Henry Hunt and others, so far differing from Lord Sidmouth's view 'as to make them think his Lordship is in the habit of *going to sleep with his eyes open'*. The editorial concludes, adapting lines from Shakespeare's *Hamlet*: 'let the abettors of the corruptionists "paint and patch their atrocities an inch thick, to the complexion of *murder* they must come at last, and that most *foul* and most *unnatural*"'.[7]

In reaction to the events in Manchester, the radical writer and bookseller William Hone produced a bitingly satirical pamphlet entitled *The Political House that Jack Built*, using the same rhythm and repetition as the *Manchester Observer*'s poem *'PETER-LOO'*, in which he described the Prince Regent as

A dandy of sixty who bows with a grace,
And has taste in wigs, collars, cuirasses and lace;
Who, to tricksters, and fools, leaves the State and its treasure,
And, when Britain's in tears, sails about at his pleasure.[8]

Soon after, Hone would publish another pamphlet lambasting the prince, this one fittingly entitled 'The Man in the Moon'.

THE
MAN IN THE MOON,
&c. &c. &c.

" If Cæsar can hide the Sun with a blanket, or put the Moon in his pocket, we
will pay him tribute for light."—*Cymbeline.*

WITH FIFTEEN CUTS.

Twenty-fifth Edition.

LONDON:
PRINTED BY AND FOR WILLIAM HONE,
45, LUDGATE-HILL.
1820.

ONE SHILLING.

17

OLDHAM

'The occasion of my death'

Jonah Andrew found John Lees some time between two and three o'clock on Monday 16 August, long after the crowd had been dispersed. He was visibly distressed, and said to his friend, 'I have been dangerously hurt, Andrew, which has affected my body very much.'[1] Andrew recalled that, rather than walk to the infirmary nearby, where some of the injured were being treated, he declared, 'I must return home, for I am getting very sick and poorly, which I think will be the occasion of my death.'

It was just before dark when Hannah Lees saw her stepson at the gate of the family home in Oldham. She had already been told by one of her sons, James, that John had been 'cut' and so she told him to come into the house so that his arm could be cleaned and dressed.[2] John entered the house and had tea and toast, after which his other stepbrother, Thomas, helped him up the stairs to bed. But, having made slow progress to reach the top of the stairs, John appeared to faint.[3] By the time they had reached the bedchamber, he had turned very pale. As Thomas tried to help him out of his clothes, he realized that John's shirt was stuck fast to his body by blood and 'the flesh was cut to the bone'.[4] He later described the wound as 'a foul cut'.[5] Having slowly removed the shirt, Thomas washed the wound as best he could, while John 'told me that was not the worst, and he desired me to look at his shoes, how they were cut off by the horses'.[6] Thomas saw how the left shoe was sliced off and the leather torn. He stayed with John the whole night, afraid to leave him alone in this severely battered condition.

Hannah recalled that John's shirt 'was cut in many a place, and his coat was cut over his shoulder and elbow', yet it was Thomas's comment that it was a 'foul cut' which alerted her that her stepson was in a very bad way. On the left shoulder, both John's coat and waistcoat had been cut through. The top of his hat had been completely removed, although she was uncertain whether it, too, had been cut with a sword. Hannah observed that the wound on John's elbow was about two inches long and opened to the breadth of her little finger. She advised him to see a doctor, which he did the following day, and the wound was dressed.[7]

Robert Lees saw his son at his factory on the morning of Tuesday 17 August, between eight and nine o'clock. John was without his coat and waistcoat and the shirt he wore was 'all over blood'.[8] Robert also recalled seeing blood on John's arm.[9] Despite this Robert was irritable with his son, still angry that John had attended the meeting against his wishes, telling him that if he could not work, he should go to the overseer. John did not utter a word in response.

Over the coming days, Robert observed his son's condition getting worse and worse, but, surprisingly, was not much concerned: 'I thought he would get better; and I did not think there was any danger.'[10] Although he had been cut and beaten, John was young, and he had fought in and survived major battles, so, with care, he might well make a full recovery.

John remained in the family home, usually in his bed, although he occasionally had strength enough to go out for a walk and take some fresh air. Over this period, Thomas and he walked into Oldham, to Middleton and to Stockport. While on their way to Middleton, the brothers drank ale at the Dusty Miller Inn and several other places and John was 'rather tipsy like; not what they call drunk; he walked well enough'.[11] The two of them even ventured to Manchester, travelling by cart there and back.[12] This might have suggested that John's strength and health were returning.

But as time passed John became less able to hold down his food, eventually vomiting every time he ate. He also complained of a violent pain in his left shoulder, where Hannah had observed the cuts through his clothing. Whenever Hannah tried to lift him up to give him water to drink, he winced and 'made faces'.[13] She said that he was 'very low and down-spirited'.[14] Then John's left leg began to swell and became mottled with purple spots from the foot upwards. At this point a surgeon, Mr Earnshaw, was called. He remained in attendance for the next few weeks. The left side of John's body gradually became completely numb. Eventually he lost the use of his left leg and arm and the sight of his left eye.[15]

William Harrison saw John on Thursday 2 September. He was lying on a couch in the kitchen, his face 'as white as a cap'. John 'told me he was at the battle of Waterloo, but he never was in such danger there as he was at the meeting; for at Waterloo there was man to man, but at Manchester it was downright murder'.[16]

The following day, Thomas observed that his brother 'had no knowledge at all of what was done or said to him',[17] and on Sunday the 5th Hannah describes him as being so poorly that he had to be carried downstairs by his brothers so he could sit in the kitchen for company, as was his habit. She also says that by this time he had difficulty responding with a 'No'.[18] James Clegg, a spinner who worked in Robert Lees's factory, sat up with him that night and confirmed that John was unable to respond to anything.[19] John's brother Thomas said that by the Sunday he had become 'speechless'.[20] From that time on John remained in his bed until, in the early hours of Tuesday 7 September, he died. He was twenty-two years old.

Mr Earnshaw, the surgeon, certified that his death had been the result of violence. Several householders were duly summoned to attend the coroner's inquest, initially conducted by George Battye (a clerk and deputy to the coroner of the Rochdale district, Thomas Ferrand), at the Duke of York Inn at Oldham, on Wednesday 8 September at half past ten.[21] The eyewitness accounts cited here come from the transcript of this inquest.

As part of the inquiry, several surgeons were asked to inspect the body. William Basnett saw John's body the day after he died and said that it 'was in a high state of putrefaction'. He also observed that the cut to John's elbow was 'livid' and that the bone 'was separated' so much so that when he bent the elbow 'the bone was protruded' and 'cut partly in two'.[22] He described the discolouration to the skin on the shoulders, back and loins. Basnett considered that this was the result of 'violence, inflicted with some blunt instrument' and that as a result of these injuries John would have been 'in excruciating pain for some days previous to his death'.[23] The loss of eyesight and the use of limbs, the sickness, low spirits and dwindling appetite were all a consequence, in his opinion, of a spinal injury. In sum, William Basnett concluded, 'the wounds and bruises caused the mortification'.[24]

John Cox also examined the body. He stated that the wound to the elbow was consistent with a sword cut, as if the victim had raised his arm to deflect a blow. He had removed a piece of loosened bone from the wound the size of a sixpence.[25] The fact that John's back was bruised rather than cut suggested that, if he had been attacked with a sword, the flat rather than the edge had been used.[26] John Cox had opened up the body, noting that the omentum, the fatty layer that covers the intestines and organs of the lower abdomen, was very inflamed and that 'on moving the body, much blood gushed from the mouth and nostrils. On opening the larynx, or windpipe, it was full of blood. The right lobe of the lungs was full of blood.'[27] Cox was asked whether, if the deceased had been bled, he might have survived. The surgeon thought this a possibility: 'if he had received proper surgical and medical assistance... if copious quantities of blood had been taken from him, as I should have done, the injury might have been checked.' Cox had not conferred with Earnshaw prior to examining the body, nor was Earnshaw requested to be present during Cox's examination, as was the usual practice.[28] Cox stated that with the injuries John had suffered, it would be expected that he would have complained more, certainly, than had been reported by various people who were with him at the time, but Cox also observed, 'I understood he was afraid of complaining to his father on account of the circumstances under which he received the injury.'[29] James Clegg was present at the autopsy, and recalled that Cox said that the bruises, rather than the cut, had been the cause of death.[30]

All this detail was vital. Was it the cuts he had suffered from the cavalry – whether Yeomanry or Hussars – that had killed John or the sustained beating he had received at the hands of the special constables, as many witnesses came forward to testify?

Betty Ireland and James Clegg laid out John's body before it had turned cold.[31] Betty, the wife of the local shoemaker, declared that 'I have seen many dead people, but I never saw such a corpse as this, in all my life'.[32] In general appearance, 'there was hardly a free place on his back; it was exactly as if he had been tied to a halberd and flogged.' She continued, 'I have often seen dead bodies discoloured, but I never saw one like this. I think his inside was putrified [sic].' She confirmed that the wounds were mainly on his back and sides, not on his front and breast.[33] One wound, she recalled, refused to heal and, while she was preparing the body, it opened up. 'He bled most when he was put into his coffin.'[34]

James Wroe, in *Peterloo Massacre*, declared the investigation into John Lees's death as being of 'extreme importance', for the 'issue of this Inquest, if it ever be suffered to come to an issue, will, we have no doubt, give a decisive blow to Lord Sidmouth and the rest of his crew: for we have no hesitation in anticipating the verdict of twelve honest men and independent men, from the nature of the evidence which has already come before them.'[35] If the inquest had the capacity, whether in and of itself or through a future prosecution, to bring someone to account for the death of John Lees, it was thanks to the efforts of two resourceful solicitors, James Harmer* of London, the son of a Spitalfields weaver, and Henry Denison of Liverpool, who had arrived in Oldham accompanied by as many witnesses to the events at St Peter's Field as would fill three or four coaches.[36] James Harmer, now representing Robert Lees, had attempted to serve indictments against several of the Manchester and Salford Yeomanry Cavalry at Lancaster the previous week, but this had been thrown out by the Grand Jury.[37] This was in the wake of an application to any Justice of the Peace in the County of Lancashire to accept charges against the Manchester magistrates, which was, unsurprisingly, rejected.[38] It was then that Harmer heard that John Lees had died from his wounds, and, after some enquiry, discovered where and when the coroner's inquest would be held.

Despite delaying tactics, several changes of venue (from the Duke of York to the Angel Inn in Oldham and then the Star Inn in Manchester), a change of coroner from Battye to Ferrand and

---

* Harmer is said to be the model for Charles Dickens' Mr Jaggers in *Great Expectations* (first serialized in 1860–1).

the exhumation of John's body as a result, and several attempts to throw out witness statements or close down the entire procedure, Harmer, Denison and their team managed to keep the inquest going, on and off, for a month. The failure, thus far, to instigate legal proceedings against the magistrates meant that this inquest became the main focus for the reformers and, as a result, carried a great burden of expectation. The evidence given by a relentless parade of witnesses, all attesting to the brutality with which John and his fellows were treated, seemed to point to one conclusion in this case: death from injuries inflicted during a prolonged and violent attack by the special constables. Murder, in fact.

However, as the first coroner, Mr Battye, admitted at the start of the inquest, the presumption had been a straightforward verdict of death caused by crushing from the crowds.[39] And despite Harmer's persistence, on 13 October the inquest was adjourned until 1 December, ostensibly because of the jury's fatigue. There was also a suggestion of intimidation, as the authorities saw it, from the unruly crowds that gathered in and around the inn. An application, with a joint affidavit from Harmer and Dennison, was made to the King's Bench to compel the coroner to proceed and the case was heard on 29 November. However, the inquest was abandoned on the technicality that, contrary to procedure, the jury and coroner had viewed John's body at different times.[40] In a petition to the House of Commons, Robert Lees declared that despite the evidence, 'the Coroner throughout evinced a manifest partiality for the Magistrates and Yeomanry Cavalry of Manchester, to whose illegal and violent conduct your Petitioner attributes the premature death of his Son.' Robert Lees was convinced 'that a verdict of Wilful Murder must and would have been given against many individuals engaged in the cruel attack... and your Petitioner has good reason to believe that the last-mentioned adjournment was made solely with a view to screen and protect the delinquents, who were likely to be affected by the verdict of the Jury'. Having no other recourse 'to bring to justice the authors of his son's death', he 'presumed to lay a simple statement of the facts before your Honourable House'.[41] The petition was presented to the House of Commons by Sir Francis Burdett and debated on 16 December.[42] But even then, the case was not reopened or re-examined.[43]

Some years later Archibald Prentice contemplated the amazing restraint displayed by the people of Lancashire, who had not retaliated against either those individuals who had actually maimed, disabled and even killed the victims of Peterloo, or the men who had ordered them into the crowd. He arrived at a simple answer: 'The population of Lancashire had faith in the just administration of the law.' The working men may have been rough in manner and 'rude in speech' but they were 'shrewd, intelligent', 'possessing much of the generous qualities of the Anglo-Saxon race'. They would not 'stoop to cowardly assassination. They had faith in their principles and greater belief in moral than physical force.'[44]

Many of the leading radicals, including Henry Hunt, now placed their faith in the courts for legal redress, rather than trying to maintain pressure on the authorities via the mass demonstrations that had formerly served them so well. As seen at Oldham, the battle ground had moved to an arena where the authorities had the upper hand.[45] Yet although the inquest into John Lees's death failed to develop into a criminal prosecution (in fact no one was ever charged with his murder), another opportunity soon arose to expose the perpetrators and bring them to account. At the Lancaster Assizes in September, ten prisoners, including Henry Hunt, Joseph Johnson, James Moorhouse, John Knight, Joseph Healey, John Thacker Saxton and Samuel Bamford, were indicted, not for high treason but on the lesser charge of conspiracy and

A Freeborn Englishman! The admiration of the world!!! And the envy of surround nations!!!!, by George Cruikshank, 1819.

(© The Trustees of the British Museum)

unlawful assembly. All were granted bail, with the trial fixed for 16 March 1820: not, however, in Salford or even Lancaster, but seventy miles away on the other side of the Pennine Hills, at York. Hunt had petitioned for this, in order, as he thought, to have any hope of a fair trial.[46]

Hunt had already begun agitating from his solitary confinement in the New Bailey. After his release on bail, with the surety provided by Sir Charles Wolseley, he paraded back to Manchester from Lancaster in triumph, led by a thousand working men – colliers, weavers and crofters. To the local magistrates, as James Norris said, it seemed that Hunt was once more 'in possession of this part of the country'.[47] But in London, moderate reformers such as Sir Francis Burdett were attempting to take advantage of the post-Peterloo environment, while also attempting to remove Henry Hunt from their deliberations: he had created too many enemies and, as the figurehead for what was viewed as a principally working-class movement, he was something of a pariah.

The beleaguered Hunt might have had some cause for cheer with the arrival at Liverpool on 22 November of William Cobbett. Cobbett did not arrive empty-handed. Amongst his baggage were the remains of the 'immortal' Thomas Paine, which he had removed from the grounds of the New Rochelle cottage in New York State that had been Paine's home between 1802 and 1806 (Paine had died in 1809). What genuine benefit Cobbett might have gained from bringing such a relic back to England is debatable. Cobbett himself declared in an open letter to Henry Hunt that their reburial in England would create a focus for the reform movement, a place of homage and even pilgrimage for the people.[48] In fact, he was widely ridiculed for this peculiar and faintly macabre gesture. Realizing his mistake, according to William Hazlitt, Cobbett had scarcely landed in Liverpool 'when he left the bones of a great man to shift for themselves'.[49] In the 1820 pamphlet *A Parody on the Political House that Jack Built*, Cobbett was caricatured carrying a coffin on his back containing what was left of the great English radical.[*]

In the meantime, Lord Sidmouth had heard that the Lord Lieutenant of the West Riding of Yorkshire, Lord Fitzwilliam, was organizing a petition for a government enquiry into the events of 16 August. With the support of the Prince Regent and the cabinet, Sidmouth quickly forced Fitzwilliam to resign. In any case, by the end of 1819, the Liverpool government had devised a sequence of bills to repress reformist activity, which became known as the Six Acts. The legislation targeted radical newspapers and mass meetings; drilling, of the kind that had been seen before the meeting on 16 August, could now result in arrest and even transportation. Through the Seditious Meetings Prevention Bill even the carrying of banners was prohibited, while attendance at political meetings was now restricted to those who lived within the parish in which the meeting was held: in future there would be no marching to Manchester from all over Lancashire. The Blasphemous and Seditious Libels Act increased the maximum sentence for such crimes to fourteen years' transportation, while the Newspaper and Stamp Duties Act extended taxation to publications that expressed opinions as well as news. This draconian legislation effectively ended the post-war radical mobilization.[50]

---

[*] Rather than abandoned, as Hazlitt's comment might suggest, they were, in fact, still in Cobbett's possession when he died twenty years later, but then disappeared.

18

HOUSE OF COMMONS

'The representation of the People'

On 29 January 1820 King George III died. The Prince Regent was now, at last, King George IV. Preparations were already well underway for his lavish coronation: a mock-Tudor extravaganza (eventually staged on 19 July 1821) with the Abbey and Palace of Westminster as the backdrop and the ageing king presented as Bluff King Hal and Gloriana rolled into one.[1] Parliament had voted £100,000 as a contribution to the costs, with a further £138,238 found from France's post-war reparations. The untimely arrival from Italy of George's estranged queen, Caroline, demanding her right to be crowned alongside her husband, threatened to cast a significant pall over his triumph. The king pressurized Lord Liverpool's government to allow him to divorce her, through the intriguingly entitled 'Pains and Penalties' Bill, but popular opposition to the queen's treatment escalated during Caroline's sensational trial in the House of Lords. Her plight became the unlikely rallying point for reformers – even Samuel Bamford penned a ditty, 'God save the Queen', in her honour – and eventually the bill was withdrawn. In the event, Caroline was barred from the coronation ceremony and, falling desperately ill, died a few weeks later.

Meanwhile, in March 1820, the trial of Henry Hunt and his fellows began in York. Much like the coroner's inquest in Oldham the year before, the event allowed for a roll-call of witnesses to be paraded, here including John Tyas, John Smith and Edward Baines junior. And, as with the trial in Oldham, the agenda was set not by the radicals, but the authorities. Hunt and his companions were on trial, not the magistrates, the Yeomanry Cavalry and the military. Indeed, months on, the testimonies of the magistrates in particular had conveniently aligned in their opinion as to cause and effect. The trial transcripts have been used extensively here, but, for this reason, with caution.

Despite the hundreds of men, women and children now known to have been affected by the events of 16 August, despite the rising death toll directly associated with it, and despite Hunt's eloquent questioning and cross-examination in his own defence and the heartfelt testimonies of his co-defendants – Samuel Bamford most notably – the result was inevitable. Hunt was found guilty of unlawful assembly and sentenced to two and a half years in Ilchester gaol, or 'Ilchester Bastille' as he described it, in Somerset. During his lengthy incarceration, in wretched conditions, and the relentless petty vindictiveness of his gaolers, the undaunted Hunt continued to agitate for redress for the victims of Manchester alongside radical electoral and parliamentary reform. He also wrote and then published his three-volume *Memoirs*. With their 'interminable concentration on self', as his biographer John Belchem admits, it is these *Memoirs* that spawned the author's reputation for vanity.[2] At the same time, Hunt's rallying cries to his fellow reformers across the United Kingdom, penned from his dank prison cell, established him as the most high-profile of the Peterloo martyrs and increased his popularity still further among the Lancastrian labouring class.

Samuel Bamford, Joseph Johnson, John Knight and Dr Joseph Healey, found guilty of the same charge, were sentenced to a year in Lincoln gaol. The rest, including John Saxton, were acquitted. Saxton's defence, that he was a journalist reporting on the event rather than a member of Hunt's party, was accepted. From the authorities' point of view, the key players, most importantly the 'demagogue' Orator Hunt, were now safely behind bars.

While in prison once again, Samuel Bamford wrote a number of poems that reflected on the events of 16 August. Percy Bysshe Shelley's *The Masque of Anarchy*, written in distant Italy just after the event but not published until 1832, is still considered the definitive poetic response to Peterloo. Yet Bamford, the working-class radical, was, after all, there on the day and had suffered greatly for his ardent belief in parliamentary reform and the rights of his fellow labouring men and women. His responses to the event, in poetry as well as prose, deserve to be better known and appreciated.[3] In addition to his 'Ode to a Plotting Parson', a barely disguised diatribe against the Reverend William Hay, Bamford wrote 'A Song of Slaughter', to be sung to the tune of the 'Sicilian Mariner's Hymn', which was first published by Henry Hunt (while in prison, it should be noted) in July 1820:

> *Parent of the wide creation,*
> *We would counsel ask of thee!*
> *Look upon a mighty nation,*
> *Rousing from its slavery!*
>
> *Thou hast made us to inherit*
> *Strength of body, daring mind;*
> *Shall we rise, and, in thy spirit,*
> *Tear away the chains that bind?*
>
> *Chains, but forged to degrade us,*
> *O, the base indignity!*
> *In the name of God, who made us,*
> *Let us perish, or be free!*[4]

317

In 1821, on the second anniversary of the 'never-to-be-forgotten 16th of August', Oldham's radical reformers, men and women, gathered at the Union Rooms in West Street to commemorate the event. According to the letter sent by their chairman, James Clegg, to Henry Hunt, flags were flown from windows and chimney-stacks across the town and the memorial event was opened and closed by the singing of Bamford's 'The Slaughter'.[5] A year later, the newspaper *Bell's Life in London* reported that the teachers and scholars of the Union Sunday School in Manchester, along with a large number of townspeople, had gathered on St Peter's Field and sung 'The Slaughter' as part of their commemorations.[6]

While Hunt, Bamford and the other reformers were awaiting trial, a plot to assassinate the entire Liverpool cabinet, while they were dining at Lord Harrowby's townhouse in Grosvenor Square, was discovered and its ringleaders arrested, including Arthur Thistlewood – the Spencean ultra-radical who had been arrested for high treason after the Spa Field meeting of 2 December 1816, but discharged – and William Davidson, a 'mulatto' from Jamaica. The event was known as the Cato Street Conspiracy, after the plotters' bolthole located off Edgware Road in London. One of the conspirators, James Ings, apparently admitted that his aim had been to behead all the members of the cabinet and then exhibit the severed heads of Lords Castlereagh and Sidmouth, among others, on spikes over Westminster Bridge. Six of the men were transported, while Davidson, Thistlewood, Ings and two others were hanged and, like Jeremiah Brandreth, posthumously beheaded for high treason on 1 May 1820.[7]

One victim of the repressive laws that had been passed in December 1819 was the *Manchester Observer*. After several arrests, imprisonment for James Wroe and the imposition of heavy fines, the newspaper closed in 1821. However, John Edward Taylor, with the support of Archibald Prentice, had already established the *Manchester Guardian*, whose first edition was published on 5 May 1821.* It was less overtly radical than James Wroe's paper, but it was a liberal publication determined to act as the voice for reform in general, and in particular to campaign against the Corn Laws. These laws were finally repealed in 1846.

In April 1822, the Lancaster Assizes heard a case brought by Thomas Redford (who had carried Middleton's green banner) against Hugh Hornby Birley, the captain of the Manchester and Salford Yeomanry Cavalry who had led his men onto St Peter's Field, and three other members of the Yeomanry, including the hot-headed Irishman Edward Meagher. The defence lawyers pursued the line that the mass meeting was unlawful – which was demonstrably not the case – and that the magistrates had therefore acted appropriately and the defendants had simply performed their duty in response to orders. They also encouraged their witnesses to repeat the accusations that members of the crowd had provoked and relentlessly attacked the Yeomanry, including by throwing stones, and they emphasized the extent of the injuries caused. By these means – almost three years after the event and with memories fading – they introduced sufficient doubt in the minds of the jury as to whether the Yeomanry's response to the situation had been excessive. All four defendants were acquitted.

Through the 1820s there were few significant advances but in 1830 the Tory government led by the Duke of Wellington (no supporter of reform) was ousted, in the wake of the Catholic Emancipation Act the previous year. Charles Grey, second Earl Grey, a Whig, took the helm under the banner of parliamentary reform. Two attempts to pass a reform bill failed, and it was

---

* The newspaper continues today under the title *The Guardian*.

rumoured that Lord Grey planned to utilize the constitutional powers of the new king, William IV (George IV's brother, r. 1830–7), to create enough new Whig peers to swing the vote in the House of Lords. The impasse was broken by Tory peers abstaining and the 'Great Reform Act' came into being. Fifty-six boroughs were disenfranchised, including the infamous Old Sarum, and a further thirty-one saw their two members of Parliament reduced to just one. Sixty-seven new constituencies were created, including two MPs each for Blackburn, Bolton, Manchester and Oldham – William Cobbett was one of those elected for the latter – and one each for Ashton-under-Lyne, Bury, Rochdale, Salford and Warrington. The franchise was extended in the counties to include small landowners, tenant farmers and shopkeepers, while in the boroughs the vote was broadened to include all householders who paid yearly rental of £10 or more. Although the changes brought about in 1832 were limited – far too limited for Henry Hunt, since 1830 MP for Preston, who considered it a sop to avoid far-reaching reform and voted against it – none the less it was a modest move in the right direction.

On 16 October 1834, a fire swept through the Palace of Westminster, reducing most of its buildings, including the House of Lords' and Commons' chambers, to smoking shells.[8] For radicals, it was a poignant symbol that the old corrupt order had gone at last – as Cobbett gleefully expressed it, 'a great event!'[9] For many Tories, however, it was a terrible manifestation of the very present danger to the nation's ancient constitution and cherished traditions.* Some even saw the fire as an act of God for the passing of the Great Reform Bill.

---

* Westminster Hall was saved and later integrated into the new Palace, designed by Charles Barry.

Given the modest expansion of the franchise, this meant that the vast majority of British working men still could not vote in general elections. The situation spawned a new labouring-class movement, Chartism. Between 1839 and 1848 three mass petitions, the People's Charters, were presented to Parliament, demanding the following: a vote for all men over the age of twenty-one; voting by secret ballot; no property qualification for MPs; payment for MPs; electoral districts of equal size; and annual general elections for Parliament. Four out of six of these issues were, sadly, very familiar – an indication of just how limited the so-called 'Great Reform Act' was. Consciously evoking the spirit of the post-Waterloo mobilization led by Henry Hunt, a hero for the Chartists, one last great 'monster' meeting, intended to accompany a petition signed by six million people, was arranged for 10 April 1848 on Kennington Common in London. The main speaker was another charismatic radical reformer, Feargus O'Connor, editor of the *Morning Star*. But, once again, the petition was rejected.

Universal male suffrage would not be achieved for another seventy years, when the property restriction for men was removed on the return of disenfranchised veterans from another terrible Europe-wide conflict, the Great War (1914–18). One hundred years after the Hampden Club convention in Westminster where the principle had first been officially championed, all men over the age of twenty-one could, at last, vote. Furthermore, so could some women – subject to age and property restrictions.* The Women's Social and Political Union had been established in 1903 by Emmeline Pankhurst, born at Moss Side, Manchester in 1858. Its members, dedicated to female suffrage, were known as 'suffragettes', as

---

* Equal suffrage for men and women, over the age of twenty-one, was achieved in 1928.

Anticipated Radical Meeting (Hunt the Matchless Reformer),
by C. E. P. Motte after John ('HB') Doyle, 1831.
(© British Library Board / Bridgeman Images)

distinct to the less militant but equally determined 'suffragists' under Millicent Fawcett. With their white dresses and banner slogans such as 'Taxation Without Representation is Tyranny', echoes of the Lancastrian Female Reform Societies, formed under the pioneering leadership of Alice Kitchen and Mary Fildes among others, can be traced in the female suffrage movement of the early twentieth century.

In 1918, this vastly expanded electorate brought in a coalition government led by the Liberal David Lloyd George, and, at the same time, saw a surge in support for a new party, originally founded by the Scotsman Keir Hardie, its first MP. This party, dedicated to the representation of the labouring class in the House of Commons, emerged from the expanded Trade Union movement in the latter decades of the nineteenth century.* The stage was now set for the Commons House in Parliament to genuinely represent the common man and, eventually, the people.

*

Did the events of 16 August 1819 have any lasting impact, beyond the collective outpouring of shock and disgust immediately following that terrible day? Peterloo certainly drew national attention to the conditions of the working man, woman and child in the manufacturing districts of Great Britain. On a local and national level, the shift in attitude by the 'middling sort' towards the plight of the disenfranchised labouring class, as Archibald Prentice had perceived in Manchester, surely assisted in bringing about the reform of Parliament and the electoral system in 1832: a change that met the reformers' demands in

---

* In 1924, the Labour Party formed the government of the United Kingdom for the first time.

part, while agonizingly deferring the full delivery of their central tenet – one man, one vote – for another century. However, the threat of insurrection, as an element of the mass-meeting tactic, had proved to be empty, and the radicals, in the immediate post-Peterloo years, were distracted by internal divisions. The Six Acts and the abrupt removal, from the public arena, of leading figures like Henry Hunt, had had the desired effect. Even so, the emergence of Chartism, Trade Unionism and the Labour Party demonstrated that the mobilization of the labouring class, as amply expressed through the tens of thousands gathered on St Peter's Field, could not be subdued.

At the same time, it is in its meaning and symbolism, and in the concept of social and political, rather than religious martyrdom, that Peterloo has continued to resonate down through the generations.[10] Even now, when a social injustice on a mass scale occurs, when national or local government is judged to have run roughshod over the rights – human as well as constitutional – of citizens, to have abrogated their basic duty of care resulting in physical harm and even death, Peterloo is evoked. Perhaps a more pertinent question is why this significant regional and national event remains so little known among the broader British public: a public that enjoys the full and precious rights of citizenship which their predecessors fought so long to attain and at such great personal cost. As for the English, often characterized as a nation of reactionaries and nostalgists – yearning for an imagined past, where everything was better – the Peterloo story offers a potent and inspiring example of progressive men and women, from across the social spectrum, honouring their country and their ancestors, whilst harnessing a deep-rooted understanding of the nation's past to the cause of a better future. With the bicentenary upon us, now is the time for the Peterloo Massacre, alongside the names of Henry Hunt, Samuel Bamford, Mary Fildes, John Bagguley and the myriad characters described in these pages, to take their rightful place in our national story.

ACKNOWLEDGEMENTS

My thanks to the team at Head of Zeus, in particular Georgina Blackwell and my fabulous editor Richard Milbank. And to my agent Bill Hamilton: ever patient, wise and (despite all manner of provocation) upbeat.

To all my Peterloo colleagues and friends, both cast and crew – what a journey – with particular thanks to Georgina Lowe (who suggested I write a book on the subject, and here it is), Helen Grearson, Gayle Egan, Mary Ann Marino, Kate Churchill, Nina Gold, Danielle Brandon, Chris Lahr, Dan Turner, Emma Parsons, Sarah Carswell, Orla Sharpe, Dick and Pat Pope, Peter Marsden, Heather Storr, Suzie Davies, Charlotte Watts, Jane Brodie, Dan Taylor, Caroline Harper, Mick Pirie, Paul Carter, Jacqueline Durran, Andrea Cripps, Sinéad O'Sullivan, Christine Blundell, Tim Fraser, Dan Channing Williams, Gayle Dickie, Tom Reynolds, Caroline Meer, Zoë Alker, Henry Woolley, Nick Ridout, George Zwier, Gary Yershon, Bek Leigh, Rachel Proudlove, Jon Gregory, Polly Duvall, Jonathan Rutter, Simon Mein and Marion Bailey.

The following institutions and their staff were crucial for both film and book research: British Library, British Museum, Chetham's Library, London Library, Manchester Central Library, National Archives, Parliamentary Archives and the University of Manchester. I am indebted to the following historians, curators and archivists for their time, support, encouragement, advice and generosity: Robert Poole, Katrina Navickas, Nathan Bend, Chris Day, Paul Carter, Tim Clayton, Michael Powell, Fergus Wilde, David Prior and Malcolm Hay; and The Guardian editor (and chum) David Teather. I am extremely grateful to John Belchem, who kindly read and commented on an early draft and who instilled in me, through his infectious enthusiasm, an admiration for Henry Hunt. The wealth of scholarship consulted is humbly acknowledged within the endnotes and bibliography.

To my family, the Ridings and the Johnsons – John, Patricia, Linda, Duncan, Christine, Karl, Joel, Ana, Sara and Susanna. To my friends and colleagues Tabitha Barber, Juliet Carey, Simon Chaplin, Amy Concannon, Jane Darcy, Nick Devison, Janet Dickinson, Timothy Duke, Susanna Eastburn, Sarah Fraser, Ruth Gill, Mark Hallett, Charlotte Higgins, Caro Howell, David Fraser Jenkins, Tim Knapman, John Lloyd, Andrew Loukes, Anne Lyles, Sarah McBryde, David McCulloch, Natasha McEnroe, Nick Merriman, Keith Miller, Steven Parissien, Matthew Plampin, Rosie Razzall, Eileen Read, Kate Retford, Imogen Robertson, James Robinson, Sara Robinson, Hallie Rubenhold, David Souden, Martin Stiles, Peter Trippi, Will Tuckett, Sarah Victoria Turner and Tim Wright.

Finally, my heartfelt gratitude and thanks to Mike Leigh, who invited me, once more, to join him on another great adventure.

BIBLIOGRAPHY

Oxford Dictionary of National Biography (online) *ODNB*

Manuscripts and Prints

British Museum1935,0522.11.147 J. Lewis Marks, "Much wanted RE-FORM AMONG FEMALES!!!", hand-coloured etching, August 1819
Chetham's Library, Manchester (CL)
MAIN Collection Hay 1–18, William Robert Hay Scrapbooks
MUN Collection Mun.A.6.30 James Weatherley, *Autobiography*, 1860
Manchester Libraries, Information and Archives (MLIA)BR F 942.7389
SC13 f. 123 Advertisement for no. 1 of "The Peterloo Massacre", 23 August 1819
The National Archives (TNA)
Home Office Papers (HO) 40, 41, 42, 79
Treasury Solicitor's Papers (TS) 11, 1125
War Office Papers (WO) 69, 97, 100
The Royal Archives, Windsor. Georgian Papers Online (http://gpp.royalcollection.org.uk., January 2017)
RA GEO_MENUS Georgian Menu Books MRH/MRHF/MENUS/MAIN/MIXED/4 Menu book for the Prince Regent, 26 January 1817 – 28 September 1818
University of Manchester Library (UML)EGR4/2/3/2/5 *"Illegal MEETING"* poster English MS 172 *Peterloo Relief Fund Account Book*, c.1820

Primary Sources (printed)

[Anon.], *An Examination of the late dreadful Occurrences at the Meeting at Manchester, on August 16, 1819; being a clear statement and review of its object, circumstances, and results*, Newcastle-upon-Tyne, 1819.
[Anon.] 'A Chelsea Pensioner', *Jottings from my Sabretasch*, London, 1847.

Adams, M., *A Parody on the Political House that Jack Built,: or, The real house that Jack built*, London, 1820.

A Full, Accurate, and Impartial Report of the Trial of John Bagguley, of Stockport, John Johnston, of Salford, and Samuel Drummond, of Manchester, Manchester, 1819.

Aikin, J., *A Description of the Country from Thirty to Forty Miles Round Manchester*, London, 1795.

An Act for Preventing Tumults and Riotous Assemblies, and for the more speedy and effectual Punishing the Rioters, London, 1715.

Aston, J., *The Manchester Guide*, Manchester, 1804.

Aston, J., *Picture of Manchester*, Manchester, 1816.

Baines, E., *History of the Reign of George III*, 4 vols, Leeds, 1820–3.

Baines, E., *History, Directory and Gazetteer, of the County Palatine of Lancaster*, 2 vols, Liverpool, 1825.

Bamford, S., *An Account of the Arrest and Imprisonment of Samuel Bamford, Middleton, on Suspicion of High Treason*, Manchester, 1817.

Bamford, S., *The Weaver Boy; or, Miscellaneous Poetry*, Manchester, 1819.

Bamford, S., *God Save the Queen. A New Song*, London, 1820.

Bamford, S., *Miscellaneous Poetry*, London, 1821.

Bamford, S., *Passages in the Life of a Radical*, London, 1844.

Bamford, S., *Early Days*, London, 1849.

Banks, I. [Mrs. George Linnaeus Banks], *The Manchester Man*, 3 vols, London, 1876.

Bell's Life in London and Sporting Chronicle

Black Dwarf

Bruton, F.A., 'Bishop Stanley's Account of Peterloo' in *Three Accounts of Peterloo, by Eyewitnesses*, Manchester, 1921, pp. 10–23.

Buchan, W., *Domestic Medicine: Or, A Treatise on the Prevention and Cure of Diseases by Regimen and Simple Medicines*, 16th edition, London, 1798.

Burn, R. and W. Woodfall, *The Justice of the Peace and Parish Officer*, 20th edition, 4 vols, London, 1805.

Burn, R. and G. Chetwynd, *The Justice of the Peace and Parish Officer*, 23rd edition, 5 vols, London, 1820.

Burke, E., *Reflections on the Revolution in France*, London, 1790.

Burton, A., *Rush-Bearing*, Manchester, 1891.

Butterworth, E., *Historical Sketches of Oldham*, Oldham, 1856.

Clark, R., *An Account of the national anthem entitled God Save the King!*, London, 1822.

Cobbett's Weekly Political Register

Coke, T. (ed.), *A Collection of Hymns for the Use of the People called Methodists. By the Rev. John Wesley*, Dublin, 1816.

Crossley, J., 'Pott's Discovery of Witches in the County of Lancaster' in *Remains Historical & Literary connected with the Palatine Counties of Lancaster and Chester published by The Chetham Society*, vol.VI, Manchester, 1845.

Crowther, J., *A Portraiture of Methodism, Or, the History of the Wesleyan Methodists*, London, 1815.

Davies, L. C. Drummond, *Recollections of Society in France and England*, 2 vols, London, 1872.

Defoe, D., *A Tour Thro' the Whole Island of Great Britain*, London, 1748.

Derby Mercury

Dolby, T., *The Trial of Henry Hunt, Esq. Jno. Knight, Jos. Johnson, Jno. hacker Saxton, Samuel Bamford, Jos. Healey, James Moorhouse, Robert Jones, Geo. Swift, and Robert Wylde, for an alledged [sic] Conspiracy to Overturn the Government, &c.*, London, 1820.

Dowling, J. A., *The Whole Proceedings before the Coroner's Inquest at Oldham on the body of John Lees...*, London, 1820.

Ethelston, Rev. C. W., *The Suicide: with other poems*, London, 1803.

Farquharson, G., *A Correct Report of the Proceedings on the Trial of Thirty Eight Men on a Charge of Administering an Unlawful Oath ... At Lancaster on Thursday 27th August 1812, with an Introductory Narrative by John Knight, One of the Defendants*, Manchester, 1812.

Fisher, H., *An Impartial Narrative of the Late Melancholy Occurrences in Manchester*, Liverpool, 1819.

Gibney, R. D., *Eighty Years Ago, or the Recollections of an Old Army Doctor*, London, 1896.

Glover, G. (ed.), *From Corunna to Waterloo: The Letters and Journals of Two Napoleonic Hussars, 1801–1816*, London, 2007.

Gentleman's Magazine

Gould, N., *Information concerning the State of Children employed in Cotton Factories*, Manchester, 1818.

Harland, J. (ed.), *Ballads and Songs of Lancashire: Chiefly Older than the 19th Century*, London, 1865.

Harland, J. and T. T. Wilkinson, *Lancashire Folk-Lore: Illustrative of the Superstitions Beliefs and Practices, Local Customs and Usages of the People of the County Palatine*, London, 1867.

Harland, J. and T. T. Wilkinson, *Lancashire Legends, Traditions, Pageants, Sports, &c.*, London, 1873.

Harrop, J., *A Report of the Trial, Redford against Birley and Others for An Assault on The Sixteenth of August 1819*, Manchester, 1822.

Hazlitt, W., *Table-Talk; or, Original Essays*, London, 1821.

Henderson, W. O. (ed.), *J. C. Fischer and his Diary of Industrial England 1814–51*, London, 1966.

Henderson, W.O. (ed.), *Industrial Britain Under the Regency*, London, 1968.

Hewitt, M. and R. Poole (eds), *The Diaries of Samuel Bamford*, Stroud, 2000.

Hibbert, S., *History of the Foundations in Manchester*, 3 vols, London, Manchester and Edinburgh, 1833–4.

Hone, W., *The Political House that Jack Built*, 26th edition, London, 1819.

Hone, W., *The Man on the Moon*, London, 1820.

Hone, W., *Report of the Metropolitan and Central Committee, Appointed for the Relief of the Manchester Sufferers*, London, 1820.

Hone, W., *The Year Book of Daily Recreation and Information*, London, 1832.

Huish, R., *Memoirs of George the Fourth*, 2 vols, London, 1830.

Huish, R., *Memoirs of the Late William Cobbett*, 2 vols, London, 1836.

Huish, R., *The History of the private and political life of Henry Hunt, Esq.*, 2 vols, London, 1836.

Hunt, E., *Charging Against Napoleon: Diaries and Letters of Three Hussars 1808–1815*, Barnsley, 2001.

Hunt, H., *Memoirs of Henry Hunt Esq*, 3 vols, London, 1820–2.

Hunt, H., *To the Radical Reformers, Male and Female, of England, Ireland, and Scotland*, London, 1820–3.

Johnson, J., *A Letter to Henry Hunt, Esq. by Joseph Johnson*, Manchester, 1822.

Kay, J. P., *The Moral and Physical Condition of the Working Classes Employed in the Cotton Manufacture in Manchester*, London, 1832.

Kipling, R., *Barrack-Room Ballads and Other Verses*, London, 1892.

Knight, J., *A Full and Particular Report of the Proceedings of the Public Meeting held in Manchester on Monday the 18th of January 1819*, Manchester, n.d.

La Trobe, J. A., *The Music of the Church*, London, 1831.

L'Estrange, G. B., *Recollections of Sir George B. L'Estrange*, London, 1874.

Leeds Intelligencer

Leeds Mercury

Liverpool Mercury

Manchester Chronicle

Manchester Comet: Or a Rap at Radicals

Manchester Courier

Manchester Guardian

Manchester Mercury

Manchester Observer

Morning Chronicle

Mutrie, Robert, 'Letter to Archibald Moore dated Thursday [19 August 1819]', transcribed by Philip Lawson in 'Peterloo: A Constable's Eye-View Re-Assessed', *Peterloo Massacre*, Manchester Region History Review (Special Issue), vol. III, no. 1, Spring/Summer 1989, pp. 39–42, p. 42.

Nodal, J. H. and G. Milner, *A Glossary of the Lancashire Dialect*, Manchester and London, 1875.

Paine, T., *Common Sense; Addressed to the Inhabitants of America*, Philadelphia, 1776.

Paine, T., *Rights of Man: Being an Answer to Mr. Burke's Attack on the French Revolution*, London, 1791.

Parliamentary Debates (Hansard) House of Commons, 1819.

Parliamentary Debates (Hansard) House of Lords, 1815 and 1817.

Pellow, G., *The Life and Correspondence of the Right Hon[oura]ble Henry Addington, 1st Viscount Sidmouth*, 3 vols, London, 1847.

Pellow, G. (transcr.), 'Sir William Jolliffe's Account' in *The Life and Correspondence of the Right Hon[oura]ble Henry Addington, 1st Viscount Sidmouth*, 3 vols, London, 1847, pp. 253–61.

Philips, F., *An Exposure of the Calumnies circulated by the Enemies of Social Order … Against the Magistrates and the Yeomanry Cavalry of Manchester and Salford*, 2nd edition, London, 1819.

Prentice, A., *Historical Sketches and Personal Recollections of Manchester*, London and Manchester, 1851.

The Public Ledger and Daily Advertiser

Pyne, W. H., *The History of the Royal Residences*, 3 vols, London, 1819.

Radcliffe, W., *Origin of the New System of Manufacture, commonly called "Power-Loom Weaving"*, Stockport, 1828.

Ray, J., *A Compleat History of the Rebellion*, York, 1749.

The Republican

Roby, J., *Traditions of Lancashire*, 2 vols, London, 1829.

Sherwin's Weekly Political Register

Siborne, H. T., *Waterloo Letters: A Selection from Original and hitherto Unpublished Letters…*, London, 1891.

The Sporting Magazine or Monthly Calendar

Stamford Mercury

Taylor, J. E., *Notes and Observations*, London, 1820.

The Times

Weatherby, E. & J. Weatherby, *The Racing Calendar for the Year 1818*, London, 1819.

Weatherby, E., & J. Weatherby, *The Racing Calendar for the Year 1823*, London, 1824.

Wheeler, J., *Manchester: Its Political, Social and Commercial History, Ancient and Modern*, London, 1836.

Whinyates, F. A. (ed.), *Letters Written by Lieut.-General Dyneley*, London, 1984.

Wooler, T. J., *A Verbatim Report of the Two Trials of Mr. T.J. Wooler, Editor of the Black Dwarf, for Alleged Libels*, London, 1817.

Wroe, J., *Peterloo Massacre, containing a faithful narrative*, 2nd edition, Manchester, 1819.

Wroe, J., *Peterloo Massacre, containing a faithful narrative*, 3rd edition, Manchester, 1819.

Wylly, H. C. (ed.), *The Military Memoirs of Lieutenant-General Sir Joseph Thackwell*, London, 1908.

Yorkshire Gazette

Secondary Sources

Athawes, P. D., *Yeomanry Wars: The History of the Yeomanry, Volunteer and Volunteer Association Cavalry; a Civilian Tradition from 1794*, Dalkeith, 1994.

Anglesey, Henry Paget, Marquess of, *A History of the British Cavalry 1816 to 1919*, 8 vols, Barnsley, 1975–97.

Bee, M. and W. Bee, 'The Casualties of Peterloo' in *Peterloo Massacre*, Manchester Region History Review (Special Issue), vol. III, no. 1, Spring/Summer 1989, pp. 43–50.

Belchem, J., *Orator Hunt: Henry Hunt and English Working-class Radicalism*, Oxford, 1985.

Belchem, J., 'Manchester, Peterloo and the Radical Challenge' in *Peterloo Massacre*, Manchester Region History Review (Special Issue), vol. III, no. 1, Spring/Summer 1989, pp. 9–14.

Belchem, J., 'Henry Hunt', *ODNB*, article 14193, 2004.

Bend, N., *The Home Office and Public Disturbance, c.1800–1832*, Unpublished Doctoral Thesis, University of Hertfordshire and The National Archives, 2018.

Bew, J., *Castlereagh: Enlightenment, War and Tyranny*, London, 2011.

Boase, G. C. and G. H. Martin, 'Henry Hobhouse', *ODNB*, article 13403, 2004.

Bourke, R., *Empire and Revolution: The Political Life of Edmund Burke*, Princeton and Oxford, 2015.

Brooke, A. and L. Kipling, *Liberty or Death: Radicals, Republicans and Luddites, 1793–1823*, Huddersfield, 2012.

Brown, C., *The Scum of the Earth: What happened to the Real British Heroes of Waterloo?*, London, 2015.

Bush, M. L., *The Casualties of Peterloo*, Lancaster, 2005.

Bush, M. L., 'The Women at Peterloo: The Impact of Female Reform on the Manchester Meeting of 16 August 1819' in *History*, 89 (2004), pp. 209–32.

Bush, M. L., *The Friends and Following of Richard Carlile*, Diss, 2016.

Bythell, D., *The Handloom Weavers: A Study in the English Cotton Industry during the Industrial Revolution*, Cambridge, 1969.

Chase, M., *Early Trade Unionism: Fraternity, skill and the politics of labour*, Aldershot, 2000.

Chase, M., 'W. J. Richards', *ODNB*, article 57111, 2004/2008.

Chase, M., *Chartism: a new history*, Manchester, 2007.

Chase, M., *1820: Disorder and stability in the United Kingdom*, Manchester, 2015.

Clark, A., *The Struggle for the Breeches: Gender and the Making of the British Working Class*, Berkeley and Los Angeles, 1995.

Clark, J. C. D., *Thomas Paine: Britain, America, and France in the Age of Enlightenment and Revolution*, Oxford, 2018.

Clayton, T., *Waterloo: Four Days that Changed Europe's Destiny*, London, 2015.

Colley, L., *Britons: Forging the Nation, 1707–1837*, New Haven and London, 1992.

Cozens, J., 'The Making of the Peterloo Martyrs, 1819 to the Present' in Q. Outram and K. Laybourn (eds), *Secular Martyrdom in Britain and Ireland from Peterloo to the Present*, Basingstoke, 2018, pp. 31–58.

Custer, P. A., 'Refiguring Jemima: Gender, Work and Politics in Lancashire 1770–1820' in *Past & Present*, No. 195 (May 2007), pp. 127–58.

Davidoff, L. and C. Hall, *Family Fortune: Men and Women of the English Middle Class 1780–1850* [Revised Edition], London and New York, 2002.

Davis, H. W. C., 'Lancashire Reformers, 1816–1817' in *The Bulletin of the John Rylands Library*, vol. X, issue 1, Manchester, 1926, pp. 47–79.

Davis, J. E., 'Sir [Samuel] Luke Fildes', *ODNB*, article 33127, 2004/2011.

Drage, S., 'Elias Hall, "The Faithful Chronicler" of Oldham Psalmody' in *Early Music*, vol. 28, no. 4, Music in Georgian Britain (November 2000), pp. 621–8 and pp. 630–4.

Donald, D., 'The Power of Print: Graphic Images of Peterloo' in *Peterloo Massacre*, Manchester Region History Review (Special Issue), vol. III, no. 1, Spring/Summer 1989, pp. 21–30.

Edwards, M. M., *The Growth of the British Cotton trade 1780–1815*, Manchester, 1967.

Elmsley, C., 'The English Magistracy 1700–1850' in *International Association for the History of Crime and Criminal Justice*, Bulletin no. 15, February 1992, pp. 28–38.

Epstein, J., 'Understanding the Cap of Liberty: Symbolic Practice and Social Conflict in Early Nineteenth-century England' in *Past and Present*, no. 122 (February 1989), pp. 75–118.

Epstein, J., 'Thomas Jonathan Wooler', *ODNB*, article 29952, 2004.

Farnie, D. A., *The English Cotton Industry and the World Market 1815–1896*, Oxford, 1879.

Fitton, R. S. and A. P. Wadsworth, *The Strutts and the Arkwrights 1758–1830: A Study of the Early Factory System*, Manchester, 1958.

Fraser, P., 'Public Petitioning and Parliament before 1832' in *History*, vol. 46, no. 158 (1961), pp. 195–211.

Frow, R. and E. (eds), *Political Women 1800–1850*, London and Winchester, Mass., 1989.

Gardner, J, 'The Suppression of Samuel Bamford's Peterloo Poems' in *Romanticism*, vol. 13, issue 2, 2007, pp. 145–55.

Gardner, J., *Poetry and Popular Protest: Peterloo, Cato Street and the Queen Caroline Controversy*, Basingstoke, 2011.

Gardner, J., 'William Hone and Peterloo' in Robert Poole ed., *Return to*

Peterloo, Manchester Region History Review (Special Edition), vol. 23, 2012/2014, pp. 79–92.

Gardner, J., 'Cobbett's Return to England in 1819' in J. Grande and J. Stevenson (eds), *William Cobbett, Romanticism and the Enlightenment: Contexts and Legacy*, London and New York, 2015, pp. 61–76.

Gardner, V. E. M., *The Business of News in England, 1760–1820*, Basingstoke, 2016.

Gildart, K., D. Howell and N. Kirk (eds), *Dictionary of Labour Biography*, Basingstoke, vol. XI, 2003.

Glasgow, G. H. H., 'The John Lees Inquest of 1819 and the Peterloo Massacre' in *Transactions of the Historic Society of Lancashire and Cheshire*, vol. 148, 1998, pp. 95–118.

Grande, J., *William Cobbett, the Press and Rural England: Radicalism and the Fourth Estate, 1792–1835*, London, 2014.

Griffin, E., *Liberty's Dawn: A People's History of the Industrial Revolution*, New Haven and London, 2013.

Hall, C., *White, Male and Middle Class: Explorations in Feminism and History*, Cambridge, 1992/2007.

Hall, R. G., Tyranny, Work and Politics: The 1818 Strike Wave in the English Cotton District' in *International Review of Social History*, vol. 34, no. 3 (1989), pp. 433–70.

Hargreaves, R. and A. Hampson, *Beyond Peterloo: Elijah Dixon and Manchester's Forgotten Reformers*, Barnsley, 2018.

Hewitt, E., *Capital of Discontent: Protest and Crime in Manchester's Industrial Revolution*, Stroud, 2014.

Hewitt, M., 'Radicalism and the Victorian Working Class: The Case of Samuel Bamford' in *The Historical Journal*, vol. 34, no. 4 (December 1991), pp. 873–92.

Hibbert, C., 'George IV', *ODNB*, article 10541, 2004/2008.

History of Parliament (online) www.historyofparliamentonline.org

Jones, G. D. B., *Roman Manchester*, Manchester, 1974.

Kidd, A. J., 'Joseph Nadin', *ODNB*, article 19717, 2004.

Lawson, P. 'Peterloo: A Constable's Eye-View Re-assessed' in *Peterloo Massacre*, Manchester Region History Review (Special Issue), vol. III, no.1, Spring/Summer 1989, pp. 39–42.

Leary, F., *The Earl of Chester's Regiment of Yeomanry Cavalry: Its Formation and Services 1797–1897*, Edinburgh, 1898.

Lee, C. H., *A Cotton Enterprise 1795–1840: A History of McConnel & Ken-*

nedy fine cotton spinners, Manchester, 1972.

Lobban, M., 'From Seditious Libel to Unlawful Assembly: Peterloo and the Changing Face of Political Crime c.1770–1820' in *Oxford Journal of Legal Studies*, vol. 10, no. 3 (Autumn, 1990), pp. 307–52.

MacDermott, K. H., *The Old Church Gallery Minstrels: An Account of the Church Bands and Singers in England from about 1660 to 1860*, London, 1948.

Mallinson, A., *Light Dragoons: The Making of a Regiment*, Barnsley, 2012.

Marlow, J., *The Peterloo Massacre*, London, 1969.

Mather, R., "These Lancashire Women are witches in politics': Female reform societies and the theatre of radicalism 1819–1820' in R. Poole ed., *Return to Peterloo*, Manchester Region History Review (Special Edition), vol. 23, 2012/2014, pp. 49–64.

Mather, R., *The Home-Making of the English Working Class: Radical Politics and a Domestic Life in Late-Georgian England, c.1790–1820*, Unpublished Doctoral Thesis, Queen Mary University of London, 2016.

Miller, I. and C. Wild, *A & G Murray and the Cotton Mills of Ancoats*, Lancaster, 2007.

Mollo, J., *The Prince's Dolls: Scandals, Skirmishes and Splendours of the First British Hussars 1793–1815*, London, 1997.

Morgan, A., 'Starving mothers and murdered children in cultural representations of Peterloo' in R. Poole (ed.), *Return to Peterloo*, Manchester Region History Review (Special Edition), vol. 23, 2012/2014, pp. 65–78.

Myerly, S. H., *British Military Spectacle: From the Napoleonic Wars through to the Crimea*, Cambridge, Massachusetts and London, 1996.

Navickas, K., *Loyalism and Radicalism in Lancashire 1798–1815*, Oxford, 2009.

Navickas, K., *Protest and the Politics of Space and Place, 1789–1848*, Manchester, 2016.

Newsam, F., *The Home Office*, London, 1954.

Oxford English Dictionary (online) www.oed.com

Pearse, H. W., *The History of the 31st Foot and 70th Foot, Subsequently the 1st and 2nd Battalions of the East Surrey Regiment*, vol. I (1702–1914), London, 1916.

Poole, R., "By the Law or the Sword': Peterloo Revisited' in *History*, vol. 91, no. 2 (302) (April 2006), pp. 254–276.

Poole, R., 'The March to Peterloo: Politics and Festivity in Late Georgian England' in *Past and Present*, no. 192 (August 2006), pp. 109–53.

Poole, R., 'French Revolution or Peasants' revolt? Petitioners and rebels from the Blanketeers to the Chartists' in *Labour History Review*, vol. 74, issue 1, (April 2009), pp. 6–26.

Poole, R. (ed.), *Return to Peterloo*, Manchester Region History Review (Special Edition), vol. 23, 2012/2014.

Porter, R. and G. Rousseau, *Gout: The Patrician Malady*, New Haven and London, 2000.

Raines, F. R. (F. Renaud ed.), *Lives of the Fellows and Chaplains of the Collegiate Church of Manchester*, 2 Parts, Manchester, 1891.

Read, D., *Peterloo: The 'Massacre' and its Background*, Manchester, 1958.

Redford, A., *History of Local Government in Manchester*, 3 vols, Manchester, 1939–40.

Reid, R., *The Peterloo Massacre*, London, 1989.

Reynolds, K. D., 'Elizabeth Conyngham [née Denison]', *ODNB*, article 45483, 2004.

Riding, C., and J. Riding (eds), *The Houses of Parliament: History, Art, Architecture*, London, 2000.

Riding, J., *Jacobites: A New History of the '45 Rebellion*, London, 2016.

Roberts, M., 'Radical Banners from Peterloo to Chartism' in R. Poole (ed.), *Return to Peterloo*, Manchester Region History Review (Special Edition), vol. 23, 2012/2014, pp. 93–109.

Rose, M. B., *The Gregs of Quarry Bank Mill: The rise and decline of a family firm, 1750–1914*, Cambridge, 1986.

Royle, E., *Revolutionary Britannia? Reflections on the threat of revolution in Britain, 1789–1848*, Manchester, 2000.

Rule, J., *The Labouring Classes in Early Industrial England 1750–1850*, London and New York, 1986/1994.

Sainty, J. C., *Office-Holders in Modern Britain*, vol. V, Home Office Officials 1782–1870, London, 1975.

Sato, S., *Edmund Burke as Historian: War, Order and Civilisation*, Basingstoke, 2018.

Spence, P., 'Samuel Bamford', *ODNB*, article 1256, 2004/2009.

Stephens, H. M. revised by J. Sweetman, 'Sir John Byng, first Earl of Stafford', *ODNB*, article 4264, 2004/2008.

Swindells, T., *Manchester Streets and Manchester Men*, 5th series, Manchester, 1908.

Thompson, E. P., *The Making of the English Working Class*, London, 1968.

Thompson, E. P., 'Thompson on Peterloo' in *Peterloo Massacre*, Manchester Region History Review (Special Issue), vol. III, no. 1, Spring/Summer 1989, pp. 67–75.

Tomlinson, V. I., 'Postscript to Peterloo' in *Peterloo Massacre*, Manchester Region History Review (Special Issue), vol. III, no. 1, Spring/Summer 1989, pp. 51–9.

Troup, E., *The Home Office*, London and New York, 1925.

Walmsley, R., *Peterloo: The Case Reopened*, Manchester, 1969.

White, J., *Waterloo to Peterloo*, London, 1957.

Wilkes, S., *Regency Spies: Secret Histories of Britain's Rebels & Revolutionaries*, Barnsley, 2015.

Wright, D. G., *Popular Radicalism: The working-class experience, 1780–1880*, London, 1988.

Wyke, T., 'Remembering the Manchester Massacre' in R. Poole ed., *Return to Peterloo*, Manchester Region History Review (Special Edition), vol. 23, 2012/2014, pp. 111–31.

Wylly, H. C., *XVth (The King's) Hussars 1759 to 1913*, London, 1914.

Young, P., *Two Cocks on a Dunghill, William Cobbett and Henry Hunt: their friendship, feuds and fights*, South Lopham, 2009.

Ziegler, P., *Addington: A Life of Henry Addington, First Viscount Sidmouth*, London, 1965.

Ziegler, P., 'Archibald Prentice', *ODNB*, article 22717, 2004/2009.

NOTES

Prelude Two Fields

1. For a detailed description of the battle see Tim Clayton, *Waterloo: Four Days that Changed Europe's Destiny*, London, 2015.

2. John Lees is reported to have said that he was present at the Battle of Waterloo by William Harrison during the inquest into John's death after Peterloo (see page 308). No further military details are given in this source. John's father, Robert, who did not deny Harrison's claim, confirmed that his son was twenty-two years old when he died in early September 1819. However, there are complications in confirming John's military history. In 1816, three 'John Lees', all born in the Parish of Oldham, were named in the War Office Campaign Medal and Award Rolls (General Series): Waterloo TNA WO 100/14. The first is listed under 'private' in the '1st Regiment of Life Guards' and recorded as 'wounded' in the battle (f. 10); the second listed as number '45' under 'drivers' in Robert Bull's Royal Horse Artillery (RHA) 'I' Troop (f. 202r); and the third listed as number '72' under 'gunners', also in Bull's RHA 'I' troop (f. 202v). The first can be discounted as the Peterloo John Lees. He was discharged aged twenty-three in 1816 (see TNA WO 97/187/64).

3. Of the two 'John Lees' both serving in Bull's RHA 'I' troop by 1816, the documentation states that the driver enlisted on 23 September 1812 (TNA WO 100/14 f. 202v) while the gunner enlisted on 22 July 1812 (TNA WO 100/14 f. 202r). Further information is provided in TNA WO 69/2 *Description Book of the Non Commiss[en]d Officers, & Privates of the Royal Horse Artillery*. Here the driver is described as 'no.14', a 'Cotton Spinner', aged fourteen years when he enlisted at Manchester on 23 September 1812, 5 feet 4 ¼ inches in height, with a 'fresh' complexion, 'brown' hair and 'grey' eyes (WO 69/2/2345, f. 157v). The gunner 'no.5' is also described as of a fresh complexion

with brown hair and grey eyes (f. 158v), but aged eighteen years, 5 feet 6 ½ inches in height and as enlisting at Rochdale on 22 July 1812 (WO 69/2/2351, f. 158v). This John Lees was a 'weaver' and assigned to 6th Battalion, 6th Brigade, 'I' troop (f. 159r) while John Lees the driver was assigned to 'RAD^{rs}' (presumably Royal Artillery Drivers) 'B' troop. Another source, TNA WO 69/4 *Description of Men in Great Britain* (L/2310–N/1315) offers similar details for both men, with the additional information that the driver (ff. 141v–142r) was 'inlisted' by 'S Wilson', first mustered in the '7th' battalion and transferred to the RHA in May 1813 (for the gunner's entry see ff. 142v–43r).

John Lees the gunner can be discounted as the man who died in 1819, as he would have been around twenty-five years old in that year (based on his given age, eighteen, in 1812) and, via further sources, appears to have been discharged in 1835 aged forty: see TNA 'Statements of Service RHA Vol. 1' WO 69/7/161 and WO 97/1243/56. In another source his discharge date is listed as 1836 and his age given as forty-one: see TNA WO 97/1243/55. The age on enlisting of John Lees the driver (fourteen in 1812) at least tallies with the age at death of the Peterloo victim. Based on this analysis, it is assumed here that John Lees, the young man who died of the wounds he received on 16 August 1819, had been present at the Battle of Waterloo as a driver in Robert Bull's 'I' troop of the Royal Horse Artillery.

4. Thomas Paine, *Common Sense; Addresses to the Inhabitants of America*, Philadelphia, 1776, p. 87.

5. For a recent appraisal of Paine's life, work and influence see J. C. D. Clark, *Thomas Paine: Britain, America, and France in the Age of Enlightenment and Revolution*, Oxford, 2018. See also E. Royle, *Revolutionary Britannia? Reflections on the threat of revolution in Britain, 1789–1848*, Manchester, 2000.

6. Philip Ziegler, *Addington: A Life of Henry Addington, First Viscount Sidmouth*, London, 1965, pp. 341–2.

7. See John Belchem, *Orator Hunt: Henry Hunt and English Working-class Radicalism*, Oxford, 1985.

8. See n. 2 and n. 3 above.

9. F. A. Whinyates (ed.), *Letters Written by Lieut.-General Dyneley*, London, 1984, p. 67.

10. Colin Brown, *The Scum of the Earth: What happened to the Real British Heroes of Waterloo?*, London, 2015, pp. 169–70.

11. Whinyates, *Letters Written by Lieut.-General Thomas Dyneley*, p. 64.

12. H. C. Wylly, *XVth (The King's) Hussars 1759 to 1913*, London, 1914, p. 243.

13. R. D. Gibney, *Eighty Years Ago, or the Recollections of an Old Army Doctor*, London, 1896, p. 149.

14. H. C. Wylly (ed.), *The Military Memoirs of Lieutenant-General Sir Joseph Thackwell*, London, 1908, p. 70.

15. Whinyates, *Letters Written by Lieut.-General Dyneley*, p. 65.

16. Gibney, *Eighty Years Ago*, p. 201.

17. Quoted in Gareth Glover (ed.), *From Corunna to Waterloo: The Letters and Journals of Two Napoleonic Hussars, 1801–1816*, London, 2007, p. 264, footnote *.

18. Allan Mallinson, *Light Dragoons: The Making of a Regiment*, Barnsley, 2012, p. 79.

19. Whinyates, *Letters Written by Lieut.-General Dyneley*, p. 65.

20. Ibid., p. 66.

21. Gibney, *Eighty Years Ago*, p. 210.

22. Both 'John Lees', the gunner and the driver, who are listed as being in Major Bull's 'I' troop of the Royal Horse Artillery are among the recipients of the Waterloo Medal and both were still stationed in France, at 'Cambray', on 28 May 1816: see TNA WO 100/14 (list of medals sent to Cambrai) ff. 235–236, f. 236r and f. 236v respectively.

23. Whinyates, *Letters Written by Lieut.-General Dyneley*, p. 67.

24. Ibid.

25. 'Prince Regent's Message Respecting an additional grant to the Duke of Wellington', *Parliamentary Debates (Hansard) House of Lords*, 23 June 1815, Vol. XXXI, cc. 977–99.

26. Samuel Bamford, *Passages in the Life of a Radical*, London, 1844, p. 51.

27. Bamford, *Passages*, p. 49.

28. Ibid., p. 47.

29. Ibid., p. 55.

30. Ibid., pp. 54–5.

31. Ibid., p. 55.

32. Ibid.

33. Samuel Bamford, *Early Days*, London, 1849, p. 241.

1 Manchester

1. Joseph Aston, *Picture of Manchester*, Manchester, 1816, p. 5. For a discussion on the origins of the name see G. D. B. Jones, *Roman Manchester*, Manchester, 1974, pp. 159–63.
2. Ibid., p. 1.
3. Ibid., p. 26.
4. Ibid., p. 28.
5. For the transition from water to steam power and its impact on Manchester see I. Miller and C. Wild, *A. & G. Murray and the Cotton Mills of Ancoats*, Lancaster, 2007, pp. 7–23.
6. J. Aikin, *A Description of the Country from Thirty to Forty Miles Round Manchester*, London, 1795, p. 211.
7. *The Times*, 24 August 1819.
8. Miller and Wild, *A. & G. Murray*, p. 25.
9. W. O. Henderson (ed.), *Industrial Britain Under the Regency*, London, 1968, p. 137. See also C. H. Lee, *A Cotton Enterprise 1795–1840: A History of McConnel & Kennedy fine cotton spinners*, Manchester, 1972.
10. Miller and Wild, *A. & G. Murray*, p. 50.
11. Aston, *Picture of Manchester*, p. 225.
12. Ibid., p. 226.
13. May's report is transcribed in Henderson, *Industrial Britain*, pp. 131–69, p. 166.
14. Henderson, *Industrial Britain*, p. 136.
15. Escher's letters are transcribed in Henderson, *Industrial Britain*, pp. 27–67, p. 34.
16. Henderson, *Industrial Britain*, p. 34.
17. W. O. Henderson, *J. C. Fischer and his Diary of Industrial England 1814–51*, London, 1966, p. 140.
18. Henderson, *Fischer*, p. 57.
19. Henderson, *Industrial Britain*, p. 48.
20. Ibid., pp. 49–50.
21. Ibid., p. 50.
22. Ibid., p. 35.
23. Ibid., p. 137.
24. Ibid., p. 136.
25. Henderson, *Fischer*, p. 142.
26. Ibid., p. 143.

27. Ibid.

28. Nathan Gould, *Information concerning the State of Children employed in Cotton Factories*, Manchester, 1818, p. 5.

29. Ibid., p. 7.

30. Ibid., p. 8.

31. See Miller and Wild, *A. & G. Murray*, pp. 7–23.

32. E. Hewitt, *Capital of Discontent: Protest and Crime in Manchester's Industrial Revolution*, Stroud, 2014, p. 40.

33. *The Times*, 24 August 1819.

34. Henderson, *Industrial Britain*, p. 35.

35. TNA TS 1125, 'A Statement exhibiting at one view the wages of Labour generally in the Town of Manchester... 25 November 1819'. My thanks to Robert Poole for bringing this document to my attention.

36. TNA TS 1125, 'A Statement exhibiting at one view the wages of Labour generally in the Town of Manchester... 25 November 1819'.

37. Henderson, *Industrial Britain*, p. 50.

38. Ibid., p. 138.

39. Aston, *Picture of Manchester*, pp. 151–86, 187–8, 116–26.

40. Ibid., pp. 86–7.

41. Edward Baines, *History, Directory and Gazetteer, of the County Palatine of Lancaster*, 2 Vols, Liverpool, 1825, Vol. II, p. 137.

42. Aston, *Picture of Manchester*, p. 102.

2 The New Bailey

1. See Jacqueline Riding, *Jacobites: A New History of the '45 Rebellion*, London, 2016, pp. 227–51.

2. Bamford, *Early Days*, p. 15.

3. Ibid., p. 22.

4. Aston, *Picture of Manchester*, p. 18.

5. Paul R. Ziegler, 'Archibald Prentice', *ODNB*, article 22717, 2004/2009.

6. Archibald Prentice, *Historical Sketches and Personal Recollections of Manchester*, London and Manchester, 1851, pp. 1–2.

7. For a detailed description and full analysis see Katrina Navickas, *Loyalism and Radicalism in Lancashire 1798–1815*, Oxford, 2009.

8. Prentice, *Historical Sketches*, p. 7.

9. Bamford, *Early Days*, p. 43.

10. Prentice, *Historical Sketches*, p. 17.
11. Ibid., p. 19.
12. Bamford, *Early Days*, pp. 43–4.
13. Aston, *Picture of Manchester*, p. 28.
14. Ibid.
15. Prentice, *Historical Sketches*, p. 34.
16. Aston, *Picture of Manchester*, pp. 194–8.
17. Bamford, *Passages*, pp. 90–1.
18. F. R. Raines (F. Renaud ed.), *Lives of the Fellows and Chaplains of the Collegiate Church of Manchester*, 2 Parts, Manchester, 1891, Pt 2, p. 313.
19. Raines, *Lives of the Fellows and Chaplains*, Pt 2, p. 307.
20. Ibid., p. 310.
21. Ibid.
22. Ibid., p. 311.
23. Ibid., pp. 311–12, citing Hay's MS Vol. H, p. 286.
24. Raines, *Lives of the Fellows and Chaplains*, Pt 2, p. 313.
25. Ibid., p. 314.
26. Aston, *Picture of Manchester*, p. 30.
27. *Manchester Mercury*, 30 January 1816.
28. Ibid., 14 May 1816.
29. Ibid., 3 November 1818.
30. Ibid., 28 July 1818.
31. Prentice, *Historical Sketches*, p. 34.
32. For a more sympathetic analysis of Nadin's career see Hewitt, *Capital of Discontent*, pp. 13, 41–8.
33. Hewitt, *Capital of Discontent*, pp. 41–2.
34. Joseph Augustus Dowling, *The Whole Proceedings before the Coroner's Inquest at Oldham on the body of John Lees...*, London, 1820, p. 60.
35. Bamford, *Passages*, p. 82.
36. Dowling, *Lees Coroner's Inquest*, p. 80.
37. Prentice, *Historical Sketches*, p. 34.
38. For the most up-to-date biography see the forthcoming article by Katrina Navickas, 'John Knight', *ODNB*. I am very grateful to Katrina for showing me a draft.
39. G. Farquharson, *A Correct Report of the Proceedings on the Trial of Thirty Eight Men on a Charge of Administering an Unlawful Oath ... At Lancaster on Thursday 27th August 1812, with an Introductory Narrative by John Knight, One of the Defendants*, Manchester, 1812, p. i.

40. Farquharson, *A Correct Report*, p. 98.
41. Ibid., p. 99.
42. Ibid., p. iii.
43. Ibid.
44. Ibid.
45. Ibid., p. vi.
46. Ibid., p. viii.
47. Navickas, *Loyalism and Radicalism in Lancashire*, pp. 4–5.
48. For more on the Middleton Hampden Club see Bamford, *Passages*, pp. 8–11.
49. Bamford, *Passages*, pp. 7–8.
50. Ibid.
51. For a survey of working-class education through personal accounts see Emma Griffin, *Liberty's Dawn: A People's History of the Industrial Revolution*, New Haven and London, 2013, pp. 165–85.
52. Bamford, *Early Days*, p. 107.
53. Ibid.
54. Ibid., p. 106.
55. Ibid.
56. Bamford, *Passages*, pp. 7–8.
57. Aston, *Picture of Manchester*, p. 139.
58. Ibid., pp. 139–40.

3 Dorset House

1. J. C. Sainty, *Office-Holders in Modern Britain*, Vol. V, Home Office Officials 1782–1870, London, 1975, pp. 47–61. The method of filing such material was unique to the department and, although it no doubt made sense to the clerks at the time, can prove utterly bewildering to the modern researcher. Nathan Bend has heroically surveyed the Home Office papers for this period and the fruits of his labour can be found in his doctoral thesis, *The Home Office and Public Disturbance, c.1800–1832*, University of Hertfordshire and The National Archives, 2018.
2. E. Troup, *The Home Office*, London and New York, 1925, p. 18; see also F. Newsam, *The Home Office*, London, 1954.
3. *Gentleman's Magazine*, June 1816, pp. 423–4 and December 1816, p. 489.

4. Sainty, *Office-Holders in Modern Britain*, V, Home Office Officials 1782–1870, pp. 47–61.
5. Troup, *The Home Office*, p. 41.
6. Ibid., p. 156.
7. TNA HO 40/3/1 ff. 82–3, 'Extract of a letter from Mr Chippindale', Oldham, 2 December 1816.
8. TNA HO 40/3/1 ff. 11–12, John Lloyd 'To the Under Secretary of State', Stockport, 7 January 1817.
9. TNA HO 40/3/2 ff. 10–11, John Knight to John Kay of Bolton, Manchester, 21 November 1816.
10. TNA HO 42/158/1 f. 54, Revd Charles Ethelston to Lord Sidmouth, Longsight, Manchester, 16 January 1817.
11. TNA HO 42/158/1 ff. 55–6, 'The Information of Peter Campbell'.
12. *Cobbett's Weekly Political Register*, Vol. XXXII, No. 3, 18 January 1817, pp. 73–4. 'Price Two Pence'. This copy was among the enclosures sent to the Home Office and filed in TNA HO 42/158/1 ff. 42–9, f. 44.

4 Westminster

1. Bamford, *Passages*, p. 31.
2. Ibid., pp. 15–16.
3. Ibid., p. 16.
4. Belchem, *Orator Hunt*, pp. 58–65.
5. See Malcolm Chase, *1820: Disorder and stability in the United Kingdom*, Manchester, pp. 50–1 and Belchem, *Orator Hunt*, pp. 61–4.
6. Bamford, *Passages*, p. 16.
7. See Penny Young, *Two Cocks on a Dunghill, William Cobbett and Henry Hunt: their friendship, feuds and fights*, South Lopham, 2009.
8. Bamford, *Passages*, p. 18.
9. Ibid.
10. *Morning Chronicle*, 23 January 1817.
11. Bamford, *Passages*, p. 18.
12. *Morning Chronicle*, 23 January 1817.
13. William Cobbett, 'A letter to Earl Grosvenor 19th February 1817' in *Cobbett's Weekly Political Register*, Vol. XXXII, No. 8, 22 February 1817, pp. 225–56, p. 236.
14. Bamford, *Passages*, p. 21.

15. For Lord Castlereagh see John Bew, *Castlereagh: Enlightenment, War and Tyranny*, London, 2011.

16. K. D. Reynolds, 'Elizabeth Conyngham [née Denison]', *ODNB*, article 45483, 2004.

17. Lucy Clementina Drummond Davies, *Recollections of Society in France and England*, 2 Vols, London, 1872, Vol. I, p. 41.

18. Robert Huish, *Memoirs of George the Fourth*, 2 Vols, London, 1830, Vol. II, p. 243.

19. Huish, *Memoirs of George the Fourth*, II, p. 243.

20. *The Times*, 16 July 1830.

21. 'It is, however, among art historian and students of patronage that his reputation has been rehabilitated', Christopher Hibbert, 'George IV', *ODNB*, article 10541, 2004/2008.

22. Roy Porter and George Rousseau, *Gout: The Patrician Malady*, New Haven and London, 2000, p. 135.

23. William Buchan, *Domestic Medicine: Or, A Treatise on the Prevention and Cure of Diseases by Regimen and Simple Medicines*, 16th edition, London, 1798, p. 356.

24. For the old palace see Christine Riding and Jacqueline Riding (eds), *The Houses of Parliament: History, Art, Architecture*, London, 2000.

25. 'The Prince Regent's Speech on Opening the Session', *Parliamentary Debates (Hansard) House of Lords*, 28 January 1817, Vol. XXXV, cc. 1–4.

26. Huish, *Memoirs of George the Fourth*, II, p. 244.

27. *Morning Chronicle*, 29 January 1817.

28. RA GEO_MENUS Georgian Menu Books MRH/MRHF/MENUS/ MAIN/MIXED/4, Menu book for the Prince Regent, 26 January 1817–28 September 1818, (Tuesday) 28 January 1817.

29. Henry Hunt, *Memoirs of Henry Hunt Esq*, 3 Vols, London, 1820, Vol. III, pp. 425–6.

30. Ibid., p. 429.

31. Ibid., p. 426.

32. Bamford, *Passages*, pp. 19–20.

33. Hunt, *Memoirs*, III, p. 429.

34. *Morning Chronicle*, 29 January 1817.

35. 'Attack on the Prince Regent', *Parliamentary Debates (Hansard) House of Lords*, 28 January 1817, Vol. XXXV, cc. 4–5.

36. TNA HO 40/3/1 ff. 140–1, 'The Information of S.F in the Parish of Manchester... taken & made before me Charles Wicksted Ethelston', 28 January 1817.

37. HO 42/158/1 ff. 149–50 'Information from "E.H" [named as John England]... before Charles Wicksted Ethelston', 31 January 1817.

38. TNA HO 42/158/1 ff. 147–8, 'Information of A.B late of the first Regiment of Manchester Local Militia... taken & made before me, C. W. Ethelston... this 31ˢᵗ day of January 1817'.

39. TNA HO 40/4/2 ff. 28–9, Report dated 4 February 1817 regarding a meeting held 3 February, also transcribed in H. W. C. Davis, 'Lancashire Reformers, 1816–1817' in *The Bulletin of the John Rylands Library*, Vol. X, Issue 1, Manchester, 1926, pp. 47–79, p. 74.

40. 'Habeas Corpus Suspension Bill', *Parliamentary Debates (Hansard) House of Lords*, Vol. XXXV, 24 February 1817, cc. 551–88.

41. *Black Dwarf*, Vol. I, No. 2, 5 February 1817, pp. 24–5. For Wooler see James Epstein, 'Thomas Jonathan Wooler', *ODNB*, article 29952, 2004.

42. Ibid., p. 25.

5 Bibby's Rooms

1. Bamford, *Passages*, p. 32.

2. Davis, 'Lancashire Reformers', p. 58.

3. TNA HO 40/5/4a ff. 21–5, Deposition of John Livesey (speeches 6 March), 7 March 1817.

4. For a full exploration of the process of petitioning in this period see Peter Fraser, 'Public Petitioning and Parliament before 1832' in *History*, Vol. 46, No. 158 (1961), pp. 195–211 and the forthcoming article by Robert Poole, 'Petitioners and Rebels: Petitioning for Parliamentary Reform in Regency Britain' in *Social Science History*.

5. *Black Dwarf*, Vol. I, No. 3, 12 February 1817, pp. 39–41.

6. TNA HO 40/5/4a ff. 11–12, John Livesey's deposition before Reverend Charles Ethelston, 4 March 1817.

7. TNA HO 40/5/4a ff. 53–4, 'Deposition of John Livesey... taken on oath at Salford the eleventh day of March 1817'.

8. TNA HO 40/5/4a ff. 19–20, 'Deposition of "J.L." [John Livesey] made before Charles Wicksted Ethelston JP, 6ᵗʰ March 1817' and another version, quoted earlier, ff. 53–5, dated 11 March 1817.

9. This meeting is recorded in two separate depositions taken by the Reverend Charles Ethelston from John Livesey: TNA HO 40/5/4a ff. 11–13, 4 March 1817, f. 11, and TNA HO 40/5/4a ff. 17–18, 5 March 1817.

10. TNA HO 40/5/4a f. 17.

11. Ibid.

12. TNA HO 40/5/4a ff. 11–13, f. 12, 'Deposition of John Livesey' before Revd Charles Ethelston, 4 March 1817.

13. Ibid.

14. Ibid., ff. 17–18, 5 March 1817.

15. TNA HO 40/5/4a f. 33, 'Deposition of John Livesey', 7 March 1817.

16. TNA HO 40/5/4a ff. 21–5, f. 22, 'Speeches March 6th Johnson [sic], Baguley [sic] & Mitchell'; also TNA HO 40/5/4a f. 34.

17. TNA HO 40/5/4a ff. 21–5, f. 23; also TNA HO 40/5/4a ff. 34–5.

18. TNA HO 40/5/4a ff. 37–8, 'Deposition of John Livesey taken 8th day of March 1817' before Revd Charles Ethelston.

19. TNA HO 40/5/1 ff. 25–8, Speeches from Friday [sic] 8 March. For Elijah Dixon see T. Swindells, *Manchester Streets and Manchester Men*, 5th series, Manchester, 1908, pp. 216–21, and R. Hargreaves and A. Hampson, *Beyond Peterloo: Elijah Dixon and Manchester's Forgotten Reformers*, Barnsley, 2018.

20. TNA HO 40/5/4a ff. 26–7.

21. TNA HO 40/5/4a 'Speeches on 8th March' ff. 25–8, f. 28.

22. TNA HO 40/5/4a ff. 29–30, W. D. Evans to Lord Sidmouth, Manchester, 6 March 1817.

23. Samuel Bamford, *An Account of the Arrest and Imprisonment of Samuel Bamford, Middleton, on Suspicion of High Treason*, Manchester, 1817, pp. 15–16.

24. Ibid., p. 16.

25. Bamford, *Passages*, pp. 30–1.

6 Cold Bath Fields

1. TNA HO 40/5/4a ff. 41–2, Revd William Hay to Lord Sidmouth, New Bailey, 10 March 1817.

2. Bamford, *Passages*, p. 32.

3. TNA HO 40/5/4a ff. 43–6, 'The Meeting at St Peters Church Mar 10th 1817 Monday 9 o'clock'.

4. TNA HO 40/5/4a f. 42, Revd William Hay to Lord Sidmouth, 10 March 1817.

5. TNA HO 40/5/2 f. 1304.

6. Bamford, *Passages*, p. 34.

7. Ibid., pp. 37–8; also Bamford, *An Account of the Arrest and Imprisonment*, pp. 17–20.

8. Bamford, *Passages*, p. 43.

9. Robert Huish, *Memoirs of the Late William Cobbett*, 2 Vols, London, 1836, Vol. II, p. 195.

10. 'Mr. Cobbett's taking leave of his Countrymen' in *Cobbett's Weekly Register*, Vol. XXXII, placed after No. 13, 29 March 1817, p. 416.

11. William Cobbett, 'To the people of England, Scotland and Ireland' in *Cobbett's Weekly Political Register*, Vol. XXXII, No. 15, 12 July 1817, pp. 449–80, pp. 462–3.

12. Ibid., pp. 462–4.

13. Hunt, *Memoirs*, III, p. 463.

14. Bamford, *Passages*, p. 44.

15. Ibid., pp. 45–6.

16. Bamford, *An Account of the Arrest and Imprisonment*, pp. 21–2; also Bamford, *Passages*, pp. 79–81.

17. Bamford, *Passages*, p. 81.

18. Ibid., p. 82.

19. Ibid., p. 87.

20. Ibid., p. 91.

21. Ibid., p. 81.

22. Ibid., p. 106.

23. Ibid.

24. Ibid., pp. 108–9.

25. Bamford, *An Account of the Arrest and Imprisonment*, p. 5.

26. Ibid., p. 42.

27. Bamford, *Passages*, p. 74.

28. TNA HO 42/163 f. 365, Samuel Bamford to Jemima Bamford, 11 April 1817.

29. Bamford, *Passages*, pp. 147–8.

30. Bamford, *An Account of the Arrest and Imprisonment*, p. 55.

31. Bamford, *Passages*, p. 153.

32. Ibid., pp. 153–4.

7 Dewsbury

1. *Leeds Mercury*, 14 June 1817, p. 3.
2. Ibid.
3. Ibid.
4. For Oliver 'the Spy' see Malcolm Chase, 'W. J. Richards', *ODNB*, article 57111, 2004/2008.
5. Edward Baines, *History of the Reign of George III*, 4 Vols, Leeds, 1820–3, Vol. IV, p. 78.
6. Baines, *George III*, IV, p. 78.
7. As quoted in the *Leeds Mercury*, 5 July 1817.
8. TNA HO 79/3 ff. 40–2, f. 41 'Private & Confidential', Lord Sidmouth to Hugh Parker, Whitehall, 31 May 1817.
9. Bamford, *Passages*, pp. 156–7.
10. My thanks to John Belchem for providing additional information on Brandreth and the Pentrich rising.
11. Baines, *George III*, IV, p. 77.
12. TNA HO 42/168 ff. 279–80, John Knight to Lord Sidmouth, Salisbury Gaol, 17 July 1817.
13. *Sherwin's Weekly Political Register*, Vol. I, No. 17, 26 July 1817, p. 269.
14. TNA HO 42/170 f. 242, Letter from Elijah Dixon, 19 September 1817.
15. Hargreaves and Hampson, *Beyond Peterloo*, p. 19.
16. Many thanks again to John Belchem for this additional information and insight into the rising.
17. Samuel Bamford, *Miscellaneous Poetry*, London, 1821, p. 66. Bamford first included this poem in his collection entitled *The Weaver's Boy*, published in April 1819 and advertised in the *Manchester Observer*, 10 April 1819.
18. Hunt, *Memoirs*, III, pp. 501–2.
19. Malcolm Chase makes this point: see Chase, 'Richards', *ODNB*.
20. Hunt, *Memoirs*, III, p. 503.
21. Ibid., p. 507.

8 Covent Garden

1. *Sherwin's Weekly Political Register*, Vol. II, No. 20, 14 February 1818, p. 187.
2. *Manchester Observer*, 3 January 1818, p. 1.

3. See 'James Wroe' in K. Gildart, D. Howell and N. Kirk (eds), *Dictionary of Labour Biography*, Basingstoke, Vol. XI, 2003, p. 292.

4. Chetham's Library, MUN Collection Mun.A.6.30 James Weatherly, *Autobiography*, 1860, ff. 33–4. Weatherley states that in 1860 two of Wroe's sons were trading in Manchester, one as a bookseller in Oxford Road and the other a sheet-music seller in John Dalton Street. He says Wroe died in 1844.

5. *Derby Mercury*, 13 November 1800.

6. *Stamford Mercury*, 1 June 1804.

7. *Leeds Intelligencer*, 1 July 1816.

8. Their address is given as 4 Canal Street, Manchester in the *Manchester Observer*, 22 May 1819.

9. *The Times*, 11 August 1819.

10. Dolby, T., *The Trial of Henry Hunt, Esq. Jno. Knight, Jos. Johnson, Jno. Thacker Saxton, Samuel Bamford, Jos. Healey, James Moorhouse, Robert Jones, Geo. Swift, and Robert Wylde, for an alledged [sic] Conspiracy to Overturn the Government, &c.*, London, 1820, pp. 187–8.

11. G. C. Boase and G. H. Martin, 'Henry Hobhouse', *ODNB*, article 13403, 2004.

12. For Sidmouth's withdrawal from the department see Ziegler, *Addington*, pp. 368–9.

13. Hunt, *Memoirs*, III, p. 528.

14. www.historyofparliamentonline.org/volume/1790-1820/constituencies/westminster.

15. Hunt, *Memoirs*, III, pp. 552–3.

16. Ibid., p. 547.

17. See R. G. Hall, 'Tyranny, Work and Politics: The 1818 Strike Wave in the English Cotton District' in *International Review of Social History*, Vol. 34, No. 3 (1989), pp. 433–70.

18. As reported in newspaper clippings from Chetham's Library, Main Collection Hay 1–18, William Robert Hay Scrapbooks Vol. 11, ff. 213–14. A version of Boulter's deposition can be found in TNA HO 42/180/1 ff. 303–6, Speeches at Stockport Meeting, 1 September 1818.

19. TNA HO 42/180/1 f. 291, Deposition of John Livesey, 'The Outlines of the different speeches made by the Reformers on Sandy Brow... the first day of September 1818'.

20. As reported in newspaper clippings from Chetham's Library, Hay

Scrapbooks, Vol. 11, ff. 213–14. Livesey offers a variation in TNA HO 42/180/1 ff. 292–4.

21. TNA HO 42/180/1 f. 292, Deposition of John Livesey. See also newspaper clippings from Chetham's Library, Hay Scrapbooks, Vol. 11, ff. 213–14.

22. Robert Reid, *The Peterloo Massacre*, London, 1989, pp. 99–100.

23. TNA HO 42/180/1 ff. 102–3, John Lloyd to Henry Hobhouse, 7 September 1818.

24. Ibid., ff. 246–7, John Bagguley to Joseph Harrison, 26 September 1818.

25. Reid, *The Peterloo Massacre*, p. 102.

9 The Spread Eagle

1. For Richard Carlile see M. L. Bush, *The Friends and Following of Richard Carlile*, Diss, 2016. For the flag see *The Republican*, II, p. 254 and V, p. 270.

2. Belchem, *Orator Hunt*, p. 92.

3. John Knight, *A Full and Particular Report of the Proceedings of the Public Meeting held in Manchester on Monday the 18th of January 1819*, Manchester, n.d.

4. Ibid., p. 6.

5. Ibid.

6. Belchem, *Orator Hunt*, pp. 86–7.

7. Knight, *A Full and Particular Report*, p. 15.

8. Ibid., p. 7.

9. Ibid., pp. 7–8.

10. Ibid., p. 9.

11. Ibid., p. 10.

12. Ibid., p. 7.

13. Hunt, *Memoirs*, III, p. 598; Knight, *A Full and Particular Report*, p. 21.

14. *Manchester Observer*, 9 January 1819.

15. Ibid., 18 January 1819; Knight, *A Full and Particular Report*, pp. 21–2.

16. Hunt, *Memoirs*, III, p. 599.

17. Ibid., p. 600.

18. *Black Dwarf*, Vol. III, No. 22, 2 June 1819, pp. 337–8.

19. For a full description of this programme of mass meetings in July and August 1819 see Belchem, *Orator Hunt*, pp. 98–112.

20. Hunt, *Memoirs*, III, p. 600.

21. *Manchester Observer*, 31 July 1819.

22. TNA TS 11/1056, Letter from Henry Hunt to Joseph Johnson, Middleton Cottage, 6 July 1819.
23. Belchem, *Orator Hunt*, p. 105.
24. TNA HO 42/190/1 ff. 64–5, f. 65, Henry Hunt to Joseph Johnson, Middleton Cottage, 29 July 1819.

10 Campsmount

1. *The Sporting Magazine or Monthly Calendar*, Vol. IX (2nd Series, or Vol. LXXXIV Old Series), London, 1834, p. 222.
2. Edward and James Weatherby, *The Racing Calendar for the Year 1818*, London, 1819, Vol. XLVI, p. 337, under 'Races to Come', 'Sir John Byng, Bart, Steward'.
3. Weatherby and Weatherby, *The Racing Calendar for the Year 1818*, pp. 339–40.
4. TNA HO 42/191/1 ff. 226–229, f. 227, Sir John Byng to Henry Hobhouse, Manchester, 2 August 1819.
5. H. W. Pearse, *The History of the 31ˢᵗ Foot and 70ᵗʰ Foot, Subsequently the 1ˢᵗ and 2ⁿᵈ Battalions of the East Surrey Regiment*, 3 Vols, London, Vol. I, 1702–1914, 1916, p. 122.
6. Ibid., I, p. 125.
7. Ibid., I, p. 125.
8. Ibid., I, p. 126.
9. G. B. L'Estrange, *Recollections of Sir George B. L'Estrange*, London, 1874, pp. 185–6.
10. Quoted in John Mollo, *The Prince's Dolls: Scandals, Skirmishes and Splendours of the First British Hussars 1793–1815*, London, 1997, p. 173.
11. L'Estrange, *Recollections of Sir George B. L'Estrange*, p. 189.
12. TNA HO 42/191, Sir John Byng to Henry Hobhouse, 2 August 1819. For the army's involvement in maintaining civil order see Chapter 7 'Civil Disorder' in S. H. Myerly, *British Military Spectacle: From the Napoleonic Wars through to the Crimea*, Cambridge, Massachusetts and London, 1996, pp. 120–138.
13. TNA HO 42/191/2 f. 280, 'Disposition of the Troops in the Northern District as intended to be on Monday 2ⁿᵈ August 1819'.
14. Wylly, *History of the XVth (The King's) Hussars*, p. 260.
15. Joseph Aston, *The Manchester Guide*, Manchester, 1804, pp. 253–4.
16. 'Sir William Jolliffe's Account' transcribed in George Pellow, *The*

Life and Correspondence of the Right Hon[oura]ble Henry Addington, 1st Viscount Sidmouth, 3 Vols, London, 1847, Vol. III, pp. 253–61, p. 253.

17. Anon, 'A Chelsea Pensioner', *Jottings from my Sabretasch*, London, 1847, pp. 127–8.
18. First published in the *Scots Observer*, 1890, then in Kipling's compilation *Barrack-Room Ballads and Other Verses*, London, 1892.
19. Mollo, *The Prince's Dolls*, p. 4.
20. Quoted in Mollo, *The Prince's Dolls*, p. 192.

11 The Union Rooms

1. Daniel Defoe, *A Tour Thro' the Whole Island of Great Britain*, London, 1748, Vol. III, p. 257.
2. James Ray, *A Compleat History of the Rebellion*, York, 1749, pp. 201–2.
3. John Harland (ed.), *Ballads and Songs of Lancashire: Chiefly Older than the 19th Century*, London, 1865, pp. 278–9. The Bodleian Library has a broadsheet version currently dated 1840–66 printed by / for J Harkness of Preston, Harding B II (2052).
4. James Crossley, 'Pott's Discovery of Witches in the County of Lancaster' in *Remains Historical & Literary connected with the Palatine Counties of Lancaster and Chester published by The Chetham Society*, Manchester, 1845, Vol. VI, p. lxxix.
5. For the working class see Anna Clark, *The Struggle for the Breeches: Gender and the Making of the British Working Class*, Berkeley and Los Angeles, 1995, pp. 141–74.
6. Bamford, *Passages*, p. 165.
7. M. L. Bush, 'The Women at Peterloo: The Impact of Female Reform on the Manchester Meeting of 16 August 1819' in *History* 89 (2004), pp. 209–32, p. 210 and p. 214.
8. For women occupying public political spaces see Katrina Navickas, *Protest and the Politics of Space and Place, 1789–1848*, Manchester, 2016, pp. 75–81.
9. *Morning Chronicle*, 1 July 1819, p. 3.
10. *Leeds Intelligencer*, 5 July 1819, p. 4.
11. *Black Dwarf*, Vol. III, No. 28, 14 July 1819, p. 453.
12. Ibid.
13. Ibid.
14. Ibid., p. 454.
15. Ibid., pp. 454–6.

16. Edmund Burke, *Reflections on the Revolution in France*, London, 1790, pp. 112–13.

17. For analysis of this famous passage see Richard Bourke, *Empire and Revolution: The Political Life of Edmund Burke*, Princeton and Oxford, 2015, pp. 703–8 and Sora Sato, *Edmund Burke as Historian: War, Order and Civilisation*, Basingstoke, 2018, pp. 93–4.

18. For an exploration of the female reform societies see also Ruth Mather, '"These Lancashire Women are witches in politics": Female reform societies and the theatre of radicalism 1819–1820' in Robert Poole (ed.), *Return to Peterloo*, Manchester, 2012, pp. 49–64 and her unpublished doctoral thesis, *The Home-Making of the English Working Class: Radical Politics and a Domestic Life in Late-Georgian England, c.1790–1820*, Queen Mary University London, 2016.

19. *Black Dwarf*, 14 July 1819, pp. 455–6.

20. Bamford, *Passages*, p. 166.

21. *A Full, Accurate, and Impartial Report of the Trial of John Bagguley, of Stockport, John Johnston, of Salford, and Samuel Drummond, of Manchester*, Manchester, 1819.

22. Bagguley spells the latter names 'Montague' and 'Woolstoncroft'.

23. TNA HO 42/188 f. 138, Letter from John Bagguley to the Female Reformers of Stockport, Chester Castle, 19 June 1819.

24. *The Public Ledger and Daily Advertiser*, 14 July 1819, p. 3.

25. The British Museum, 1935,0522.11.147.

26. *Manchester Observer*, 31 July 1819, No. 31, Vol. II.

27. Ibid., 31 July 1819.

28. Ibid., also in Henry Fisher, *An Impartial Narrative of the Late Melancholy Occurrences in Manchester*, Liverpool, pp. 10–11.

29. James Wroe, *Peterloo Massacre, Containing A Faithful Narrative of the Events which preceded, accompanied, and followed the fatal Sixteenth of August 1819 ...*, 2nd edition, Manchester, 1819, pp. 21–2.

30. Ibid., p. 22.

31. TNA HO 42/191/1 ff. 41–2, Mr Wright to [Lord Sidmouth?], Manchester, 11 August 1819.

12 Smedley Cottage

1. TNA HO 42/161 f. 10, Anthony Molyneux to Lord Sidmouth, and TNA HO 42/164 f. 11.

2. TNA HO 42/164 f. 510, William Hay to Lord Sidmouth, Police Office Manchester, 26 April 1817.

3. *Manchester Mercury*, 24 June 1817.

4. Prentice, *Historical Sketches*, p. 70.

5. Ibid.

6. *Manchester Observer*, 17 July 1819.

7. Ibid., 7 August 1819.

8. Francis Philips, *An Exposure of the Calumnies circulated by the Enemies of Social Order... Against the Magistrates and the Yeomanry Cavalry of Manchester and Salford*, 2nd edition, London, 1819, pp. 17–18.

9. James Wroe, *Peterloo Massacre*, 3rd edition, Manchester, December 1819, p. 164.

10. Philips, *An Exposure of the Calumnies Circulated*, p. 17.

11. Hunt, *Memoirs*, III, p. 600.

12. TNA HO 41/4 ff. 358–60, Henry Hobhouse to James Norris, 17 July 1819.

13. Hobhouse's dealings with the magistrates to date are summarized in TNA HO 41/4 ff. 424–5, Henry Hobhouse to the Attorney General, Whitehall, 2 August 1819.

14. TNA HO 42/191/1 and another copy at Manchester University EGR4/2/3/2/5.

15. TNA HO 41/4 ff. 431–2, Henry Hobhouse to James Norris, Whitehall, 3 August 1819.

16. TNA HO 41/4 ff. 434–5, Henry Hobhouse to James Norris, Whitehall, 4 August 1819.

17. This information was printed and distributed by James Wroe, dated Manchester Observer Office, 4 August, a copy finding its way to the Home Office, TNA HO 42/191/2 f. 325.

18. *Manchester Observer*, 7 August 1819.

19. TNA HO 42/191/2 f. 327, Sir John Byng to Henry Hobhouse, Pontefract, 5 August 1819.

20. TNA HO 42/191/2 f. 327, Sir John Byng to Henry Hobhouse, Pontefract, 5 August 1819.

21. TNA HO 41/4 f. 441, Henry Hobhouse to James Norris, Whitehall, 7 August 1819.

22. *Manchester Observer*, 17 July 1819.

23. Joseph Johnson, *A Letter to Henry Hunt, Esq. by Joseph Johnson*, Manchester, 1822, p. 6.

24. Hunt, *Memoirs*, III, p. 601.

25. Ibid., pp. 601–2.

26. Ibid., pp. 602–3.

27. Ibid., p. 603.

28. Ibid., p. 604.

29. Swindells, *Manchester Streets and Manchester Men*, p. 47.

30. Hunt, *Memoirs*, III, p. 605.

31. Ibid.

32. Dolby, *Trial of Henry Hunt*, p. 214.

33. Hunt, *Memoirs*, III, pp. 606–7.

34. *The Times*, 16 August 1819, Henry Hunt's letter to the Editor of *The Star* dated Smedley Cottage, near Manchester, 12 August 1819.

35. Ibid.

36. Bamford, *Passages*, pp. 191–2.

37. Ibid.

38. Hunt, *Memoirs*, III, pp. 609–10.

39. TNA 41/4 ff. 454–5, Henry Hobhouse to James Norris, Whitehall, 11 August 1819.

40. TNA HO 42/191/2 f. 384, Sir John Byng to Henry Hobhouse, York, 10 p.m., 11 August 1819.

41. TNA HO 42/191/2 f. 386, William Hay to Sir John Byng, Police Office Manchester, 8 o'clock, 10 August 1819.

42. Hunt, *Memoirs*, III, p. 610.

43. Bamford, *Passages*, pp. 194–5.

44. Ibid., pp. 191–2.

45. Ibid., p. 196.

46. Hunt, *Memoirs*, III, p. 610.

47. John Edward Taylor, *Notes and Observations*, London, 1820, p. 53; letter from James Norris to Lord Sidmouth, Manchester, 11 p.m., 15 August 1819.

13 Middleton

1. Dolby, *Trial of Henry Hunt*, p. 52.

2. Ibid., p. 53.

3. TNA HO 79/3 f. 356, Henry Hobhouse to Colonel Ralph Fletcher, 2 March 1819.

4. Dolby, *Trial of Henry Hunt*, pp. 76–9, p. 141.

5. For a full exploration see Robert Poole, 'The March to Peterloo: Politics and Festivity in Late Georgian England' in *Past and Present*, No. 192 (August 2006), pp. 109–53.

6. Dolby, *Trial of Henry Hunt*, p. 181.

7. Ibid.

8. Bamford stated this in his petition to the House of Commons, see 'Manchester Meeting-Petition of Samuel Bamford', *Parliamentary Debates (Hansard) House of Commons*, 30 November 1819, Vol. XLI, cc. 509–13.

9. Dolby, *Trial of Henry Hunt*, p. 53.

10. Ibid.

11. J. Harland and T. T. Wilkinson, *Lancashire Legends, Traditions, Pageants, Sports, &c.*, London, 1873, p. 83. See also A. Burton, *Rush-Bearing*, Manchester, 1891.

12. Ibid., pp. 110–11.

13. Ibid., p. 113.

14. Correspondence from 'J.L.' dated Rochdale, Lancashire, 31 May 1825 and quoted in William Hone, *The Year Book of Daily Recreation and Information*, London, 1832, p. 553.

15. Jonathan Crowther, *A Portraiture of Methodism, Or, the History of the Wesleyan Methodists*, London, 1815, p. 259.

16. Thomas Coke ed., *A Collection of Hymns for the Use of the People Called Methodists. By the Rev. John Wesley*, Dublin, 1816, p. 217.

17. John A. La Trobe, *The Music of the Church*, London, 1831, p. 91. See also K. H. MacDermott, *The Old Church Gallery Minstrels: An Account of the Church Bands and Singers in England from about 1660 to 1860*, London, 1948.

18. Bamford, *Early Days*, p. 150.

19. 'J.L.' in Hone, *The Year Book of Daily Recreation*, p. 553.

20. Harland and Wilkinson, *Lancashire Legends*, p. 113.

21. Bamford, *Early Days*, pp. 146–51.

22. Ibid., p. 149.

23. Ibid., p. 150.

24. 'J.L.' in Hone, *The Year Book of Daily Recreation*, p. 553.

25. Bamford, *Passages*, p. 196.

26. Ibid., pp. 197–200.

27. Dolby, *Trial of Henry Hunt*, p. 178.

28. Bamford, *Passages*, p. 198.

29. Dolby, *Trial of Henry Hunt*, p. 178.
30. Bamford, *Passages*, pp. 198–200.
31. Dolby, *Trial of Henry Hunt*, pp. 178–9.
32. Ibid., p. 181.
33. Bamford, *Passages*, p. 200.
34. Dolby, *Trial of Henry Hunt*, p. 179.
35. Ibid., p. 185.
36. Ibid.
37. Bamford, *Passages*, p. 81
38. Ibid., p. 200.
39. Ibid., pp. 220–1.
40. Dolby, *Trial of Henry Hunt*, p. 187.
41. Ibid., p. 185.

14 St Peter's Field

1. J. Harrop, *A Report of the Trial, Redford against Birley and Others for An Assault on The Sixteenth of August 1819*, Manchester, 1822, p. 49.
2. Dolby, *Trial of Henry Hunt*, p. 265.
3. Ibid., pp. 204–5.
4. *The Times*, 19 August 1819.
5. Harrop, *Redford against Birley*, p. 23.
6. Dolby, *Trial of Henry Hunt*, p. 106.
7. Harrop, *Redford against Birley*, p. 45, William Hulton's testimony: 'The meeting on the 9th being illegal, placards were issued to prevent it; there were no such placards on the 16th, the requisition being legal; The illegal passages were taken out.'
8. Ibid., p. 44.
9. See Reid, *The Peterloo Massacre*, p. 166.
10. Dolby, *Trial of Henry Hunt*, p. 101.
11. Harrop, *Redford against Birley*, p. 30.
12. Ibid., pp. 46–8.
13. Ibid., p. 48.
14. Ibid., p. 37.
15. Ibid., p. 40.
16. Ibid., p. 41.
17. For the whole description see Harrop, *Redford against Birley*, pp. 40–1.
18. Harrop, *Redford against Birley*, p. 41.

19. Dolby, *Trial of Henry Hunt*, p. 101.
20. Harrop, *Redford against Birley*, p. 30.
21. *Manchester Chronicle*, 21 August 1819.
22. For Tatton see Harrop, *Redford against Birley*, p. 46.
23. 'Bishop Stanley's Account of Peterloo' transcribed in F. A. Bruton, *Three Accounts of Peterloo, by Eyewitnesses*, Manchester, 1921, pp. 10–23, p. 21.
24. Harrop, *Redford against Birley*, p. 30.
25. Bruton, 'Bishop Stanley's Account', p. 18.
26. Harrop, *Redford against Birley*, p. 14.
27. Dolby, *Trial of Henry Hunt*, p. 192.
28. Ibid., p. 193.
29. Prentice, *Historical Sketches*, p. 159.
30. Bruton, 'Bishop Stanley's Account', p. 18.
31. Harrop, *Redford against Birley*, p. 46.
32. Anon., *An Examination of the late dreadful Occurrences at the Meeting at Manchester, on August 16, 1819; being a clear statement and review of its object, circumstances, and results*, Newcastle-upon-Tyne, 1819, p. 7.
33. Bamford, *Passages*, pp. 200–1.
34. Dolby, *Trial of Henry Hunt*, p. 188.
35. Bamford, *Passages*, p. 201.
36. Ibid., pp. 200–1.
37. Ibid., p. 202.
38. Ibid., p. 203.
39. Harrop, *Redford against Birley*, p. 46.
40. Lucy Morville described herself as thirty-nine years old. Apparently she 'appeared much older, and excited a smile at her declaration of age', Dolby, *Trial of Henry Hunt*, p. 190.
41. Dowling, *Lees Coroner's Inquest*, p. 12.
42. Ibid., p. 74.
43. Ibid., p. 38.
44. Ibid., p. 57.
45. Hunt, *Memoirs*, III, p. 611.
46. Ibid.
47. Bush, *The Friends and Following of Richard Carlile*, p. 96.
48. *Sherwin's Weekly Political Register*, Vol. V, No. 16, 21 August 1819, p. 240.
49. Dolby, *Trial of Henry Hunt*, pp .103, 216.

50. *Sherwin's*, 21 August 1819, p. 240.
51. Hunt, *Memoirs*, III, p. 612.
52. Ibid.
53. *The Times*, 19 August 1819.
54. Ibid.
55. Dolby, *Trial of Henry Hunt*, p. 86.
56. *Manchester Chronicle*, 21 August 1819.
57. Hunt, *Memoirs*, III, p. 611.
58. *Sherwin's*, 21 August 1819, p. 240.
59. Ibid.
60. Bamford, *Passages*, p. 203.
61. *The Times*, 19 August 1819.
62. Hunt, *Memoirs*, III, pp. 619–20.
63. Dolby, *Trial of Henry Hunt*, p. 206.
64. Ibid.
65. Bamford, *Passages*, pp. 203–4.
66. Jemima Bamford's account in Bamford, *Passages*, p. 221.
67. Bamford, *Passages*, p. 204.
68. Bruton, 'Bishop Stanley's Account', p. 17.
69. Ibid.
70. Dolby, *Trial of Henry Hunt*, p. 101.
71. Harrop, *Redford against Birley*, p. 44.
72. Dowling, *Lees Coroner's Inquest*, p. 73.
73. Bamford, *Passages*, p. 205.
74. Ibid.
75. Richard Clark, *An Account of the national anthem entitled God Save the King!*, London, 1822 and Riding, *Jacobites*, pp. 285–6.
76. Dolby, *Trial of Henry Hunt*, p. 192.
77. Bamford, *Passages*, p. 205.
78. Hunt, *Memoirs*, III, pp. 612–13.
79. Ibid.
80. Ibid., pp. 613–14.
81. Dolby, *Trial of Henry Hunt*, p. 217.
82. *The Times*, 19 August 1819.
83. Dolby, *Trial of Henry Hunt*, p. 217.
84. *Sherwin's*, 21 August 1819, p. 241.
85. Dolby, *Trial of Henry Hunt*, p. 196.
86. Ibid.

87. Ibid., p. 191.
88. Bamford, *Passages*, p. 203.
89. Bruton, 'Bishop Stanley's Account', p. 18.
90. Dolby, *Trial of Henry Hunt*, p. 217.
91. Ibid., p. 192.
92. Bruton, 'Bishop Stanley's Account', p. 18.
93. Dolby, *Trial of Henry Hunt*, p. 102.
94. Harrop, *Redford against Birley*, p. 44.
95. Dolby, *Trial of Henry Hunt*, p. 102.
96. Ibid., p. 105.
97. TNA HO 42/192 f. 174 (original ff. 348–50), William Hay's account, 16 August 1819.
98. Dolby, *Trial of Henry Hunt*, p. 106.
99. Ibid., p. 102.
100. Harrop, *Redford against Birley*, p. 45.
101. TNA HO 42/198 f. 636. With thanks to Robert Poole for bringing this document to my attention.
102. Dolby, *Trial of Henry Hunt*, p. 102.
103. Harrop, *Redford against Birley*, p. 31.
104. Ibid., p. 41.
105. Ibid., p. 44.
106. Ibid.
107. Ibid., p. 45.
108. *Manchester Chronicle*, 21 August 1819.
109. Harrop, *Redford against Birley*, p. 45.
110. Ibid.
111. Ibid.
112. *An Act for Preventing Tumults and Riotous Assemblies, and for the more speedy and effectual Punishing the Rioters*, London, 1715. By 1819, with the third King George on the throne, it was usual to clarify the date of the act with 'in the first year of King George the First'.
113. Harrop, *Redford against Birley*, p. 46.
114. Ibid., p. 45.
115. J. T. Saxton (pub.), 'A Striking Resemblance of the Swearing Parsons, Hay and Ethelstone, Reading the Riot Act, on St. Peter's Plain, August 16th, 1819', Manchester, 1822, used as a frontispiece to the copy of the 3rd edition of James Wroe's *Peterloo Massacre*, Manchester, 1819, held in the collections of the University of Minnesota (WILS CLS 942.073 P44).

116. Harrop, *Redford against Birley*, p. 45.
117. Ibid., p. 19.
118. Ibid., p. 46.
119. Pellow, 'Sir William Jolliffe's Account', pp. 254–5.
120. Harrop, *Redford against Birley*, p. 49.
121. M. L. Bush, *The Casualties of Peterloo*, Lancaster, 2005, p. 94.
122. Bruton, 'Bishop Stanley's Account', p. 18.
123. Dolby, *Trial of Henry Hunt*, p. 187.
124. Weatherley, *Autobiography*, f. 27.
125. Dowling, *Lees Coroner's Inquest*, p. 179.
126. Harrop, *Redford against Birley*, p. 31.
127. Ibid., p. 41.
128. Ibid., p. 31.
129. *Manchester Chronicle*, 21 August 1819.
130. Bamford, *Passages*, p. 206.
131. *The Times*, 19 August 1819.
132. Hunt, *Memoirs*, III, pp. 614–15.
133. Ibid.
134. James Wroe, *Peterloo Massacre*, 3rd edition, Manchester, 1819, p. 3.
135. Dolby, *Trial of Henry Hunt*, p. 214.
136. Hunt, *Memoirs*, III, p. 615.
137. Dolby, *Trial of Henry Hunt*, p. 220.
138. Ibid., p. 219.
139. Ibid., p. 102.
140. Ibid., p. 108.
141. Bamford, *Passages*, p. 206.
142. Dolby, *Trial of Henry Hunt*, p. 107.
143. *Manchester Chronicle*, 21 August 1819; see also *Manchester Observer*, 21 August 1819: The Yeomanry 'put to death one of the Special Constables, and wounded many more.' See also Bush, *Casualties of Peterloo*, p. 65.
144. Dolby, *Trial of Henry Hunt*, p. 103.
145. Harrop, *Redford against Birley*, p. 49.
146. Hunt, *Memoirs*, III, p. 615.
147. Ibid.
148. *The Times*, 19 August 1819.
149. Weatherley, *Autobiography*, f. 27.
150. *Sherwin's*, 21 August 1819, p. 242.
151. Dolby, *Trial of Henry Hunt*, p. 193.

152. Dowling, *Lees Coroner's Inquest*, p. 75.

153. Bamford, *Passages*, p. 206.

154. Ibid., p. 207.

155. Bruton, 'Bishop Stanley's Account', pp. 18–19.

156. Dowling, *Lees Coroner's Inquest*, p. 44.

157. Ibid., p. 180.

158. Bruton, 'Bishop Stanley's Account', p. 19.

159. Harrop, *Redford against Birley*, p. 48.

160. Bruton, 'Bishop Stanley's Account', p. 19.

161. Dowling, *Lees Coroner's Inquest*, p. 179.

162. Ibid., p. 180.

163. *The Times*, 19 August 1819.

164. Dowling, *Lees Coroner's Inquest*, p. 461.

165. *Manchester Observer*, 21 August 1819.

166. *The Times*, 19 August 1819.

167. Ibid.

168. Harrop, *Redford against Birley*, p. 19.

169. Matthew Roberts says that some banners were 'ritually destroyed', see 'Radical Banners from Peterloo to Chartism' in R. Poole (ed.), *Return to Peterloo*, Manchester Region History Review (Special Edition), Vol. 23, 2012/2014, pp. 93–109, p. 97.

170. Bamford, *Passages*, p. 210.

171. Dowling, *Lees Coroner's Inquest*, p. 179.

172. University of Manchester Library, English MS 172 *Peterloo Relief Fund Account Book*, c.1820, p. 1; Bush, *Casualties of Peterloo*, p. 94.

173. 'Mrs. Fildes, hanging suspended by a nail in the platform which had caught her white dress, was slashed across her exposed body by one of the brave cavalry.' See Isabella Banks [Mrs George Linnaeus Banks], *The Manchester Man*, 3 Vols, London, 1876, Vol. II, p. 32. The author refers to this anecdote in the appendix to Volume 3, with the comment that the 'female sabred on the hustings was a Mrs Fildes when I knew her. Her son, Henry Hunt Fildes, was in my father's employ.' Banks, *The Manchester Man*, Vol. III, p. 304.

174. University of Manchester Library, English MS 172 *Peterloo Relief Fund Account Book*, p. 1.

175. *Sherwin's*, 21 August 1819, p. 242.

176. Ibid.

177. Bruton, 'Bishop Stanley's Account', p. 19.

178. Ibid.

179. Hunt, *Memoirs*, III, p. 616.

180. Harrop, *Redford against Birley*, p. 50.

181. Hunt, *Memoirs*, III, p. 617.

182. Ibid., pp. 617–18.

183. Ibid., p. 618.

184. *Manchester Chronicle*, 21 August 1819.

185. Letter quoted by Hunt in *Memoirs*, III, p. 619.

186. Hunt, *Memoirs*, III, p. 617.

187. Ibid., p. 619.

188. Bruton, 'Bishop Stanley's Account', p. 20.

189. Harrop, *Redford against Birley*, p. 49.

190. Pellow, 'Sir William Jolliffe's Account', p. 255.

191. Harrop, *Redford against Birley*, p. 49.

192. Dolby, *Trial of Henry Hunt*, p. 103.

193. Ibid.

194. Harrop, *Redford against Birley*, p. 48.

195. Ibid., p. 49.

196. Ibid., p. 45.

197. Dolby, *Trial of Henry Hunt*, p. 108.

198. Harrop, *Redford against Birley*, p. 45.

199. Dolby, *Trial of Henry Hunt*, p. 109.

200. Harrop, *Redford against Birley*, p. 49.

201. Pellow, 'Sir William Jolliffe's Account', pp. 255–6.

202. Ibid., p. 256.

203. Harrop, *Redford against Birley*, p. 45.

204. Pellow, 'Sir William Jolliffe's Account', p. 257.

205. Ibid.

206. Harrop, *Redford against Birley*, p. 49.

207. Ibid., p. 54.

208. Robert Mutrie's letter to Archibald Moore dated Thursday [19 August 1819], transcribed by Philip Lawson in 'Peterloo: A Constable's Eye-View Re-Assessed', *Peterloo Massacre*, Manchester Region History Review (Special Issue), Vol. III, No. 1, Spring/Summer 1989, pp. 39-42, p. 42.

209. Dowling, *Lees Coroner's Inquest*, p. 38.

210. Ibid., p. 41.

211. Ibid., p. 55.

212. Ibid., p. 57.

213. Ibid.

214. Ibid., p. 180. (Joseph Wrigley heard an officer of the 15th say, 'for shame, won't you give the people time to get away. Don't you see them down?', Dowling, *Lees Coroner's Inquest*, p. 38. See also ibid pp. 40 and 271.)

215. Ibid., p. 271.

216. Harrop, *Redford against Birley*, p. 14.

217. Dowling, *Lees Coroner's Inquest*, p. 267.

218. Pellow, 'Sir William Jolliffe's Account', pp. 257–8.

219. Harrop, *Redford against Birley*, p. 54.

220. Anon, *Jottings from my Sabretasch*, pp. 125–6.

221. Bamford, *Passages*, p. 210.

222. Harrop, *Redford against Birley*, p. 55.

223. Pellow, 'Sir William Jolliffe's Account', p. 258.

224. TNA TS 11/1056, Account of events at St Peter's Field by Major Dyneley, 16 August 1819.

225. Bamford, *Passages*, p. 208.

226. Pellow, 'Sir William Jolliffe's Account', p. 259.

227. Bruton, 'Bishop Stanley's Account', p. 21.

228. Dolby, *Trial of Henry Hunt*, p. 110.

229. *The Times*, 19 August 1819.

230. Bruton, 'Bishop Stanley's Account', p. 21.

231. *Manchester Chronicle*, 21 August 1819.

232. Bruton, 'Bishop Stanley's Account', p. 21.

233. *Manchester Chronicle*, 21 August 1819.

234. Bruton, 'Bishop Stanley's Account', p. 21.

235. Hunt, *Memoirs*, III, p. 620.

236. Bruton, 'Bishop Stanley's Account', p. 19.

237. *The Times*, 19 August 1819.

238. Ibid.

239. TNA TS 11/1056, Account of events at St Peter's Field by Major Dyneley, 16 August 1819.

15 New Cross

1. *The Republican*, Vol. V, p. 272.

2. James Wroe, *Peterloo Massacre*, 2nd edition, Manchester, December 1819, p. 16.

3. MLIA BR F 942.7389 SC13 f. 123 Advertisement for No. 1 of 'The Peterloo Massacre', 23 August 1819. I am extremely grateful to Robert Poole for providing me with a transcript of this document.

4. Wroe, *Peterloo Massacre*, 2nd edition, p. iii.

5. *Manchester Observer*, 28 August 1819.

6. Bamford, *Passages*, p. 211.

7. Ibid.

8. Ibid., p. 213.

9. *Manchester Observer*, 21 August 1819.

10. Mutrie, 'Letter to Archibald Moore', p. 42.

11. *Manchester Mercury*, 17 August 1819.

12. Bamford, *Passages*, p. 214.

13. Ibid.

14. Prentice, *Historical Sketches*, p. 163.

15. Ibid.

16. *The Times*, 19 August 1819.

17. Reid, *The Peterloo Massacre*, pp. 190–1.

18. *Manchester Observer*, 28 August 1819.

19. *Morning Chronicle*, 28 September 1819, p. 3.

20. Prentice, *Historical Sketches*, p. 167.

21. Ibid., p. 168. For example, James Lees, a weaver from 'Stone-wood, near Delph' when asked by 'Dr. Ransome' whether 'he had had enough of meetings?' replied 'in the negative' and was 'ordered to leave the place immediately'; see the appendix 'List of Persons Wounded at St. Petersfield' in W. Hone, *Report of the Metropolitan and Central Committee, Appointed for the Relief of the Manchester Sufferers*, London, 1820.

22. Ibid., pp. 166–8, 169–70; and Hone, *Report of the Metropolitan and Central Committee*.

23. University of Manchester Library, English MS 172, *Peterloo Relief Fund Account Book*.

24. Prentice, *Historical Sketches*, p. 171.

25. Ibid., p. 170.

26. Bamford, *Passages*, pp. 226–32.

16 HMY *Royal George*

1. TNA HO 41/4 ff. 484–5, Lord Sidmouth to William Hay, Whitehall, 18 August 1819.

2. TNA HO 41/4 f. 486, Lord Sidmouth to Sir John Byng, Whitehall, 18 August 1819 and TNA 42/192 f. 339, Lieutenant Colonel L'Estrange to Sir John Byng, 16 August 1819.

3. *The Times*, Monday 16 August 1819.

4. Ibid., 21 August 1819.

5. TNA HO 41/4 f. 494, Lord Sidmouth to the Earl of Derby and the Earl of Stamford and Warrington, 21 August 1819.

6. TNA HO 41/4 ff. 496-8, ff. 497-8 Henry Hobhouse to William Hulton, Whitehall, 23 August 1819.

7. *Manchester Observer*, 28 August 1819.

8. William Hone, *The Political House that Jack Built*, 26th edition, London, 1819.

17 Oldham

1. Dowling, *Lees Coroner's Inquest*, p. 58.

2. Ibid., p. 15.

3. For Hannah Lees' testimony see Dowling, *Lees Coroner's Inquest*, pp. 15–21 and for Thomas's statement see p. 35.

4. Dowling, *Lees Coroner's Inquest*, p. 35.

5. Ibid., p. 15.

6. Ibid., p. 35.

7. Ibid., p. 16.

8. Ibid., p. 12.

9. Ibid., p. 13.

10. Ibid.

11. Ibid., p. 36.

12. Ibid., p. 37.

13. Ibid., p. 17.

14. Ibid.

15. Ibid.

16. Ibid., p. 73.

17. Ibid., p. 37.

18. Ibid., p. 18.

19. Ibid., p. 34.

20. Ibid., p. 38.

21. Ibid., pp. 1–2.

22. Ibid., p. 24.

23. Ibid., p. 25.
24. Ibid.
25. Ibid., p. 27.
26. Ibid., p. 28.
27. Ibid., p. 29.
28. Ibid., p. 31.
29. Ibid., p. 32.
30. Ibid., p. 34.
31. Ibid., p. 23.
32. Ibid., p. 22.
33. Ibid., p. 23.
34. Ibid., p. 22.
35. Wroe, *Peterloo Massacre*, 3rd edition, p. 161.
36. For a legal/procedural analysis of the inquest see G. H. H. Glasgow, 'The John Lees Inquest of 1819 and the Peterloo Massacre' in *Transactions of the Historic Society of Lancashire and Cheshire*, Vol. CXLVIII, 1998, pp. 95–118.
37. Dowling, *Lees Coroner's Inquest*, p. 9.
38. Glasgow, 'The John Lees Inquest', p. 101.
39. Dowling, *Lees Coroner's Inquest*, p. 3 and p. 6.
40. Glasgow, 'The John Lees Inquest', pp. 110–11.
41. Dowling, *Lees Coroner's Inquest*, pp. 34–7.
42. 'Manchester Meeting. – Petitions of Messrs. Redford, Bowker, Barlow, and Lees', *Parliamentary Debates (Hansard) House of Commons*, 16 December 1819, Vol. XLI, cc. 1180–9.
43. Glasgow, 'The John Lees Inquest', p. 113.
44. Prentice, *Historical Sketches*, p. 169.
45. Belchem, *Orator Hunt*, p. 113.
46. Ibid., p. 116.
47. Ibid., p. 114.
48. James Grande, *William Cobbett, the Press and Rural England: Radicalism and the Fourth Estate, 1792–1835*, London, 2014, p. 1.
49. William Hazlitt, 'Character of Cobbett' in *Table-Talk; or, Original Essays*, London, 1821, pp. 115–34, p. 132; also John Gardner, 'Cobbett's Return to England in 1819' in J. Grande and J. Stevenson (eds), *William Cobbett, Romanticism and the Enlightenment: Contexts and Legacy*, London and New York, 2015, pp. 61–76, p. 62.
50. Belchem, *Orator Hunt*, p. 118.

18 House of Commons

1. See Riding and Riding, *Houses of Parliament*, Chapter 4.
2. See Belchem, 'Henry Hunt', *ODNB*, and Belchem, *Orator Hunt*, pp. 133–43.
3. For an appraisal of Bamford's Peterloo poetry see John Gardner, 'The Suppression of Samuel Bamford's Peterloo Poems' in *Romanticism*, Vol. 13, Issue 2, 2007, pp. 145–55.
4. Henry Hunt, 'To the Radical Reformers', dated 25 July 1820 [p. 8] in T. Dolby, *Hunt's Addresses to Reformers*, London, 1820–2.
5. Henry Hunt, 'To the Radical Reformers', dated 24 September 1821 [p. 29] in Dolby, *Hunt's Addresses to Reformers*.
6. *Bell's Life in London and Sporting Chronicle*, 24 August 1823.
7. For a full account see Chase, *1820*, pp. 76–84 and pp. 138–41.
8. See Riding and Riding, *Houses of Parliament*, pp. 13, 29, 49, 83, 106, 146, 198; and Caroline Shenton, *The Day Parliament Burned Down*, Oxford, 2012.
9. Cobbett's Weekly Political Register, Vol. 86, No. 5, 1 November 1834, pp. 262–9, p. 269.
10. For a recent exploration of this see J. Cozens, 'The Making of the Peterloo Martyrs, 1819 to the Present' in Q. Outram and K. Laybourn (eds), *Secular Martyrdom in Britain and Ireland from Peterloo to the Present*, Basingstoke, 2018, pp. 31–58.

INDEX

References in italics denote illustrations

A NEW PLAN OF
Manchester & Salford.
1819.

STRANGE WAYS

College

Collegiate Church

GREE...

Bedford Street

Ravald Street

Hudson Street

YORK STREET

KING STREET

STREET

Trinity Church

Hulme

Shaw

Street

Peru

Street

Street

Grey

Street

Street

Ackers Square

Street

Rose

Street

Adelphi

Drew

Str

CHA

St Stephens

Church

Broken Bank

Bank

Parade

Park

Street

ISLINGTON

Rodney

Street

RIVER

BRIDGE STREET

PARLIAMENT STREET

GARSIDE

QUAY STREET

JOHN

Charles

Real

Street

St JOHN'S STREET

BYROM STR

Church

St John's Church

ST JOHN'S STREET

LOWER BYROM STREET

St JOHN'S MARKET

LIVERPOOL

ROAD

Castle Field

Castle St

Coal Wharf

ORFORD ROAD

ORFORD ROAD

BOLTON CANAL

Hampson Street

NEW ROAD FROM ECCLES

New Bridge

THE RIVER

PETER

STREET

Lloyd

Street

Dickinsons Street

Windmill Street

Bridgewater

DEANS

ROCHDALE

KNOT MILL

HULME

BRIDGEWATERS CANAL